The Bumper Book of
COMIC SPEECHES
●●●●●●●●●●●●●●●●●●

D0733201

The Bumper Book of
COMIC
SPEECHES

● ● ● ● ● ● ● ● ● ● ● ● ● ● ● ●

Comic Speeches for Sportsmen

● ● ● ● ●

Comic Speeches for Social Occasions

● ● ● ● ●

Comic Speeches for the Legal Profession

● ● ● ● ●

Comic Speeches for the Sales Force

● ● ● ● ●

CHANCELLOR
PRESS

Comic Speeches for Sportsmen, *Comic Speeches for Social Occasions*, *Comic Speeches for the Legal Profession*, *Comic Speeches for the Sales Force* all first published by Futura Publications in 1986

This collected volume first published by Chancellor Press
an imprint of Reed International Books Ltd
Michelin House, 81 Fulham Road, London SW3 6RB
and Auckland, Melbourne, Singapore and Toronto

ISBN: 1 85152 675 7

A CIP catalogue record is available for this book from the British Librai

Printed and bound in Great Britain
by Cox & Wyman Ltd, Reading, Berkshire

CONTENTS

● ● ● ● ●

Comic Speeches for Sportsmen
●●●●●

Contents

PART ONE

How to make a comic speech

Ground Rules

Be heard. Be understood. Be enjoyed! Believe it or not, those three simple rules hold the key to making a successful public speech. Observe them and you have nothing to fear. It couldn't be much easier, could it?

Unfortunately, as hundreds of public speakers have found to their cost, standing up in front of an audience of strangers and trying to make them laugh can be a nerve-shattering experience. There are those speakers who mumble and falter and forget their words, leaving the audience without the faintest idea of what they are talking about. There are those who tell unsuitable jokes and stories which, at best, embarrass those listening and, at worst, provoke uproar. And there are those who don't bother to prepare their material and just drone on for as long as the fancy takes them about anything that comes into their heads — and then they wonder why their audience has fallen asleep!

The chapters that follow will show you how to avoid these common pitfalls. But much more than that, you'll find in them all you'll need to make a successful comic speech — everything from how to assess your audience and the material that will entertain them, to how to prepare and organize your speech and deliver it with confidence. And, of course, there are pages of stories, anecdotes and quotations to ensure that you're never at a loss for a joke.

Know your Audience

No matter how nervous you feel about it, remember that it's an honour to be invited to speak in front of an audience — so acknowledge the fact by creating a speech specially designed for the occasion. A rambling, irrelevant performance that has nothing to do with the occasion or those listening to you verges on the insulting. What your audience will want to hear, and you should aim to provide, are effortless, amusing stories and ideas — stories and ideas that are of direct interest and relevance to them.

Some speakers like to think that they have perfected a kind of general-purpose speech; a speech which, with a few minor alterations and additions, will go down with any audience and on any occasion. It may be useful to have a few ready phrases and jokes to hand if you suspect that you're going to be asked to make an impromptu speech, but this kind of general-purpose material won't set an audience alight. They'll sense its general nature and the fact that no great imagination or thought has gone into it — and if the speaker is unlucky some of them will have heard him perform it elsewhere!

What this means is that for every occasion and every audience you need to create a new speech. But before you sit down and start to write it, spare a few seconds' thought to work out just what's required.

The Audience

You may be keen on cricket and your cricketing jokes may have gone down brilliantly at the sports club dinner — but they are unlikely to have the same appeal for the guests at a wedding or the ladies of the Townswomen's Guild. Obvious? It doesn't seem to occur to a great number of speakers that it's the audience who will determine whether their material is funny or not. And if the audience don't like your jokes you might as well give up. So make sure that you choose the right material by finding out about the people you'll be speaking to.

Age is an important factor. If you know that your audience will be young and sophisticated, choose some of the more sophisticated material in this book and, if necessary, update some of the details. Likewise, if your audience is past retiring age adapt the jokes and stories to suit them. Try not to tell jokes about Boy George to audiences who remember Victor Sylvester!

An all-male gathering is likely to enjoy rather more robust material than an all-female gathering — but that doesn't mean that you can feel free to tell dirty jokes simply because the audience is all-male. Never offend those who are listening to you. If you suspect that your material might prove offense to anyone at all, then cut it. And if *you're* embarrassed by any of your material, leave it out. Your embarrassment will communicate itself to the audience and then *they'll* feel embarrassed for you.

The members of the local bird-watching club will want to hear a speech that reflects their interests. This doesn't necessarily mean that every word you utter must be about birds, but don't be tempted to throw in a completely irrelevant joke just because it's funny. Most jokes can be adapted to fit almost any topic, but if you can't slide a story neatly into your speech you'd do better to leave it out. You don't want your audience to be worrying about your joke about cannibals — and what it has to do with

11

them — as you try to continue with the rest of the speech!

If you have been asked to speak at a formal function where you don't know the audience, find out as much as you can about the people expected to attend — particularly, if it's appropriate, the names and titles of those on the organizing committee. Do a little homework and see if you can come up with any interesting or amusing stories about them or other guests, and weave these into the fabric of your speech. This will prove that you've worked hard to create a special speech for the occasion and your audience will respond to the personal touches.

The Occasion

Different occasions require different kinds of speeches, and you'll find details about what kind of speech is most appropriate for the major social occasions in the last part of this section of the book. But it isn't just the formal requirements of an occasion that matter when it comes to preparing your speech.

The tone of the occasion is all-important too. A vote of thanks at a rugby club when the team has just topped the local league will be quite different in tone to a vote of thanks at an afternoon business meeting. Try to assess what the mood of your audience will be. Will they be ready for a belly-laugh and a funny story about the chairman, or will a more wry and sophisticated kind of humour best suit the occasion? Make up your mind which to go for and choose your material accordingly.

It's also worthwhile bearing in mind the fact that if you've been asked to speak it's probably for a purpose. Whatever that purpose — whether it's to present a prize or propose a toast — you should never get so carried away with your own words that you forget to do it. Learn from the story of the speaker who, having stood up to give a five-minute presentation speech, sat down again still holding the award half an hour later! The best way of avoiding this kind of embarrassment is to plan your speech carefully and then stick to it. Try to resist the temptation, no matter how well you're being received, to improvise. It's improvisation that is likely to throw you off your stride.

Here's a simple check list of 10 Do's and Don't's which you should bear in mind as you sit down to prepare your speech.

Do's

1 Do check the age and sex ratio of the audience.
2 Do find out what your particular function is to be. Have you been asked to propose a toast or make an after-dinner speech? Make sure that you prepare the right kind of speech.
3 Do find out how long you will be expected to speak.
4 Do some homework on any special guests or members of the audience.
5 Do adapt your material to suit the occasion.

Don't's

1 Don't use old material.
2 Don't risk offending anyone with blue jokes.
3 Don't speak for too long and don't try to improvise.
4 Don't include irrelevant material.
5 Don't forget to fulfil your function. If you've been asked to make a toast or offer a vote of thanks then remember to do so.

Perfect Preparation

Once you know the kind of speech you're going to make and the sort of audience you'll be entertaining, you can begin to prepare your material. Preparation is absolutely vital if you're going to give a polished performance, so allow as much time as possible to work on the speech.

Start by reading through this book and jotting down all the jokes, quotes, anecdotes and so on that you like and that you feel are directly relevant to your audience. Be ruthless and cut out anything that isn't related in some way to your subject and anything that can't be adapted to fit. On a separate sheet, put down all the things that you *have* to say in the speech and all the points that you particularly want to make.

With any luck you'll begin to see the material falling into place, with the quotes leading into the points you want to make and the stories illustrating the theme. This is exactly what you're aiming for — a seamless speech with one idea moving into the next without any effort. You'll probably have to adapt some of the material if it's to fit in perfectly, so change the names and locations and details to suit the occasion. For example, if you're going to be speaking in Newcastle and you're using a joke set in London, change the location and add some Geordie colour. Most importantly of all, put everything into your own words. You'll feel more comfortable when you come to use the material if it's written in the kind of language and the style you're used to, and it will make your speech seem that much more personal to the audience.

Sir Thomas Beecham once said of his orchestra that the important thing was 'to begin and end together, what happens in between doesn't matter very much.' Pretty much the same can be said of making a speech. If you can capture the attention of the audience with your first line, you're likely to have them with you for the rest of the speech. And if they're going to remember anything when they get home it's likely to be your final line — so make sure that it's worth remembering.

Some speakers like to work on the opening and closing lines of their speech together, linking them so that the last line finishes what the first line started. Whatever you decide to do, make sure that both the beginning and the end of your speech are absolutely relevant — both to the occasion and the central part of the speech. Nothing irrelevant should be allowed in at all or you'll begin to look as if you're rambling.

Opening and closing a speech are the two most difficult things of all. If a brilliant opening occurs to you then use it — but if nothing original springs to mind, try using one of these opening gambits.

Quotations

You'll find dozens of useful quotations in this book and one of them should be ideal for opening your speech. When you're looking for it, bear in mind that it should allow you to move straight into the main part of your speech without any stress. If you have to force a quotation to fit your theme then forget it. Always inform your audience that it *is* a quote and not your own words. It's quite likely that someone in the audience will have heard it before and they might think you a fraud if you don't name the person who said it first.

Questions

A question can be a very effective way of getting your

speech off the ground. Try asking an apparently serious one and following it up with a ridiculous answer. Or ask a ridiculous question to which there's no answer. Whichever kind you choose, aim to raise a laugh from the audience and break the ice.

The 'Did you know?' gambit is also a useful one. Find an amazing fact in the relevant section of this book and ask your audience if they knew it. It's bound to start your speech off with a bang!

Jokes

A joke may seem the obvious way of starting a speech, but in fact jokes can go badly wrong. If they work you'll have the audience eating out of your hand — but if they fall flat you'll have everyone in an agony of embarrassment and praying that you finish quickly.

The best kind of joke to look out for is one that has something to do with a member of the audience or with something directly relevant to the occasion. You may find that simply by changing a few details in one of the jokes in this book you've got the ideal opening gag — in which case use it. But never use a joke simply because *you* think it's funny.

Ending a speech with a joke is even more risky than opening with one. After all, even if your opening joke falls flat you have the rest of your speech to regain the audience's interest. If you end with a damp squib, however, no matter how good the speech the audience will remember you for only one thing — your failure to pull it off. Only finish with a joke if you can think of nothing better and if you're absolutely certain that it will work.

Exactly the same advice can be applied to ending a speech. No speech, no matter how well-received can be counted a great success unless it ends on a high note. Looking for a new screenplay, Sam Goldwyn once remarked, 'What we want is a story that begins with an earthquake and builds up to a climax.' That's what you have to aim for too!

Never end with an apologetic, 'Well, folks, that's about it,' line. That only suggests that you've run out of ideas or that you couldn't be bothered to finish the job off properly, and there's really no excuse for that. Even if you can't find the kind of climax that Goldwyn was looking for, you *can* end you speech in an amusing and tidy way.

Quotations

Don't use a quotation for the opening *and* closing of your speech because that would look too much like cheating, but a quote can round off a speech perfectly. Again, you'll find something suitable in the relevant section of this book — and again, make sure that it ties in completely with the main subject of your speech.

Anecdotes

There's bound to be an anecdote in this book that will encapsulate and illustrate your theme perfectly. You can use it to finish your speech in classic style, but beware of using anything too long or rambling. You don't want to lose your audience's attention in the last few moments. If you're speaking about friends, family or colleagues at work, try to uncover an amusing story about them; nothing embarrassing, of course, just something to show what nice people they are. This is *guaranteed* to bring your speech to a successful conclusion.

When you're preparing your speech, take an occasional look at this checklist of 10 Do's and Don't's just to keep your aims in mind.

Do's

1 Do check your material to ensure that it's suitable for the audience you assessed in the last section.
2 Do make sure that you have included all the things you *have* to say — your vote of thanks or the toast, for example.
3 Do adapt all the material to ensure that it's relevant.
4 Do aim to start and finish your speech on a high note.
5 Do credit any quotations you use.

Don't's

1 Don't use any material that isn't relevant to the occasion or will cause offence.
2 Don't start your speech with a joke unless you feel confident that it will work.
3 Don't tail off at the end of the speech; finish properly.
4 Don't use too many quotes or anecdotes from the lives of other people.
5 Don't speak too long; make sure that your speech is the right length.

If, when you finish preparing your speech, you feel confident that you've observed these guidelines, you can be sure that you're halfway towards success. Now all you need to know is how to deliver the speech you've written!

Successful Delivery

Preparing your speech is one thing — and the most important of all — but delivering it is something else. The best speech can be ruined by poor delivery and the thoroughly mediocre made to pass muster by good technique. Fortunately just a few simple measures will ensure that your delivery does your speech justice.

Rehearsal

You don't need to learn your material like an actor, but rehearsal will help you to become familiar with it and iron out any problems that weren't apparent on paper. For example, you may find that a particular sequence of words turn out to be difficult to say, or you might have problems pronouncing certain words — in which case find alternatives. Try to learn half a dozen key phrases which will take you smoothly from one part of your speech to the next so that you don't keep having to refer to your notes; no matter how nervous you're feeling, this will make your speech seem smooth and practised.

While you're rehearsing, experiment by using your voice to emphasise different points of the speech. Try changing your tone and volume, too, for effect. If you have a tape recorder then use it to tape the various versions of your speech — then you can play them back and decide which sounds the most interesting and lively. Don't, by the way, worry about your accent. Lots of speakers try to iron out their natural accent, but they forget that the way they speak is all part of their personality. Without it they seem very dull. As you listen to yourself speaking you'll begin to recognise the most successful ways of delivering certain parts of your speech. For example, the best way of telling your jokes is to do it casually, without labouring them too much. If you feel that there's a rather dull patch in the speech try animating it by changing your tone or emphasis, or even just speeding it up a bit. It's this kind of preparation that will give you polish on the day.

Body language

No matter how nervous you feel about speaking in front of an audience, you should try not to let them know — and it's the body which most often gives the secret away.

Begin by standing easily with your weight on both feet so that you feel balanced. This way you'll look steady, even if you don't feel it. Your main problem will be what to do with your hands. If you have notes, hold them in front of you at about waist level with one hand. With your free hand, lightly grasp the note-holding wrist. If you're lucky, there will be a lectern of some sort at which you can stand. Rest your hands on either side of it and you'll look very much at ease. Only royalty can get away with holding their hands behind their backs, and you'll look sloppy if you put your hands in your pockets, so don't adopt either of these postures. If you've no notes and no lectern, just stand with your left hand lightly holding your right wrist in front of you. It looks surprisingly natural and relaxed. Next time you switch on the TV you'll notice how many presenters and comedians use the position!

Notes

The very worst thing you can do is *read* your speech. Comic speeches need a touch of spontaneity, even if they've been prepared weeks in advance and you've been rehearsing for days. Reading a speech kills it dead. It makes the material seem dull, even if it isn't; it prevents eye contact, which is very important in breaking down the barrier between speaker and audience; and it destroys that important sense of a shared occasion, with speaker and audience responding to each other. On top of all that, the very fact that you are reading will indicate a lack of confidence — and your audience will be alerted to your discomfort and share in it.

That said, it's equally inadvisable to stand up and speak without the aid of any notes at all. Nerves can affect the memories of even professional speakers, so don't take any risks. Many people like to write their notes on postcards, using a single main heading and a couple of key phrases to prompt them. If you decide to do this, make sure that you number the cards clearly. You are bound to drop them if you don't, and reassembling them in the wrong order could create all kinds of chaos! Make sure, too, that you write your headings in large capital letters. When you're standing up and holding the cards at waist level you need to take in all the information at a single glance.

If cards seem too fiddly, write the main headings of your speech on a single sheet of paper, again using a few key words underneath to jog your memory. You'll know, from your rehearsals, those things you find difficult to remember and those which come easily. Jot down the point you get stuck on.

If you're going to use quotations then write them clearly on postcards and read them when the time comes. This ensures that you get them absolutely right and, far from doubting your competence, your audience will be impressed by your thoroughness.

Don't try to hide your notes. Simply use them as inconspicuously as possible. They prove that you have prepared a speech specially for the occasion and that you care about getting it right — and there's no need to be concerned about that.

On the day

On the day of your speech there are a number of simple precautions you can take to ensure that everything goes smoothly. Some of them may seem quite painfully obvious, but it's the most obvious things that are overlooked, particularly when you're nervous.

The most basic precaution of all is to ensure that you arrive at the right place at the right time. If you can get there a little early you'll be able to check out the acoustics and the arrangements. For example, will you be speaking from a podium or simply standing up at the table? Is there a microphone — and if so, do you know how to work it? If you've had time to think these things through you're less likely to be flustered by them.

Wear the right kind of clothes. You'll feel very uncomfortable if you turn up to a black-tie dinner in your second-best suit, so make sure that you're correctly dressed for the occasion and that everything about you is neat and tidy. You don't have to look like a fashion plate; you simply have to avoid anything distracting. It's a good idea to slip off to the cloakroom before your time comes and check your appearance. There's nothing like a tuft of hair sticking up from the top of your head to take the audience's mind off what you're saying.

While you're in the cloakroom, use the chance to go to the loo. Nerves affect different people in different ways, but it's better to be safe than sorry!

If you know that you tend to put your hands in your pockets while you're speaking, remove all your loose change and keys so that you're not tempted to jangle them. And make sure that you have a clean handkerchief somewhere about you. A scrap of well-used tissue isn't going to impress the audience when you need to blow your nose.

If you've worked hard to make the opening words of your speech interesting and funny, it would be a great shame to waste them by starting to speak while the audience is still talking and settling down in their seats. So wait for silence, even if it seems to take an age, and when you've obtained it start confidently and loudly so that everyone can hear what you have to say. Whatever you do, don't be hurried. Public speakers talk quite slowly and allow plenty of pauses so that the audience can respond. Take it at a leisurely pace, making sure that you're heard throughout the room, and you'll win the audience's attention immediately.

Some people, but only a *very* few, are at their best after a few drinks. Unless you know for certain that alcohol will improve your performance, it's probably best not to drink before you speak. Drinking tends to dull reactions and instil a false sense of confidence — and you need to be completely in control of yourself and your material if you're going to make a success of the occasion. Naturally, once you've made your speech and it's been greeted with success and laughter, you can reward yourself!

Whether you've been drinking or not, accidents do happen. Cope with them by acknowledging them and turning them to your advantage. For example, the speaker who knocked a glass of water over himself brought the house down with the throwaway line, 'Whoops! For a moment there I thought my trousers were on fire!' If someone in the audience drops a glass or falls off their chair, acknowledge it and pause for laughter rather than ploughing on as if nothing has happened. Although you have prepared your speech in advance, you should be aware of things happening around you and flexible enough to add a topical observation or funny remark if necessary. And the better-rehearsed and more at ease you are with your material, the more confident you'll be about including the odd spontaneous line.

If you follow these guidelines you really can't go far wrong. But here, as a last minute reminder, is a checklist of Do's and Don't's that will ensure that your delivery will do justice to all the work you've put into your speech.

Do's

1 Do rehearse your material.
2 Do work on your posture so that you look relaxed and comfortable.
3 Do prepare your notes and quotations carefully.
4 Do take simple precautions — like dressing correctly and checking your appearance.
5 Do anticipate any accidents and interruptions and be prepared for them.

Don't's

1 Don't read your speech.
2 Don't make any last-minute attempts to change your accent or your appearance.
3 Don't arrive late or unprepared.
4 Don't start your speech before everyone is ready.
5 Don't drink before you make your speech.

The Right Speech for the Right Occasion

The kind of speeches that sportsmen and women are most likely to have to make fall into two categories — after-dinner speeches and presentation speeches. Of course, you can use the jokes in this book for all kinds of purposes and not just for sporting events — but the most common sporting occasions when speeches are required are dinners and presentations.

After-dinner speeches

The after-dinner speaker doesn't have to propose toasts or give votes of thanks. He or she has only one job to perform, and that's to entertain the audience with an amusing speech for fifteen minutes or so after dinner. After-dinner speeches are difficult because the speaker is entirely alone when he stands up and he has to be entertaining for some time. But they can also be very rewarding, giving you a chance to show your skill in front of a willing audience.

Preparation is the most important ingredient of an after-dinner speech, because if you can't speak confidently and amusingly for the prescribed time you're stuck. The moment a speaker gets boring or begins to ramble, he has failed in his task — which is to entertain. So for the after-dinner speaker above all others, the section on preparation which you'll find earlier in this book is vital reading.

The second most important ingredient is wit. Although after-dinner speakers can include a serious moment in their material, no one will want to hear anything too downbeat. Keep it funny — and you'll find no shortage of suitable jokes and anecdotes in this book.

The final ingredient is brevity. However well your speech seems to be going, don't be tempted to extend it. A short but wickedly amusing speech that keeps the audience spellbound is far better than a longer but only occasionally funny performance. If you should find that your speech doesn't seem to be going down as well as you'd hoped, and if after ten minutes or so things haven't picked up, then cut it short, conclude properly, and sit down. If an audience is determined not to enjoy you then there's no point in ploughing doggedly on. However, if you've done your preparation properly and practised your delivery, you should have no reason to fear a cool reception.

Presentations

Sportsmen and women seem to spend much of their time participating in competitions of one sort or another, so if you're in line to win an award or to present a trophy you'll be pleased to hear that presentation speeches are very simple indeed.

The most important thing about this kind of occasion is to give the audience the basic information it needs to understand what's going on — and very little more than that. If you're presenting the award, try not to go on for too long about it. The spotlight should fall on the sportsman or woman, not on you. By all means, if you know the recipient and you have a personal story to tell about him, then do so — just don't take too long.

There's a simple formula to follow for making a presentation:

1. Name the trophy or award and some details about it:
   The Puddleton and District Challenge Cup was first awarded in 1966 as a memorial to that great Puddleton and England darts player, Norman Pippin.
2. State the reason for the presentation:
   Each year the Cup is awarded to the team that tops the Puddleton and District Darts League.
3. State what the recipient has done to deserve the award:
   This year's winning team, who were an astounding eleven points clear at the top of the league, are from the Ferret and Firkin in Lower Puddleton. Eric Flight, their captain, is here this evening to receive the trophy on their behalf.
4. Present the award:
   It gives me great pleasure, Eric, to present you with this magnificent cup. Congratulations to you and to all the team.

If you're to be the recipient at this kind of presentation your reply should follow this pattern:

1. Say thank you:
   Thank you, Mr Smith and all the organisers of the Puddleton and District Darts League, for this lovely cup.
2. Acknowledge the donors or origins of the prize:
   Every darts player in Puddleton knows all about that great player Norman Pippin, and I and my team are very honoured to have won this trophy.
3. Say what you intend to do with the award:
   We will hang this cup up in pride of place above the bar at the Ferret and Firkin, and every time we look at it we will remember Norman Pippin.

Don't try to be modest if you've won an award and don't say that you can't think what you've done to merit it. People will either agree with you or think you're telling lies.

Should you be asked to speak at any other kind of function, the general guidelines offered in this section will still apply.

Find out from the organisers how long you'll be required to speak for and if there is any specific task that they want you to fulfil. Then, using this book, assess the kind of speech the audience and the occasion will require, prepare it using the jokes and anecdotes in the next section, and practise it until you feel confident. And good luck!

Here's a final checklist of Do's and Don't's to be considered when you're working out what kind of speech is required for a particular occasion.

Do's

1 Do consider the audience and the occasion.
2 Find out how long you're expected to speak for and, if necessary, on what subject.
3 Find out what kind of speech you are required to make.
4 Research all the necessary information including names, titles and clubs.
5 Be prepared, be witty, be brief.

Don't's

1 Don't, if you're making a presentation, hog the limelight.
2 Don't forget to thank and acknowledge everyone who needs to be thanked and acknowledged.
3 Don't be over-effusive or falsely modest.
4 Don't forget to make clear notes of important names, facts and details.
5 Don't extend your prepared speech unless it's absolutely necessary.

PART TWO

The Material

In this part of the book you'll find all the material you need to create a comic speech for any kind of sporting occasion. There are jokes, quotes, facts and stories about almost every sport you can name, from football and cricket through to some more unusual recreations like croquet and curling, to ensure that you're never at a loss for a witty word.

Just Joking

Somewhere in this section you'll find the ideal jokes for your speech. When you find them, don't just lift them straight from the page. Adapt them so that they are completely relevant to the theme of your speech and add your own personal touch to the details. Last of all, rewrite them in your own words. By the time you've finished, you won't simply have borrowed them from this book — you'll have made them your own.

The coach of a local football team decided to take drastic measures to improve his players' performance. He lined up 11 dustbins on the pitch and told the players to dribble and pass the ball around them as if they were opponents. The dustbins won 3-2 after extra time.

Two men were trying to get into a crowded football stadium minutes before kick-off at a vital cup tie. One of them turned to the other and asked, 'Do you think we'll make it in?'

'I certainly hope so,' said the other. 'I'm the bloody ref!'

In the dying minutes of the jungle soccer match the grasshopper bounded down the left wing looking for the winning goal. Quick as a flash a defending rhinoceros lunged out at the insect and pulverised him into the ground. The crowd went berserk and the referee, a wise old owl, called the offending rhino over. 'Right,' said the owl sternly, 'you've killed a player — you're off!'

'But ref,' protested the rhino, sobbing, 'it was an accident. I only meant to trip him!'

What do you call a brain surgeon who specialises in treating footballers?
A chiropodist.

The Irish football manger was explaining tactics to his side before the big cup final. 'Sure,' he said, 'we just have to make sure that we equalise before the other team scores.'

Did you hear about the soccer player who was stopped by the police for drinking and driving? The police officer went up to him and asked him to blow up a balloon. 'Certainly,' said the driver, 'who's playing goalie?'

An Irish goalkeeper was explaining why he never stopped a shot. He said he thought that was why the net was there.

The Irish football team had a poor season. The only success they had was when the pools panel chose them for a win.

A Liverpool fan was asked how he thought his team would fare in an upcoming cup tie.
'I think it will be three each,' he said confidently.
'Really,' said the reporter, 'three each?'
'Indeed,' said the fan. 'Three for Kenny Dalglish, three for Ian Rush, three for ...'

The goalie was having another poor day and had just let in his fifth goal of the match. One fan in particular was disgusted by the performance.
'How much does that joker get paid for doing his job?' he shouted. A fellow fan thought it was about £100 a week.
'Good God,' cried the first man, 'I know a carpenter who'd board the whole goal up for a tenner!'

The opposition crowd were giving the hard-pressed goalie in front of them a lot of useful advice.

'Move out to it,' 'Punch it clear,' 'Stay on your line,' they kept yelling. In the dying moments of the game a dashing forward bore down on the goal and threatened to score. The crowd was partly hushed in the tension of the moment when one of them called out loud and clear, 'Use your own discretion!'

Animals can be great sports fans. A man went to the pub with his dog just as the soccer results came up on TV. When the commentator announced that the local side had lost heavily, the dog started an almighty howling and could not be comforted.

'What's got into the animal?' asked a fellow drinker.

'He supports Rovers,' explained the dog's owner, 'and he always gets upset when they lose.'

'What happens when they win?'

'I've no idea,' said the man. 'I've only had him for 18 months.'

After 25 years of loyal support, a soccer fan gave up going to watch his local team. He claimed it was a complete waste of toilet paper.

Did you hear about the patriotic Brazilian woman who named her first-born son after the entire national football team? Apparently she wasn't sure which was the father . . .

And did you hear about the soccer team that bought a highly-rated Jewish striker? They had to sell him because he wouldn't give anyone the ball.

A football fan was bragging about his team's abilities to his rather dim girlfriend. 'We've got a great team — no losses, no draws and not a single goal conceded.'

'That's fantastic,' said his girlfriend. 'How many

matches have they played?'

'None yet,' said the fan. 'The season starts next week.'

The local prison has a great football team but there's just one small problem — they don't play away games.

An occasional supporter of a struggling lower division soccer team rang up the ground on match day. 'When's the kick-off?' he asked.

'When can you make it?' came the reply.

Deep in the tropical jungle the army patrol was in a tight spot. Pursued by enemy troops they had to cross a crocodile-infested river. The first three volunteers who tried to swim across were eaten by the crocs. In desperation the sergeant turned to one of his men. 'Private Wilkins, swim across with this rope.'

At this the captain, who was standing nearby, protested that this was not cricket, as the Private had not volunteered for the duty. 'It's all right, sir,' said the sergeant. 'Private Wilkins is a Bristol soccer fan.'

And before the captain could reply, they saw the soldier swim safely across with the rope. The crocodiles glanced at him only briefly as he splashed under their noses. 'What do you mean, he's a Bristol soccer fan?' asked the baffled captain.

'Look at his bum, sir,' said the sergeant. Both men looked across the river and saw, neatly tattooed on Wilkin's buttocks, *Bristol Rovers for the Cup* and *Bristol City for the League*.

'I see what you mean,' said the captain. 'Not even a crocodile could swallow that!'

A life-long Merseyside soccer fan joined the committee of Everton Supporters Club. His friend was disgusted.
'What the hell have you done that for?' he demanded.
'You've always been a Liverpool fan like me!'

'I know, I know, but I've just been to the doctor and he says that I've only got three months to live.'

'What's that got to do with it?' his friend asked.

'Well, I thought that if someone had to lose a member I'd rather it was those bastards at Everton!'

A striker who had a good reputation as a scorer both on and off the field, finally decided to hang up his boots and look for new employment. Although he was keen to get a job he was also rather fussy about what he took on — and the Job Centre had a lot of trouble finding work for him. Eventually they called him up and asked him if he'd mind working abroad.

The player umm-ed and aah-ed and finally said he'd give it a go. Did they have any more details? The official said they didn't; all they knew was that it was well-paid work, with expenses, somewhere in the Middle East.

So the soccer player flew out and arrived at a luxurious palace in the middle of the desert, where he was greeted by the chief adviser to the local Arab prince.

'You are here,' said the adviser, 'to impregnate 80 maidens of my master's choice. For each of them you will be paid £20 plus expenses.'

'That's bloody typical of the Job Centre, isn't it?' the striker said bitterly. 'They send you all this way for two days' work!'

Two old pals, Bill and George, had been going to watch Spurs play for donkey's years. One season however, Bill failed to turn up at their usual spot on the terraces. This happened four times in a row, so George went round to see Bill and find out what was the matter.

'I'm very sorry, George,' said Bill, 'but over the summer I married a very randy woman. Just as I'm about to leave for the match she grabs hold of me and ...'

George was furious. 'Don't let yourself be bossed around like this,' he instructed. 'Next time she tries that move, pick her up, take off her knickers and spank her hard. Then go to the game.' Bill agreed to try this.

The next week there was another home match and, once again, Bill failed to turn up for it. George stormed round to his friend's house. 'Why didn't you do what I said?' he demanded.

'But I did!' Bill protested. 'When she grabbed me I put her over my knee, took down her knickers and ... Well, Spurs haven't been playing too well lately, have they?'

An elderly sportsman, in his day a great athlete and performer, loyally supported his local football side through thick and thin. Alas, their record became so bad that they were regarded by many as little more than a joke side.

As the old chap lay on his death bed he called the club president to him. 'Look here,' he gasped, 'I've been a loyal fan and always come up with the cash when you've needed it, haven't I?'

'Oh yes!' said the president. 'You've always been a faithful patron to us.'

'In that case,' the dying man said quietly,' would you do a favour for me?'

'Of course, what is it?'

'I'd be very grateful if the players would all gather on my grave when I'm gone, as a sign of remembrance.'

'That's a fine idea!' cried the club president. 'Where are you to be buried?'

'At sea,' the old man murmured. 'At sea ...'

Overheard on a golf course ...
GOLFER: My wife says golf is my religion.
FRIEND: Why's that?
GOLFER: I always play on Sundays.

A young priest was on the golf course — and having great difficulty in hitting the ball. Try as he might he couldn't make contact. In desperation he began to pray for help, but still he missed the ball. Once more he launched into a prayer as he lined up the shot yet again — but still the ball didn't move. His wily old caddie sidled up to him.

'Look, father,' he whispered, 'when you pray, keep your head down!'

To broaden his game a young American golfer came to Britain to try out some famous British courses. His first was St Andrews and he arrived on the first tee expecting a great game. He positioned himself, took a great swipe — and missed the ball. He tried again, took a huge swing, and missed once more. 'Gee,' he said, turing to his embarrassed companion, 'is this a tough course!'

Another poor golfer was hacking his way around a course, digging out divots as he went. About half-way round, as he removed another massive piece of turf as he tried to hit the ball, he turned suddenly to his caddie. 'You know,' he said, 'I'd move heaven and earth to break 100 this round.'

'Then you'd better try heaven,' muttered the caddie. 'That's all that's left.'

Members of a golf club were horrified to see one of their players carrying the dead body of his companion on his shoulders as he came back from the links. The club president spoke for all of them when he said, 'It must have been a terrible experience, having to bring him back dead like that.'

'Oh, it wasn't that so much,' said the surviving golfer. 'It was having to pick him up and put him down again between holes.'

Bored with heaven, Moses and Jesus came down to earth for a round of golf. On the third hole part of the fairway was covered by a lake and Jesus decided to make an approach shot over it with an eight-iron.

'You're nuts' said Moses. 'It will never reach.'

'What do you mean?' asked Jesus. 'Arnold Palmer uses

an eight-iron, doesn't he?' And with that he chipped the ball
— which fell straight into the lake. 'Okay, Moses,' said Jesus,
'just part the waters so that I can go and fetch the ball, will
you?'

'Forget it,' said Moses. 'I told you it wouldn't reach. Go
and do your walking on the water bit and fetch it yourself.'

Jesus refused and tried the shot again. 'If Arnold Plamer
can do it, so can I.' But once more the ball plonked straight
into the water. He tried again, but still couldn't make the far
shore. Finally, worried about the number of balls he was
losing, he agreed to fetch them himself and walked out onto
the water to collect them. Just then a bemused couple who
have been playing a few holes behind them came up and
stood near Moses. 'Who the hell does that guy think he is?'
asked the man, 'Jesus Christ?'

'No,' exclaimed Moses turning round. 'Ruddy Arnold
Palmer.'

Two men who have been golfing buddies for years were
finally parted by death. One night the ghost of the dead
golfer appeared to his friend. 'Good news,' said the ghost.
'They've got a fantastic course up here. The bad news is
you're booked in there first thing tomorrow!'

The colonel and the vicar were playing golf together for the
first time. Trying to drive off at the first tee the colonel
missed the ball. 'Sod it, missed!' he exclaimed. The vicar
took a very dim view of this language and told the colonel so.
But some minutes later the colonel failed with an important
putt and again exclaimed, 'Sod it!'

This time the vicar was really furious. 'I'm telling you,
Colonel, God is not mocked. If you can't control your
language something terrible will happen.'

His companion took the point and, deciding that
discretion is the greater part of valour, managed to control
himself. Then, on the final green, he found himself faced
with an easy six-inch putt to win the game. He approached it

carefully — and fluffed it. Then he began swearing like a demon.

Suddenly there was a tremendous thunderclap and the vicar was hit by a bolt of lightning, which killed him where he stood. In the distance the colonel heard a deep rumbling sound ... 'Sod it, missed!'

Did you hear about the Irish golfer who managed to lodge his ball in an oak tree? He used a tree iron to get it down.

After they had unsuccessfully searched the rough for nearly an hour and still not found their balls, the two young golfers were about to give up when an old lady, who had been watching them, came nervously over.

'Forgive me for intruding,' she said, 'but would it be against the rules if I were to tell you where the balls are?'

Two friends were enjoying a round of golf. One of them took from his bag a new invention which he had just come across — an unloseable golf ball.

'If you hit it into the trees or the rough and can't find it, you just yell and it will give out a little bleeping noise,' he explained.

'Is that all?' said the other man.

'Not at all. It can float on water and for evening games it glows in the dark.'

'That's terrific,' exclaimed the other man, impressed. 'Where did you buy it?'

'Buy it?' asked the first man. 'I didn't *buy* it, I found it!'

Two sports entrepreneurs were travelling in Africa when they were shown a remarkable sight by the local witch doctor — a gorilla which could play golf. The African explained that he had taught the creature how to hit the ball from birth, and with its natural strength it could propel the ball for miles. The two Americans, sensing a great publicity coup, paid the witch doctor a huge sum to allow them to take the gorilla back to the USA. After a few strings were pulled, the gorilla was entered for the US Open — and as it arrived on the course it caused the desired stir. The animal lined up on the first tee, a par five hole, and hit a magnificent shot which travelled 450 yards down the fairway to lie right next to the hole.

The crowd were amazed and watched delightedly as the gorilla walked to the hole and, taking a putter from the caddie, prepared for its next shot. The animal took aim, swung the putter . . . and hit the ball another 450 yards to the next hole.

A golf news item: 'As in previous years, the evening concluded with a toast to the new president, in champagne provided by the retiring president, drunk as usual at midnight.'

Two Jewish golfers decided to go on a golfing tour of South America. Alas, things began to go disastrously wrong from their very first day on tour, and after serious problems at customs they found themselves in front of a firing squad at dawn.

As they were being tied to the posts the captain came up to the first golfer and asked if he had a last request. He said that he hadn't. The captain then went to the second golfer and asked if he had a last request. Instead of replying, the man spat in his face.

'Stop it, Arnie,' whispered his golfing companion. 'Do you want to get us in trouble or something?'

A young girl from a poor country family was taken to visit rich relatives, a wealthy middle-class couple. As she entered the house she saw two old golf balls lying in a box.

'What are those?' she asked.
'They're golf balls,' her uncle explained. The girl took note of this information, and about a year later when she visited

once more she noticed that there were now four golf balls in the box.

'Oh look, everyone!' she exclaimed. 'Uncle's shot another golf!'

A young British golfer on the world circuit went to play in a small Arab state in a little-known tournament. One day, after finishing a round, he met a fellow countryman who was working there in an oil refinery.

'What do you do with all your spare time out here?' asked the golfer. 'You must go out of your mind with boredom.'

'Not at all,' replied his new friend. 'We have a great time. For instance, today if Tuesday when they bring in the booze. Want to come round for a piss-up tonight?' The golfer explained that he rarely drank.

'Hang on until Thursday, then' said the oil worker. 'That's the day they bring in the women.' The golfer went red and said that he wasn't interested. 'You're not gay, are you?' asked the man.

'Certainly not,' said the golfer indignantly. 'The very thought of it disgusts me.'

'In that case,' said the oil man, 'you'd better not hang around for Saturday night . . .'

Two anglers, who'd established a bet of £30 on who would catch the first fish, were sitting side by side on the river bank. Suddenly one of them saw his float twitch, but he got so excited that he managed to fall in the water.

'Christ!' shouted his companion in disgust. 'If you're going to dive in after the buggers the bet's off!'

An angler was lying seriously ill in hospital with injuries to his legs when the doctor came up. 'First the bad news,' said the doctor. 'You're going to lose both legs.'

The angler groaned. 'And what's the good news, Doctor?'

'A patient two beds along wants to buy your wellies.'

41

Two likely lads went fishing one day. As teatime approached one asked the other, 'What did you bring for supper then?'

'Let's see.' He looked in his bag and reported, 'Two bottles of whisky, a bottle of rum, a crate of beer and three lettuce sandwiches.'

'Good God,' said the other, 'what are you going to do with all that food?'

Two anglers were sitting on a bank waiting for a bite. One said, 'I pity that poor Noah. He was never able to fish.'

'Why not?' asked the other.

'With only two worms?'

The mourners were following the coffin of an angler's wife through the cemetery. On top of it lay a long rod and some tackle.

'That's odd,' said one mourner to his bereaved friend. 'I didn't know that your Elsie was interested in fishing.'

'She wasn't,' said the widower. 'I've got a match at three o'clock.'

A scruffy young boy was sitting on the kerb, apparently fishing from a rusty old bucket. A kindly old man came up and asked him what he was doing.

'I'm fishing,' said the child.

'How silly of me not to realise,' said the old chap, feeling sorry for the boy. He tossed a coin into the bucket. 'And how many have you caught today?'

'You're the fourth so far,' said the boy.

FIRST ANGLER: I hooked a mermaid the other day: What a figure!

SECOND: Really? What were the measurements?

FIRST ANGLER: 36-22 and 80 pence a pound.

A man met his old fishing pal walking down the street, his arm in a sling and using crutches.

'What happened?' he asked.

'It was my wife,' said his friend. 'She found out about that fishing trip I went on.'

'So?'

'She found out I didn't go on it.'

Two men were fishing at sea when one of them hooked a mermaid. He hauled her aboard, examined her beautiful body for a moment, then threw her back into the waves.

'Why?' asked his friend.

'How?' he replied.

'I've had terrible news,' said a man in the pub. 'My wife has just run off with my best mate.'

'That's awful,' sympathised the man next to him. 'What'll you do?'

'I suppose I'll have to go fishing without him.'

A fisherman's story . . . 'I caught the most marvellous pike,' said one fisherman to another. 'You should have seen it — ten inches.'

'Ten inches? That's nothing, I've caught plenty that size,' his friend replied.

'Between the ears?'

Despite hours of preparation the angler failed to get a single nibble all day, so on the way home he went into the pub to drown his sorrows. Sitting there and drinking more than was good for him, he became more and more angry with the world in general. As he stood to leave his eyes fell on a massive stuffed fish in a glass case above the bar.

'And whoever caught that fish,' he yelled drunkenly, 'is a bloody liar!'

43

An Englishman went to Ireland to do a spot of fishing. He came upon a suitable spot by a river and prepared to wade into the murky water with his wellies. But before he did so he asked a farmer who was mending a fence nearby if the water was shallow.

'Sure, that water's quite shallow,' came the reply. With this the angler walked straight into the river — and found himself up to his neck.

'You said it was shallow!' he cried as he waded out, completely soaked.

'To be sure,' said the farmer, 'and I thought it was. It only comes up to the waists of the ducks, and they're only six inches tall!'

Did you hear about the Irish Test match that had to be abandoned the other day? Both teams turned up in white.

A batsman's wife was very upset after listening to the cricket commentary on Radio Three. However, she was later reassured that the commentator had actually said that the wicketkeeper had whipped her husband's *bails* off ...

A young boy rushed up to a spectator at a Yorkshire cricket match. 'Dad, Dad,' he yelled, 'I've got terrible news for you. Jimmy's got tetanus, grandma's dead and mother's run off with the postman!'

The man looked down at his son. 'Ay, lad, and I've got even worse news for thee — Hutton's out!'

The batsman sidled up to the bowler. 'Ere, mate,' he whispered, 'how about bowling a nice slow one I can hit? My wife's over there watching, see?'

'I'd be glad to help,' said the bowler, 'but I don't reckon you'll hit her from here.'

Just as the bowler was about to run up to bowl, the batsman put out his arm to stop him, stood bolt upright and took off his cap. Puzzled by this behaviour the bowler and fielders looked round and saw a hearse slowly drawing past the ground. They all joined in this tribute and after a minute everyone resumed training.

At the end of the over the bowler went up to the batsman. 'I must say,' he said, 'I thought that was a very touching and respectful gesture. Very touching indeed.'

'Well it was the least I could do,' said the batsman. 'After all, we were married for 25 years.'

Just before a vital cricket match a Cambridge college side discovered that they were one man short. They scrounged around and managed to find a brilliant local player who was, unfortunately, not very bright.

'Make sure that the opposition don't get to speak to you for too long and you'll be all right,' the skipper told him. 'No one will notice.'

Next day the game went ahead and, sure enough, the new recruit scored a splendid hundred for the college team — and won them the match. During drinks afterwards both teams got chatting and the opposition skipper came over to congratulate the young player on his fine innings. Then he asked what he was studying at university. The young man racked his brains for a moment, then inspiration struck. 'I'm studying sums,' he said.

The manager of a potentially rowdy cricket tour made a strict rule about keeping a diary on his team's behaviour. One day the captain of the team had a few drinks too many and the manager duly recorded, 'Captain drunk today.' When the captain complained he defended himself saying, 'It was the truth and I had to write it down.' A few days later the captain asked to make an entry in the diary. The manager, anxious to be fair, agreed — and was appalled to read, 'The manager was sober today.' Furious, he rushed to the captain and demanded an explanation. 'Well,' said the captain, 'it was true and I had to write it down.'

The tearaway fast bowler flew in to the wicket and hurled a delivery which hit the nervous young batsman plumb in front of the stumps. Everyone appealed loudly but to the bowler's amazement the umpire declared it not out. So the bowler tried again and delivered an even faster ball which once more only failed to bowl the batsman by hitting his pads. Again, the umpire turned down the appeal.

The bowler, furious by this time, took an even longer run, stormed in and bowled a ball that knocked all three stumps clean out of the ground. The bowler immediately turned around on the umpire. 'Nearly had him that time,' he snarled.

Ireland were playing England at Twickenham and the usual contingent of fans came over from the Emerald Isle for the weekend. One fan, staying at a London hotel, called the maid to his room to complain.

'It's my sleeping bag,' he said. 'I can't find the zip.'

'I'm not surprised,' said the maid sharply. 'It's a duvet.'

As expected, the crucial rugby match between the Archbishop's XV and the Pope's XV proved to be a finely-balanced contest. The Archbishop's side had all the tries, while the Pope's team had all the conversions.

A beery rugby player got home after a lengthy session in the pub with the team. 'Is my dinner warm?' he asked his wife as he burst into the bedroom where she was lying asleep.

'Only if the dustbin's on fire,' she growled.

An Irish rugby player visiting London for the weekend phoned the Salvation Army. 'Do you really save fallen women?' he asked.

'Yes, that's part of our work,' said a kindly voice on the other end of the phone.

'Great,' said the Irishman. 'Would you save a couple for me on Friday night?'

A vicar stood watching his first-ever rugby match. Pretty soon things got a bit nasty and at a line-out one forward turned round and punched the other right in the balls. The vicar turned to his companion on the touchline and said, puzzled, 'I wonder, can you tell me . . . How did one player know the other was a bar steward?'

A superstitious fly-half went to consult a fortune-teller about the prospects for the next day's crucial rugby match. 'Tell me, what do you see in the crystal ball?' he asked her.

'I see a large white van,' said the woman.

'What else?'

'I can also see a man standing there in a white coat.'

'This doesn't sound too good,' said the player. 'Is there anything else?'

'Yes, I see you lying on a stretcher.'

'That's it,' said the fly-half, 'I'm not playing tomorrow, it's far too dangerous.' And despite great attempts by the rest of the team to get him to play, he stayed at home all day. Inevitably they lost.

Later that evening he decided that it was safe enough to venture out and made his way to the pub. On his way he was run over by an ice-cream van.

Sign in an Irish rugby club: 'We open at 9.30 a.m. and close at 11 p.m. on the dot. If you still haven't had enough to drink in that period the proprietors feel you can't have been trying.'

An Irish weightlifter was given a dope test at the World Championships — and passed.

Did you hear about the unfortunate hurdler? He mistook the high hurdles for the low hurdles and shattered his personal best.

And have you heard about the unfortunate athlete who shot himself shortly after winning the Olympic marathon? It was a false start.

The organisation EXIT has arranged two new events for the next Olympics — catching the javelin and heading the shot.

Did you hear about the cyclist who collapsed and died after winning the Tour de France! It wasn't the race that killed him — it was the lap of honour.

Darts players are famous for their interest in food and drink. The girlfriend of one large player said one night, 'Say something soft and sweet to me, darling.'
'Black Forest Gateau,' he whispered.

A well-oiled darts player staggered home one evening to be met in the hall by his furious wife. 'I demand an explanation — and I want the truth,' she shouted.
'Well make up your mind,' said the darts player.

One darts player to another: 'Would it cause problems if you went home late and drunk again tonight?'
'Not really. I was planning to have my front teeth out, anyway.'

'No swimming on a full stomach,' the swimming coach warned his team after lunch. Five minutes later he returned to the pool — to find them all swimming on their backs.

A sportsman went to the doctor, saying he thought his diet wasn't healthy enough and was making him ill. 'What do you eat in the mornings?' asked the doctor.
'Snooker balls,' said the sportsman. 'Two reds, a yellow, and a brown.'
'Lunch?'
'Two pinks, a red and a blue.'
'Tea?'
'A black and three reds.'
'It's obvious what the matter is,' said the doctor.
'What is it?' asked the sportsman.
'You're not getting enough greens.'

A travelling salesman's car broke down and stranded him in a remote little town, so he booked himself into the only hotel for the night. It was a seedy old place; the TV was broken and there was no one in the bar, but as he passed one door he noticed an old snooker table and decided to have a solitary game.

When he asked about balls and cue the barman handed over a set of balls so old and dirty that they were a uniform grey in colour. 'How do you expect me to play with these?' the guest asked. 'I can't even tell the white from the black.'

'That's all right,' said the barman. 'You'll soon get to know them by their shape.'

Two Irish snooker players were on a national tour giving exhibition matches. One evening, with no game to play, they found themselves stuck in a small country town with nothing to do. Patrick suddenly got up and left the pub in which they were sitting, declaring that he was going to confession. Mick told him he was mad, but off Patrick strolled.

In the confessional, he told the priest that he'd made love to a local girl. Naturally concerned, the priest quizzed him as to who this girl was — but Patrick refused to say and eventually left.

'Well, Pat,' said his friend when he returned to the pub, 'did you get absolution?'

'Indeed I didn't,' said Patrick. 'But I got some useful names and addresses!'

Bill was pleased to discover that one of the new secretaries in his department was a good-looker and that she seemed to be giving him the eye. One night they both worked late, and he offered to take her for a meal — and soon one thing led to another and they ended up in bed at her place. By this time it was pretty late and Bill was worried about what his wife would say, so he rubbed some chalk into his hands, took a slug of whisky and made his way back home to face the music.

'And where do you think you've been?' were his wife's first words as he entered the house.

'If you must know, I've just had sex with the new secretary,' Bill muttered.

'Rubbish,' said his wife. 'You've got chalk all over you and you reek of whisky — you've been playing bloody snooker down at the club again!'

Did you read about the man who had some bad luck with the horses the other day? He put £200 on the Grand National winner each way. Unfortunately the bookie insisted that the horse had only gone *one* way.

Just this morning a table tennis player was taken to hospital after trying to jump the net at the end of the game ...

A famous fox-hunting man was at a party — and being lectured by a large lady who objected to the sport on grounds of its cruelty. For half an hour she went on about poor innocent foxes being torn apart by savage hounds, until finally the hunter's patience deserted him.

'Madam,' he cried, 'I can't agree with you. I have killed many foxes, but I have always spared them the ultimate cruelty — not one did I bore to death!'

An expert hunter took his young son out shooting for the day. Soon the man spotted a pheasant breaking cover, aimed, fired, and the bird fell with a thud at their feet. 'That was a waste of a shot,' said the boy. 'It would have died in the fall, anyway.'

Irish TV got into a terrible mix-up with their programme schedules the other day. They ordered ten episodes of Pot Black thinking that it was a cookery series.

A Chinese athlete recently set a terrific record for running over mountain, vallies, woods and swimming across lakes, but it was all in vain. He was recaptured.

The young boxer, facing his first fight, turned nervously to his opponent as they entered the ring. 'It's a long way from the changing rooms to here, isn't it?' he asked, trying to make conversation.

'It sure is,' said his massive opponent. 'But you don't have to worry about it. You won't be walking back.'

A young karate expert seemed set for a promising career in the Royal Marines. However things went wrong on his first day when he saluted — and knocked himself out.

'I've seen a wonderful game,' said the bowls umpire as he ushered the two players off the green, 'but that wasn't it.'

A pigeon-racer was having problems with his birds and wrote to the sport's board of control for advice.

'Dear Sir,' he wrote, 'I have difficulty with my pigeons. Every day I go up into the loft and find one or two of them lying stiff on the floor with their feet pointing up. Can you tell me what is wrong?'

He waited and waited for a reply, and eventually a letter came back from the board. 'Dear Sir,' it read, 'Your pigeons are dead.'

Did you hear about the failed sky-diver? He kept on missing the ground ...

There was a sad story about an unlucky driver in the last Irish Grand Prix. He was two legs ahead and within sight of the finishing line when he clocked up 50,000 miles and had to make a pit stop to change his oil.

And then there was the tale of the poor Irish racing driver who had to stop 25 times in another Grand Prix. Once for petrol, twice for tyres, and 22 times to ask for directions.

An unfit man went to see the doctor and was told to take up jogging. 'You should run at least ten miles a day,' said the doctor. Two weeks later the man rang up the doctor to tell him he was feeling much better. 'That's excellent,' said the doctor. 'But you'd better come in and see me this afternoon so I can examine you properly.'

'But that's impossible,' said the man, 'I'm 150 miles away!'

A sportsman returned home after a lengthy tour of the world to find his wife pregnant. 'It can't be true,' he insisted to the doctor. 'I've been away for nearly twelve months!'

'I'm afraid,' said the doctor sympathetically, 'it's what we know in the profession as a grudge pregnancy.'

'What does that mean?'

'Put simply — someone had it in for you.'

The traditional Scottish sport of curling has had its fair share of dramatic moments. A player once fell through thawing ice as he was playing a vital shot. However, he managed to send the stone on its way before he fell in and as he sank he had made a near-perfect shot.

'Make sure that you put that on my headstone,' he called out as he disappeared under the icy waters.

A Jewish skier was enjoying a spell in the mountains one day when he got stuck in a drift. Soon the mountain rescue team were out looking for him. Night was beginning to close in as cries of 'Red Cross! Red Cross!' reached the freezing skier's ears.

'Oh, go away,' he yelled back to them. 'I already gave twice this year.'

Strong Stuff

*Although one of the first rules of speechmaking is not to use any material that will offend your audience, there are some occasions when a saucy joke will go down well — and you'll find some in this section. There's just one thing to remember. If **you** don't feel comfortable with the material don't use it, because your audience will sense your unhappiness. Be guided by your own taste and, if in doubt, leave it out.*

An ageing British soccer manager came out to the Middle East to do some coaching. When he arived he discovered that his home was to be a small all-male village in the centre of the desert. As he was exploring the place on his first day he came across a small hut in a quiet corner in which was kept a scruffy, ill-looking camel. He asked his companion what the camel was for and the man looked rather apologetic. 'Er,' he muttered, 'it's for the men when they get desperate. We're a long way from any women, you know.'

The soccer manager was horrified. 'That's the most disgusting thing I've ever heard,' he said, and stormed out.

The months passed and though the coaching went well the manager began to get very lonely. One day he could resist it no more. He went to the hut where the camel was kept, pulled up a stool and was just undoing his trousers when his earlier companion rushed in.

'No, no! You've made a big mistake,' he screamed. 'We use the camel for riding to the nearest brothel!'

The team's star footballer had mysteriously lost form only weeks before the cup final. The skipper after much questioning, learned that the player was depressed about his lack of sex life. This puzzled the captain because the striker was a fine athlete and very attractive to women. Again, after much probing, he found out that the player had a very strong foot fetish and that when it came to the crunch, few women were prepared to put up with his demands.

Desperate to satisfy his best player, the skipper dug deep into his own pocket and sent him to Soho where he would find someone who would tolerate him.

A week or two later a London doctor approached a nurse and said, 'It's amazing, Nurse Jenkins, but this job has its surprises even after 25 years. Only today I had two unique cases — a soccer player with VD of the big toe and a prostitute with athlete's foot of the fanny!'

There was a young soccer player who insisted on turning out for his club only a day before his wedding. Sure enough, within ten minutes of the kick-off he was kicked in the crotch and carried off to hospital. There surgeons carried out repairs and did him up in splints and bandages. The wedding itself went smoothly enough and the newlyweds arived at their honeymoon hotel. The bride, stunning but shy and wearing only a transparent negligee, lay down on the bed. 'Here I am, darling,' she whispered, 'untouched by man.'

'I can do even better than that,' said the bridegroom as he removed his pants. 'Look, mine hasn't even been unwrapped!'

Moira had been a golf widow to her Scots husband for many years — until one day he died and she became the real thing. His body was cremated and Moira took the ashes home with her in a box. In the solitude of her home, she opened the box and began talking to her husband in a way she had never been able to when he was alive. 'For years you kept me under control. You were too mean to buy me things for the house, you refused to let me play golf and you made unreasonable sexual demands on me.'

'Well,' she continued, 'now you've gone — and I'm going to have a new washing-machine, a dish-washer and carpets. And I've made friends with the president of the golf club and I'm going to play a round of golf every day.'

'And as,' she said, holding the box closer to her face, 'for that bloody blow job you were always pestering me for — *whoosh!'*

A bad golfer is like a bad lover — several strokes of foreplay, then he fails to enter the hole.

The Scottish rugby club president had just taken on the club's star player, a fly-half, at his firm. Several weeks went by, and someone asked the president how the player, who was having a brilliant season, was getting on at work. 'Well he's seduced my daughter, made love to my wife and touched up my secretary,' said the president.

'How awful — what are you going to do?'

'Don't worry,' said the president sternly. 'If I catch him fiddling the petty cash I'll be down on him like a ton of bricks!'

A powerful rugby forward seemed to lose his strength and had to be dropped from the side. Greatly perturbed at this loss of form, the team manager sent him to see a psychiatrist. The shrink asked the man about his dreams.

'Every night it's the same, Doctor,' he said. 'I dream I'm at Paddington with a wheelbarrow of concrete blocks and I have to push them to Maida Vale. I wake up knackered.'

The psychiatrist said that he could help. The player was to take a pill that he would prescribe. If he took it each night he would soon feel better. The player went home and took the pills and continued to have the same dream, except that before long the psychiatrist appeared and pushed the wheelbarrow to Maida Vale for him. So the rugby player woke up more refreshed than usual and pretty soon was able to regain his place in the team.

Naturally the whole club was impressed by this quick return to form and so when another player, a fly-half, began to play poorly they sent him to see the psychiatrist too. The fly-half explained his dreams. 'It's like this, Doctor. Each night I'm in this amazing bedroom when 12 lovely women walk in. They climb all over me, and they're so attractive that I make love to them all. When I wake up I'm exhausted!' Again the psychiatrist prescribed the pills, but this time the player's form got worse, not better. The skipper asked what was wrong. The fly-half said that now the shrink appeared and took six of the girls off his hands.

'Yes,' agreed the skipper. 'I suppose six girls are still rather a lot.'

'You don't understand,' said the player. 'When I get outside, having finished with the girls, I find some bugger's left a wheelbarrow full of bricks that I have to wheel all the way to Maida Vale!'

A young housewife was confessing her secrets to a good friend. 'Some very odd things have been happening lately. On Tuesday this young athlete who was jogging past the house knocked on the door and asked, 'Is your husband Jack in?' I said no, so this chap grabbed me, took me upstairs and made love to me for hours.'

'On Wednesday it was the same thing. He knocked on the door, asked if Jack was in and when I said no, took me upstairs again. Yesterday, exactly the same — "Is Jack in?" No, I say, so we go upstairs and make love all morning. There's just one thing I don't understand.'

'What's that?' asked the amazed friend.

'What on earth does he want with our Jack?'

A Scottish athlete travelled over to Athens for a major championship and one evening went to a brothel. He asked for one of the girls in particular, had sex, then gave her £200. The next evening he was back again for a repeat performance with the same girl and for the same sum. For two more nights he repeated the routine. On the fourth night the girl, who had thoroughly enjoyed her encounters with him, begged him to return the next night.

'I can't,' said the Scot. 'My events have ended and I must go back to Glasgow. Anyway, I know your uncle there. He gave me £800 to give to you.'

Three Olympic athletes, all fine specimens of young manhood, were boasting about their prowess in bed. The German said he made love to his wife once every hour, on the hour, making eight or nine times a night. The others asked what his wife said to him in the morning.

'Ah, she says it was wunderbar, wunderbar!'

Next the Frenchman described how he made love to his mistress. 'Many times I make love to her. Then I rest and do it again and again. Perhaps twenty times in one night,' he boasted. The other two asked what she said to him in the morning.

'She says I am magnifique, simply magnifique.'

Finally it was the turn of the Englishman to describe how he made love to his wife. 'I just do it once,' he said simply.

'Once?' the other two cried in unison. 'What does your wife say in the morning?'

'I think you'd better get off now and give us both a rest.'

One morning a young athlete was up in court for stealing a bike. The magistrates told him to describe what happened.

'Well, your worships,' he began, 'I was jogging through the woods when this pretty young girl came up on a bike and persuaded me to sit down with her. I wasn't tired, but I did so. Then she took off her blouse, though it wasn't very warm, then she said, "Kiss me," so I did.'

'And then?' the magistrate asked.

'Then she lifted up her skirt and told me I could have anything I wanted.'

'And then?' asked the magistrate.

'So I took her bike.'

Sporting Life

Sporting stories say a great deal about the human condition, and you're bound to find one in this collection that will illustrate your speech perfectly. After all, if life is a game of cricket, as Lord Dorset said in 1777, it's no wonder that the world's a mess. How many people do you know who know the rules of cricket?

The legendary Everton forward Dixie Dean was a formidable header of the ball. Once he was walking down a street on the day of the big local derby when he saw the Liverpool goalie on the other side of the road. Out of courtesy Dean nodded his head to him — and legend has it that the goalie, out of habit, dived to make the 'save' . . . straight through the window of a shop.

In the days when the two lower soccer divisions were divided regionally into North and South, Liverpool had just been relegated into Division Two and were having a bad season. During one game their centre forward rose to head the ball but instead gave his head a nasty smack on the cross bar. He was immediately carried off and taken to the Royal Northern Hospital. When the striker eventually came round he was disorientated and called out to the nurse, 'Where the hell am I?'

'It's okay,' she replied comfortingly, 'you're in the Northern.'

'Blimey,' said the concussed footballer, 'we weren't long in the Second, were we?'

The football club chairman made a morale-boosting visit to his team, who had not been doing too well of late. As he arrived in the changing rooms he was peeved to find only four players and a ball-boy waiting to hear him. He turned on the manager who was cowering behind him. 'Did you tell them all that I was coming?' he asked fiercely.

'Oh no,' said the manager in a whisper. 'Someone must have leaked it.'

Ipswich Town had just beaten Arsenal in breathtaking style in the FA Cup final. The club's president, Lady Blanche Cobbold, was asked by an official if she wanted to go and meet the guest of honour — Mrs Thatcher.

'Frankly,' replied Lady Cobbold, 'I'd much rather have a gin and tonic.'

Bill Shankley, the former Liverpool manager, was utterly dedicated to football. He was once asked by an impertinent journalist if it was true that he had taken his wife to see a reserve team match as a wedding anniversary treat.

'It's not true at all,' said Shankley vehemently. 'That's a lie.' Then he paused and added. 'It was her birthday.'

The secretary of an Irish football club asked his wife to take a presentation tankard to the engravers and dictated the inscription to her. She wrote it down and handed it over with the tankard. Unfortunately the inscription had been written on a shopping list and the tankard was returned bearing the words 'One bottle of shoe cleaner and a pair of white laces.'

Few journalists have ever got the better of Bill Shankley. His team was once beaten 5-1 in a European cup match. A cocky reporter put it to Shanks that he had to admit his team had been well and truly smashed this time.

Shankley turned on the young man. 'We canna play football against defensive teams,' he said. And he meant it.

After his team's famous and unexpected win over arch-rivals Manchester United in 1968, Colin Bell, the Manchester City player, was asked how he felt.

'Chuffed,' came the simple reply.

The newspaper man persisted. 'Look, this was a fantastic victory and you played a blinder. How do you really feel?'

Bell paused and then said quietly, 'Very chuffed.'

Fred, an ageing football fan, finally achieved his ambition of going to Wembley to see his team play in the Cup Final. He was very distressed to see that the two seats next to him were empty only minutes before kick-off. Eventually, seconds before the start, a man raced up and took one of the seats.

Fred took no time in engaging him in conversation. 'I think it's scandalous,' he told his new companion. 'I've tried for tickets in the past and never got one, and what do I find when I eventually get here but an empty seat next to me.'

'I agree with you entirely,' said his neighbour. 'The truth is that the other seat was for my wife, who sadly died three days ago.'

Fred was only slightly taken aback. 'Well, you could have given the ticket away to a friend or relative.'

'No chance,' said his neighbour. 'They're an unsporting family. They've all gone to the funeral instead.'

There was once on the golf circuit an explosive young player called Tommy 'Thunder' Bolt. Although he was usually a happy guy, he was liable to explode if things went wrong on the links. People took bets not on how many shots he'd take but how many clubs he'd have left when he finished a round. He once came to the final hole and asked his young caddie what club was needed for a difficult tee shot. 'A six-iron,' replied the caddie.

'What?' exploded Bolt, 'A six-iron? But it's more than 200 yards to the flag! How can you say it's a six-iron?'

'Because that's all that's left in the bag,' sighed the caddie.

An Australian golfer mis-hit his tee shot and, cursing, went to fetch it from the river. Imagine his surprise when he found the ball had hit and killed a two-pound fish! The lucky golfer took it home and had the fish for his lunch.

The foxy Argentinian golfer Roberto de Vicenzo fooled his Australian companion Noel Ratcliffe as they played a practice round before the British Open. They were just about to tee-off on one hole, a dog-leg with a massive row of trees in the corner when de Vicenzo said, 'When I was your age, I used to hit the ball over those trees.' Naturally Ratcliffe could not resist the challenge and tried to smash the ball over the top of them. But he didn't make it and drove right into the thicket.

'But then,' finished the wily old pro, 'those trees had only just been planted.'

Australian cricket commentator Alan McGilvray, once put his foot in it when he described the fate of Aussie test batsman Kim Hughes. 'It's been a weekend of delight and disappointment for Hughes,' said McGilvray to millions of listeners. 'His wife presented him with twins yesterday ... and a duck today.'

W.G. Grace, the master batsman, was not one to keep quiet about his crowd-pulling potential. Playing on a tour of Australia, he faced a young bowler from a local district team. Amazingly, the very first ball beat his guard and knocked over the stumps. Bowler and fielders celebrated. However, Grace stayed his ground and replaced the bails.

'I never could play the practice ball,' he said casually, taking guard. Not surprisingly the bowler was not prepared to leave the matter there and demanded that Grace leave the crease.

'Now look here,' retorted the master, 'these people have paid to see me bat, not you bowl — so let's get on with it!'

The Yorkshire spinner Hedley Verity, normally a difficult bowler to hit, was once collared by a big South African hitter. The batsman clobbered him for two sixes and three fours in one over. At the end of it one of Verity's colleagues came over to him. 'It's okay, Hedley,' said the player. 'Reckon you've got him in two minds.'

'How do you mean, in two minds?' puzzled the spinner.

'He doesn't know whether to hit you for four or six.'

At one time in cricket the bowling team could claim a new ball when 100 runs were on the board instead of after a set number of overs. Once, an Australian touring team in India were being introduced to important local dignitaries. 'This is the Maharajah of this area,' said the team manager as he introduced him to the side. 'He is one of the wealthiest men in the world — and he also has 199 wives.'

'Crikey,' remarked one of the players. 'One more and he'd need a new ball.'

That tough cricketer Brian Close was fielding close to the wicket at short leg when the batsman produced a full-blooded pull shot and the ball hit the fielder hard on the side of this face. Amazingly it flew straight up in the air and the batsman was caught at slip.

'My God,' said a worried fielder going to check up on Close. 'What would have happened if he'd hit you right between the eyes?'

'In that case,' growled Close, 'the bugger would have been caught at cover.'

John Wisden, the founder of the famed cricketer's almanack and no mean cricketer, was once sailing across the Atlantic as part of a tour. A furious gale blew up and the seas were running very high. Turning to a colleague he said, 'What this pitch needs is ten minutes with a heavy roller.'

During the festival week of cricket at Weston-Super-Mare, the visiting team, Surrey, stayed at a large local hotel. The Surrey skipper, Percy Fender, pointed out to the management that there wasn't 'enough room to swing a cat, in his bedroom. 'I'm very sorry, sir,' said the manager. 'I didn't realise you'd come to Weston for the cat-swinging.'

The prolific Hampshire batsman Phil Mead found a novel way of getting out. His captain, Lord Tennyson, relying on Mead to occupy the crease, would take a leisurely bath in the pavilion while his team batted. He would get dressed and put on his pads before summoning a Post Office messenger boy to dictate a message.

A few minutes later a telegram would be hurried out to the middle with an 'urgent message' for one of the batsman. It would simply read, 'Mead. Get out at once. Tennyson.'

Those two great cricketing stalwarts Bomber Wells and Sam Cook were batting for Gloucestershire when they made an almighty mess of going for a run.

'Call, Bomber!' cried Sam.

'Heads!' replied his companion.

Many forget that W.G. Grace was a respected doctor besides being a cricketing legend. One day a timid man turned up at the surgery and asked, 'Is the doctor in?'

'Of course he's in,' snapped the assistant. 'He's been batting since Monday.'

The Duke personally organised his side's annual circet match with a neighbouring village team. The game was played at his own grounds and took place in perfect surroundings. The Duke had just come in to bat when his partner, wanting to give his Lordship a chance, called for a quick single. Alas, half-way down the pitch the Duke tripped and fell, leaving him stranded helpless and yards from the crease.

The opposing wicket keeper whipped off the bails and loudly appealed, 'Howzat?' The umpire was the Duke's own butler, drafted in as a late replacement. Naturally the butler was in something of a dilemma and paused to give thought about what to do. Eventually, after what seemed an age, he lifted himself up to his full height and grandly declared, 'His Lordship is not in.'

Fred Price, the Middlesex wicket keeper, had just taken a record seven catches in one innings. A woman approached him afterwards in the bar and said, 'Oh, Mr Price, I was so excited by your wicket keeping today I nearly fell out of the balcony.'

'And had you done so, madam,' said Fred, 'on today's form I'd have caught you!'

The Fijians, entertaining rugby players, were often amused by the interest their 'humble' origins caused. On the 1970 tour of Britain a novice journalist asked one of the massive Fijian forwards how they celebrated after a game in their country. 'The winners eat the losers,' he replied.

Players on the 1980 Lions tour of South Africa were doubtless encouraged by this piece of advice from their coach, Noel Murphy, before a game. 'Right, lads,' he said, 'I want 80 per cent concentration for 100 minutes.'

The Blantyre rugby club from Malawi were about to make a tour to Mauritius when the secretary of the rugby club in that country sent an urgent telegram. 'Please bring your own ball,' it read. 'We have lost ours.'

Blackheath player Arnold Alcock was surprised to receive a letter asking him to play for England against South Africa in a rugby international in 1906. After all, even by his own admission Alcock was just an ordinary club player. He turned up on the day, but when he did so the team secretary realised he'd made a ghastly mistake. The letter *should* have been sent to Andrew Slocock. However, it was too late to change things, so Alcock got his cap — but was never picked again!

An All Black full-back was taking part in a charity rugby match when he caught the ball from a clearance, ran through a gap in the defence and scored with a flourish under the posts. The only problem was that he was *supposed* to be the referee!

On their 1982 tour of the States, England's three-quarters were developing a good movement in the middle of the field when to their amazement the referee blew his whistle and halted the game. He explained to the baffled players that the game was being sponsored by a TV station and therefore he had to stop for commercial breaks. 'I wore a bleeper,' he said. 'Three bleeps and I had to stop for precisely one minute.'

In 1968 a student revolt broke out in Paris and for one week the French capital was cut off from the outside world. The phones were cut off and the airports were closed. By chance at this time an English rugby team were visiting Paris for a brief tour and one journalist, a dour northern sportswriter called Fred, was with them.

Oblivious of all the momentous events going on around him, Fred spent all day trying to phone his office. Finally, with minutes to spare before his deadline, he managed to get a line through to his northern newspaper office. His call caused an incredible stir and he was passed straight through to the news editor.

'What the hell's going on over there?' asked the editor. 'Do you realise you're the only journalist who's been able to get through to us? What's happening?'

The bemused Fred told him that some strange things had been happening. 'A tank's just come through the wall of the hotel as I'm speaking to you,' he reported.

'This is brilliant,' said the news editor excitedly, foreseeing all kinds of exclusives. 'I'm going to put you straight through to a copy typist. Give us all you've got, Fred.'

So Fred was passed over to the copy department while the editor planned how to handle the world scoop. Slightly baffled, Fred began to dictate his copy over the phone. 'Eric Jenkinson, the Widnes forward, is to have a fitness test on his suspect left knee . . .'

A couple of hundred words later and Fred put down the phone, his job well done, and wandered off happily to look for a drink.

And meanwhile the revolution went on all round him . . .

Welshman Keith Jarrett had a memorable day in 1967 when, aged only 19 and on his international debut, he scored 19 points to help the Welsh side defeat the English at Cardiff by 34-21.

After the celebrations Jarrett had to catch a bus to Newport where he lived. Unfortunately when he got to the bus station the last bus had gone and it was an eight-mile walk to Newport. Luckily a driver who was knocking off recognised Jarrett from his sterling deeds at the Arms Park that day and offered him a lift in a bus. As they moved off an inspector stopped them. 'What are you doing?' he asked the driver.

'I'm taking Mr Jarrett home — he scored 19 points against England.' The inspector checked, recognised Jarrett and said to the driver, 'You fool! Go and get a double decker — the lad might want to smoke!'

At a charity gala athlete Alan Pascoe was talking to Prince Philip about a stomach injury he had sustained hurdling. 'I don't know what's wrong with you athletes,' said Prince Philip. 'You get more injuries than my bloody horses.'

'Perhaps you ought to put me in touch with a vet,' said the hurdler.

'If I did that, you'd end up in the knacker's yard!'

At the end of the third round boxer Max Baer returned to his corner after another mauling from Joe Louis. His corner-man, Jack Dempsey, greeted him. 'Keep going, you're doing fine. The other guy hasn't even hit you yet.'

'In that case,' mumbled Baer through swollen, blood-stained lips, 'you'd better keep an eye on the referee next round, cause some guy is sure beating the hell out of me.'

The true story is told of when an Irish farmer bet one hundred pounds with a bookie called Finnegan on a horse at 7-1. The animal duly cantered in to pass the post first and the farmer, no lover of bookies, went to collect his £700. As he did so he was heard to repeat several times, 'You've heard of Finnegan's Wake, well this is your wake, Finnegan.'

That brilliant jockey Lester Piggott was known to put his hardness of hearing to good effect. He was accosted by a down-and-out fan, who appealed for assistance one day. 'Please,' said the old man feebly, 'just a couple of quid for a life-long fan,' Lester seemed not to hear and continued on his way, but the man was persistent. 'Please, Mr Piggott,' he hollered in his ear, 'just a fiver for an old and loyal fan.'

'What's that?' said Lester. 'Just now it was only a couple of quid!'

There are strict rules about the kind of clothing that darts players may wear at major competitions where television cameras are present — and jeans are not allowed. One year this caused quite a stir at the British Open. A player was about to begin playing in the quarter finals wearing jeans when he was dragged off the stage by two large officials, taken out of view of the TV cameras, debagged — and given another more acceptable pair of trousers to wear!

Darts star John Lowe strolled into the bar after losing a semi-final in an important championship. 'I want nineteen brandies, a double vodka and a whisky,' he called to the barman. 'All in the same glass.'

Tennis ace Ilie Nastasie admitted he had failed to report that his American Express card had gone missing. As he put it, 'Whoever stole it is bound to be spending less than my wife.'

An Australian snooker player decided to invent a new shot, to be called after him, and had himself suspended upside down over the table with helium balloons attached to his wrists and his legs fastened to the rafters of the building. Sadly his arrangements went wrong and while making his shot he fell head-first onto the table and died.

Sporting Talk

In this section of sporting quotes you'll find the famous and the not-so-famous — words of unforgettable wisdom and appalling slips of the tongue that sports commentators have been hoping we'll all forget!

Players who lose are worse than bank robbers.

Bill Shankley

I've got no time for shirkers. I want a man who'll go through a wall of fire, break a leg, and still come out shooting for goal.

Bill Shankley

All a manager had to do is keep 11 players happy — the 11 in the reserves. The first team are happy because they're the first team.

Rodney Marsh

There are only two basic situations in football — either you have the ball or you haven't.

Ron Greenwood

Our problem is that we have tried to score too many goals.

Gordon Lee, manager of Everton

It's those buggers on the sports pages I hate most.

Brian Clough

Brains? There's a lot of players who think manual labour is the Spanish president.

Tommy Docherty

I'd give my right arm to get back into the England team.

Peter Shilton, goalkeeper

For those of you watching in black and white, Spurs are in the all-yellow strip.

John Motson, sports commentator

Remeber now, postcards only, please. The winner will be the first one opened.

Brian Moore, announcing a soccer quiz

I'm convinced that the greatest contribution that Britain has made to the national life in Uruguay was teaching people football.

Prince Philip

I have this book with players' names in it. If I get the chance to do them I will. I'll make them suffer before I pack it in. If I can kick them four yards over the touchline I will.

Jack Charlton

Asked if he would name his side for that night's match against Milan, *Bill Shankley* said: 'I'm not going to give any secrets like that to Milan. If I had my way I wouldn't even tell them the time of the kick-off.'

The rules are very simple, basically it is this; if it moves, kick it. If it doesn't move, kick it till it does.
US soccer promoter Phil Woosnam, on suggestions that the Americans might find the rules of soccer difficult.

Professionalism, if you like, is not having sex on Thursdays and Fridays.

Don Revie

Say nowt, win it, then talk your head off.
Brian Clough on how to manage the media

If you watch a game, it's fun. If you play it, it's recreation. If you work at it, it's golf.

Bob Hope

Someone sent a shilling towards W.G. Grace's testimonial with a note that said: 'It's not in support of cricket, but as an earnest protest against golf.'

Golf is so popular simply because it's the best game in the world at which to be bad.

A.A. Milne

All I've got against golf is that it takes you so far from the clubhouse.

Eric Linklater

If a woman can walk she can play golf.

Louise Suggs

The least things upset him on the links. He missed short putts because of the uproar of butterflies in adjoining meadows.

P.G. Wodehouse

Golf — a good walk spoiled.

Mark Twain

Statistics indicate that, as a result of overwork, modern executives are dropping like flies on the nation's golf courses.

Ira Wallach

I am sure that the Almighty never intended that cricket should be played in anything but glorious sunshine, especially if the wicket was doing a bit.

Ray Illingworth

Try explaining cricket to an intelligent foreigner. It is far harder than trying to explain Chomsky's generational grammar.

Lord Snow

If they don't cooperate they'll walk straight into a meat mangle.

Kerry Packer on the Australian Cricket Board

It won't take much work to get me psyched up to hating anyone.

Jeff Thomson

I have always imagined cricket as a game invented by roughnecks in a moment of idleness by casually throwing an unexploded bomb at one another. The game was observed by some officer with a twisted and ingenious mind who devoted his life to inventing impossible rules for it.

Peter Ustinov

Personally I have always looked on cricket as organised loafing.

William Temple (later Archbishop of Canterbury)

It's a funny kind of month, October. For the really keen cricket fan it's when you discover your wife left you in May.

Dennis Norden

What is life but a game of cricket?

Duke of Dorset

A cricketer — a creature very nearly as stupid as a dog.

Bernard Levin

I would have got a better mention in Pravda.
Kerry Packer, on his bad press

I have nightmares about having to become an umpire.
John Snow

One fact seems sure;
That, while the Church approves, Lord's will endure.
Siegfried Sassoon

He played his cricket on the heath,
The pitch was full of bumps:
A fast ball hit him in the teeth —
The dentist drew the stumps.

Anon

I tend to believe that cricket is the greatest thing that God
ever created on earth.
Harold Pinter

Rugby is a beastly game played by gentlemen; soccer is a
gentlemen's game played by beasts; and American football
is a beastly game played by beasts.
Henry Bahia

Fishing, with me, has always been an excuse to drink in the
daytime.
Jimmy Cannon, sportswriter

If you want to be happy for a day, get drunk.
If you want to be happy for a week, get married.
But if you want to be happy for life, go fishing.

Anon

Angling — I can only compare it to a stick and a string with a
worm at one end and a fool at the other.

Dr Johnson

All men are equal before fish.

Herbert Hoover, US president

Fishing is a delusion entirely surrounded by liars in old clothes.

Don Marquis

Angling — the name given to fishing by those people who can't fish.

Stephen Leacock

A good darts player who can count can always beat a brilliant player who can't.

Leighton Rees

Boxing is showbusines with blood.

David Belasco, US impresario

I must be the greatest — am I immortal too?
And . . . I'm not an ordinary mortal, I'm bigger than the sport itself. And . . . I don't believe all the stuff I say.

Muhammed Ali

Boxing is not a sport, it is a criminal activity.

Prof. Ernst Johl

Boxing is the best and most individual lifestyle you can have in society without being a criminal.

Randy Neumann, US boxer

Boxing is sort of like jazz. The better it is the fewer people can understand it.

George Foreman

A lot of boxing promoters couldn't match the cheeks of their own backsides.

Mickey Duff, entrepreneur and promoter

You're damn right I know where I am — I'm in Madison Square Gardens getting beaten up!
Willie Pastrano, boxer, when knocked down in the ring and asked by the referee if he knew where he was

Clay can't insult me. I'm too ignorant.

Brian London, boxer

I'm only a prawn in this game.

Brian London

If you hadn't been there it wouldn't have been much of a fight.

Harry Carpenter to Ken Norton after a bout

I lost it by default, not de punch.

John Conteh, stripped of his title

My plans usually work. If they don't I resort to brutality.

George Foreman

My first priority is to finish racing above rather than beneath the ground.

James Hunt

In my sport (motor racing) the quick are often listed among the dead.

Jackie Stewart

It is necessary to relax your muscles when you can. Relaxing your brain is fatal.

Sterling Moss

To play billiards well is a sign of misspent youth.

Herbert Spencer

There's more tension and electrification in snooker as a sport than in any other kind, even motor-racing.

John Pulman, snooker champion

If someone died in the ring, they'd say it was faked.

US professional wrestler

The Americas Cup is as exciting as watching grass grow.

US sportswriter

It's Oxford! No, it's Cambridge. I can't see. It's Oxford. No . . . well, one of them must be winning.

John Snagge commentating on 1954 Boat Race

The fascination of shooting as a sport depends almost wholly on whether you are on the right or wrong end of the gun.

P.G. Wodehouse

The English country gentleman galloping after a fox — the unspeakable in pursuit of the uneatable.

Oscar Wilde

Pro football is like nuclear warfare. There are no winners, only survivors.

Frank Gifford

I never did say that you can't be a nice guy and win. I said that if I was playing third base and my mother rounded third with a winning run I'd trip her up.

Leo Durocker, US baseball manager

I gave George Allen unlimited patience and he exhausted it.

US team owner on firing his coach

I sometimes get birthday cards from fans. But it's often the same message — they hope it's my last.

Al Norman, US baseball umpire

Asked whether he preferred astroturf to grass, *Joe Namath*, US pro footballer, said: 'I don't know. I never smoked astroturf.'

When I was 40 my doctor advised me that a man in his forties should not play tennis. I heeded his advice carefully and could hardly wait until I reached 50 to start again.
Hugo Black

Running for money doesn't make you run fast. It makes you run first.
Ben Jipcho, Kenyan runner

Look at that tremendous flexibility of the ankles. They really are an extension of the legs.
Ron Pickering, sports commentator

This game is passionate enough without money.
Richard Rodgers, composer and croquet player

What I like best about bullfighting is the big money and small bulls.
Spanish matador

To win is everything. To be second is even worse than being secondary.
David Broome

To win is worthless if you don't get paid for it.
Reggie Jackson, US sportsman

Winning is not everything. It's the only thing.
Vince Lombardi, US pro football coach

Winners aren't popular. Losers often are.
Virginia Wade

The problem with good losers is they get into the habit of losing.

Knute Rochne, US pro football coach

Serious sport has nothing to do with fair play.

George Orwell

As I understand it, sport is hard work for which you do not get paid.

Irvine S. Cole

If you are fit, you don't need it. If you aren't, you shouldn't risk it.

Henry Fonda on exercise

Sporting Feats

Sport seems to have more than its fair share of amazing facts and bizarre feats, so make your audience laugh with some of these incredible snippets of information. Believe it or not, they're all true!

Oxbarn Social Club, a football side from Wolverhampton, had an unnerving experience when they went on a brief tour of Germany in 1973. They arrived in the city of Mainz where, to their surprise, they were booked to play in a large stadium. Even odder, and very flattering, they heard rumours that the opposition were on an £80 per man bonus to beat them. These Germans certainly take the game seriously, they thought.

On the day of the game there were queues of fans outside the stadium — and when the match started it was a massacre. The amused crowd cheered each time the English side managed to cross the half-way line, which wasn't often. The final result was 21-0 to the Germans.

Club secretary Ron Parker explained later how the posters outside the ground had revealed the extent of the confusion. They read SVW Mainz V Wolverhampton Wanderers.

Fans at Sicilian football match were outraged when the referee sent off a local player during a heated incident. One, particularly incensed, rushed home and fetched a shotgun. He then fired several warning shots in the air and pointed the gun at the ref while he demanded the player be reinstated. Not having any wish to die, the referee agreed. Unfortunately the visiting side's goalie was so upset by the gun-toting display and the fact that the fan was still waving the weapon in his direction, that he tactfully let in seven goals.

The great footballer Pele was probably the only player in history to stop a war. Both sides agreed on a truce during the Biafran conflict so that they could watch the genius play on his African tour.

A resourceful referee once managed to get his own back on a hostile crowd and players in that graveyard of sports officials, Italy. The soccer official, Senor Benedetti, disallowed two penalties for the home side and was chased through the streets by an angry mob. Fortunately he found sanctuary in a quiet restaurant. He was just about to tuck into a meal when the owner, a football fan, recognised him and threw him out.

The ref took his revenge by phoning the restaurant in a disguised voice, claiming to be the manager of the home side and saying that he was bringing the whole team there in an hour. He then rang the team manager, pretending to be the restaurant owner, and invited the team to come round for a cheap meal to compensate for being robbed in the match. The team arrived and ate and drank enormous amounts. When they were presented with the bill there was a fracas which resulted in the team manager being imprisoned ...

It was the rowdiness of the adults and not the players that led to the cancellation of Northamptonshire Scout troop matches in 1977. During the finals of the tournament a gang of parents began to fight each other at the touchline and two brawling mothers chased a linesman across the pitch.

Imposing a six-year ban on Scout football, the Scout District Commissioner said: 'I have blown the whistle for the last time.'

Lady golfer Mrs Bobby Pritchard faced a novel problem one morning as she played a round at her local course in Rhodesia. Her ball had settled among the coils of a ten-foot long python. Wisely deciding not to rush the shot, and too honest just to use another ball, she consulted the club secretary. His ruling was authoritative — shoot the creature and then play the stroke. And this she did.

An Australian golf course near Darwin was so prone to invasion by local wildlife that the club was compelled to introduce a new rule. It read: 'Where a hawk, lizard, crocodile, snake or wallaby takes the ball, another shall be dropped.'

On an American golf course near Washington there was a problem one year with a black bear on the fairway. New rules were accordingly drafted, which ran as follows. 'If a ball is picked up by a bear, people may replace and take one penalty stroke. If the player gets the ball back from the bear, take an automatic par for hole.'

Perhaps the most unusual reason ever for stopping a cricket match occurred in Fiji some years ago. Heavy rain had prevented any play, but when the sun came out the players turned up for a practice game . . . only to find the entire pitch covered by little green frogs which had taken advantage of the moisture to pop up from the turf.

In 1911 Nottingham cricketer Ted Alletson scored the fastest sustained innings ever in the first-class game — 189 in just 90 minutes. Remarkably, the last 142 of these came in only 40 minutes! During his savage knock he lost five balls as he hit them past the boundaries of the Hove ground. But even more incredibly, this was Alletson's first and only century and after failing to score more than 11 in subsequent innings he was eventually dropped.

The following appeared on a cricket scoreboard in Australia in 1979. Lillee caught Willey bowled Dilley 19.

In 1949 a powerful batsman hit a six into a field and killed a goose.

In Adelaide during a Test match a more formidable bird, a large seagull, swooped onto the field to save England two runs from an Australian shot. The ball hit the bird and stopped dead — and the gull was treated for shock and a leg injury.

W.G. Grace once hit a ball 37 miles — quite a feat, even for him. It happened when he was playing at Hull and smashed a ball into a passing railway truck. Its next stop was Leeds!

A determined Lancashire angler was found by a Rochdale policeman fishing through the grating of a drain. 'I'm fighting for the right of anyone to fish where they like,' he explained. The court nevertheless fined him £15 for obstruction.

A Norfolk fisherman caught a 12-pound cod whose stomach contained a packet of salt and vinegar flavour crisps.

Angler Mr E. Curry was doubtless disappointed when, in a fishing competition at Walton-on-the-Naze, he caught only one fish, a measly 9oz flounder. But he needn't have worried because the fish was still enough to win. None of the other anglers caught a thing.

After five hours of dedicated fishing the 200 competitors in the 1972 National Ambulanceman's Championship were slightly baffled that no one, not one person, had caught a single fish. Just then a local man walked past and told them why. 'Didn't you know that the local authority drained that stretch of water three weeks ago — they've only just refilled it!'

Opponents of one Yugoslavian rugby team were disconcerted to find themselves playing against a second row called Arsenic and a prop called Panic!

Radford School's rugby team once beat their opponents from Hills Court 200-0, including 38 tries.

On one remarkable rugby occasion in Argentina in 1920 all 30 players and the entire crowd of 2,500 were arrested and jailed by the police. Apparently the authorities thought that it was some kind of political gathering ...

In 1984 an Abertillery rugby player was helped off the pitch at the end of the game — suffering from exposure.

During an Olympic bout a young boxer had his gumshield knocked out. He immediately knelt down and began to scramble around on his hands and knees to pick it up in his boxing-glove — not an easy task.
   As he did so the referee began counting, and ten seconds later counted the unfortunate boxer out!

A large man came out of an American bank one day carrying an official-looking bag. Just then another man pulled a knife on him and told him to hand over the bag. The big man did so — and the weight of $400 in coins knocked the attacker backwards. As he stumbled and fell the big chap, otherwise known as heavyweight boxing champ Alex Venettis, knocked him out cold with a right hook.

At the 1972 Olympics, held in Germany, a British kayak pair got stuck in the rapids during the slalom event. They were trapped upside down in the water against a rock. 'I don't wish to appear pessimistic,' said the BBC commentator, 'but I sense our medal chances are slipping away.' Having righted themselves, one of the men discovered that he had lost his watch during the mishap. The entire artificial course was drained to look for it!

In 1912 a Japanese runner named Shizo Kanakuni stopped during the marathon to ask for a cool drink. Finding himself still some miles from the finishing line in Stockholm, Kanakuni decided he had had enough and took a tram back to the Swedish capital. Then, without telling anyone, he took a boat back to Japan. His disappearance remained a mystery until 1963, when a Swedish reporter traced the runner back to Japan and persuaded him to return to the spot where he had quit the marathon. So finally Kanakuni finished the race he had started — and it only took him 50 years!

Surinam only sent one athlete to the 1960 Rome Olympics, an 800 metre runner. After his arrival by plane in Italy he was natually tired and decided to take a nap. He slept right through the morning, rose and took a light meal, then made his way to the stadium — only to discover that the event was over.

Three US athletes were watching afternoon television at the Munich Olympics in 1972 when, to their horror, their second round 100m sprint was announced. They checked the times and found that they had confused 15.00 hours with 5 p.m. All three dashed to the stadium but only one made it on time. He at least had the satisfaction of winning the silver medal.

The official starter for the sprints at the 1904 Olympics at St Louis, Missouri, was so annoyed at three false starts in one race that he punished the four runners by making them run an extra metre. The winner, Archie Hahn, now holds a unique record — the 201m won in 21.6 seconds.

Just four men took part in the 400m Olympic finals held in London in 1908, one Briton and three Americans. As they came round the bend heading for home, one of the Americans appeared to impede the Briton, Lieutenant Wyndham Halswelle, and to the astonishment of all a British official named Dr Badger ran to the finishing line and ordered the judge to cut the tape. This meant that the race was void and a re-run was ordered, with the offending American excluded. So furious were the other two American runners that they refused to participate — so Halswelle ran on his own . . . and naturally he won.

An American runner named Billy Jones made athletics history when in 1955 he ran the 100 yards in 9.0 seconds dead. The crowd were ecstatic and Jones himself was overjoyed until officials checked the track — and found that it was only 90 yards long.

A Swedish runner, Dan Waern, caused controversy in the sport when questions were asked about the true nature of his supposedly amateur status. His own athletics board opted to back him, but eventually he was suspended and took the only course left open to him — and turned professional. His first exhibition race in Sweden attracted a large and expectant crowd. They were not disappointed. Waern had decided to run 1,000m against a team of schoolgirls and a team of schoolboys. The race began and after a tough battle the newly-professional athlete managed to out-run the girls. Alas, however, the schoolboys beat him by an entire lap.

Although he had come all the way from Guinea Bissau in Africa, a long-distance runner from the country refused point blank to take part in the 3,000m steeplechase at the Moscow Olympics. It seemed that the problem concerned the water jump.

'You don't just jump into water in Guinea Bissau,' he explained. 'There might be crocodiles!'

Pity the poor Russian oarsman who, in 1956, won the single sculls in the Melbourne Olympics. So excited was he at getting the gold that he threw the medal high into the air — and down it plunged into the nearby lake, never to be seen again. The authorities later gave him a duplicate medal.

In 1980 an official at a haggis-throwing competition in Scotland was measuring a throw when he was hit on the head by a flying haggis and knocked out.

A north Rhodesian bar was full of men playing darts and drinking, listening to the heavy rain outside. Suddenly one of the men froze as he saw a deadly puff adder slithering across the floor towards him. Things looked dangerous — then Colin Browne, the local darts champion gave a flick of the wrist and pinned the snake to the floor with a single dart. Naturally everyone was much relieved, except for Browne; rules being rules, he lost his match for missing the board.

An American football coach was ordered to stop chewing heads off frogs in front of his young players in his pre-match pep talk. He complained, saying that the kids loved it.

A tennis competition was held up by heavy rain in Calcutta in 1975 — a table tennis competition. Thieves had stolen the lead from the roof and the rain poured in and onto the tables.

Frisbee thrower Julius T Nachazel went into the woods at Eagle Harbour in California to retrieve his frisbee — and was never seen again. To this day no one knows what happened to him. His sad fate caught the imagination of fellow frisbee enthusiasts and now there is a championship named after him.

The Front Line

The best way to start your speech is with a quick joke or quote that will break the ice and establish contact between you and your audience — and for this a one-liner is ideal. When you tell a one-line joke don't labour it too hard, just drop it casually into your speech and leave it to the audience to find the humour. They'll be flattered to think that you can afford to risk wasting lines on them!

Did you hear about the Division Four football manager who was taken to hospital suffering from a bad side?

Our local football team was so bad that when they won a corner they took a lap of honour.

Another football team knew they shouldn't have appointed a goalkeeper called Cinderella. He kept missing the ball.

Why did the Irish football team play a blushing young virgin as goalkeeper? They knew she wouldn't let one in all season.

Graffiti: Joe Jordan kicks the parts other beers don't reach.
　　　　　Liverpool are magic — Everton are tragic.

Spurs striker Garth Crooks once announced to the press, 'The goal surprised many people, least of all myself.'

A soccer commentator talking about Ian Rush said: 'Deadly ten times out of ten — but that wasn't one of them.'

The local football manager is teaching his side speedway. He reckons that's the only way they'll reach Wembley.

Did you hear about the man who thought that Sheffield Wednesday was the beginning of Lent?

Jesus may save — but Shilton is better.

The local paper recently reported on a man who gave up golf to become a catholic. He said the rules were easier to follow.

Definition of a devotee: someone who keeps hitting the earth with his golf swing.

Someone once asked a bad golfer what his handicap was. 'Honesty,' he said.

Scientific law of golf. The hole is always greater than the sum of the constituent putts.

The trouble with golf is that by the time a player can afford to lose the ball he can't hit that far!

The golf course consists of 18 holes, 17 of them unnecessary but included simply to multiply frustration.

If the universe if finite, as some people claim, how come golfers never find all those balls they lose?

Mind may be control over matter, but not when it comes to golf.

Would you say that golf is just another way of beating around the bush?

Golf is unlike politics insofar as you can't improve your lie in golf . . .

Old golfers never die, they simply lose their balls.

Golf is like a love affair. If you don't take it seriously it's no fun. If you do it breaks you heart.

Would you say a golfer is a man who putts it around?

Did you hear about the fat golfer? When he put the ball where he could see it he couldn't hit it and when he put it where he could hit it, he couldn't see it!

A cricket commentator on the radio once said, 'And 33 runs have been scored, shared equally between the two batsmen.' He later followed it up with, 'The batsman throws his head back and it goes through to the keeper.'

The local cricket club is like an old bra — no cups and hardly any support.

Did you hear about the Irish rugby match? The players swapped jerseys at half time.

Sign in the toilets of a Scottish rugby club: Please don't put cigarette ends in the urinals. It makes them soggy and difficult to light.

Would you say that rugby is a game played by gentlemen with odd shaped balls?

Have you heard about the new self-help group called Anglers Anonymous? You phone them up and listen to a pack of lies.

To have good fortune when fishing, you have to get there yesterday when the fish were biting.

An optimist may be defined as a person who takes a camera with him when he goes fishing.

Anglers catch their biggest fish by the tale ...

A fisherman has a whole year of fun — ten days fishing and 355 days fiddling with his tackle.

All fish gain weight slowly, except for those that got away.

Fishing is generally better before you get there or after you leave.

How far a fisherman stretches the truth depends on the length of his arms.

Did you hear about the snooker player who set out to improve his game? He started smoking pot.

Another snooker player arrived home after a very successful evening during which he'd managed to sink seven pints and three double whiskies ...

Would you say the SAS smoke more embassies than Hurricane Higgins?

Don't believe that swimming is good for the figure. Have you ever seen a whale?

Did you see the big boxing match on TV last night? The boxer in the black shorts did so much bobbing and weaving that by the end of the fight he'd made a carpet.

In the loos of Wimbledon some bright spark has written on one wall, *For the rules of tennis see wall opposite.* And on the other wall, *For the rules of tennis see wall opposite.*

Snoopy on tennis: It doesn't matter if you win or lose — until you lose.

Nothing keeps an athletics crowd's attention more than a cross-eyed javelin thrower.

Gambling can be a messy business. Did you hear about the pigeon that put all he had on Lester Piggott?

What about the man who started manufacturing boomerangs? He said the sport was making a comeback.

The chap who kept racing pigeons was a bitterly disappointed man. He never caught one.

An Irishman who heard about the latest craze for ice hockey began to make his own sticks. Problem was, they kept melting in his hands ...

Pity the unfortunate sailor who was thrown out of the singlehanded yacht race for using both hands ...

Seen in a newspaper: One-armed tennis title changes hands.

Graffiti: Mallet rules, croquet?

The reason a woman can't catch a ball as well as a man is that a man is much bigger and easier to catch.

If at first you don't succeed, so much for sky-diving.

Comic Speeches for Social Occasions

● ● ● ● ●

Contents

PART ONE

How to make a comic speech

Social Occasions

Sooner or later it happens to almost everyone. It could be a wedding or a presentation at work; it could be an after-dinner speech to a paying audience or a family celebration; it could be an introduction at a social club or a toast at a civic dinner. What is it? It's an occasion on which you need to make a witty speech.

Most people are terrified at the prospect of having to stand up in front of an audience and try to make them laugh — and rightly so. How many times have you squirmed in your seat as a work colleague has told a string of off-colour jokes at a company dinner, or yawned as a relative has umm-ed and err-ed his way through some feeble gags? Fortunately, you *don't* have to be a professional comedian to make a success of your speech. This book contains everything you'll need to make an amusing comic speech on every kind of social occasion. It will show you how to assess your audience and the kind of speech you'll need to make for every situation. It will show you how to write and prepare the material and how to deliver it with confidence. And it will even give you tips on how to perform successfully on the day.

And naturally, because it is a *complete* guide to comic speech-making you'll find a wide selection of jokes and anecdotes, quotes and one-liners to ensure that you're never at a loss for something funny to say.

Know your Audience

No matter how nervous you feel about it, remember that it's actually an honour to be invited to speak in front of an audience — so acknowledge the fact by creating a speech specially for the occasion. What your audience will want to hear, and you should aim to provide, are effortless, amusing stories and ideas — stories and ideas that are of direct interest and relevance to them.

Some speakers like to think that they have perfected a kind of general-purpose speech; a speech which, with a few minor alterations and additions will go down with any audience and on any occasion. It may indeed be useful to have a few jokes to hand if you suspect that you're going to be asked to make an impromptu speech, but this kind of general-purpose material won't set an audience alight. They'll sense its general nature and the fact that no great imagination has gone into it — and if the speaker is very unlucky there'll be someone in the audience who's heard it all before on another occasion!

What this means is that for every occasion and every audience you need to create a new speech. But before you sit down and start to write it, spare a few seconds' thought to work out just what will be required.

The audience

You may be keen on the theatre, and your theatrical anecdotes may have gone down brilliantly at the local amateur
drama society party, but those stories are unlikely to have
the same appeal for the guests at a wedding or the ladies
of the Townswomen's Guild. Obvious it may be, but it
doesn't seem to occur to a great number of speakers that
it's the audience who decide whether the material is
funny or not. And if the audience don't like your jokes
you might as well give up. So make sure that you choose
the right material by thinking carefully about the people
you're going to be speaking to.

Age is an important factor. If you know that your
audience will be young and sophisticated, choose some of
the more sophisticated material in this book and make
sure that the details are right up to date. Similarly, if your
audience is past retiring age adapt the jokes and stories to
suit them. Try not to tell jokes about the war to an
audience who only vaguely remember the Beatles!

While an all-male gathering is likely to enjoy a rather
more robust sort of humour than a female gathering, that
doesn't mean that you can say what you like in front of a
male crowd. Never offend those who are listening to you.
It's bad enough if everyone in the audience is a stranger,
but if you're going to have to see them next weekend at
the golf club or even in the office on Monday morning,
ensure that nothing about your speech is offensive. And if
anything in your material embarrasses *you*, leave it out.
Your unease will communicate itself to your listeners and
they'll feel embarrassed on your behalf.

The members of the local astronomy club will probably
want to hear a speech that in some way reflects their
interests. This doesn't mean that every joke you tell them
must be about stars and star-gazing but try to ensure that
at least some of your material is directly relevant. For
your speech to work well, you'll need a theme and your

11

material will have to fit into it. Most jokes can be adapted to fit almost any topic, but if you can't slide a story neatly into your speech you'd do better to leave it out, no matter how funny it is. This may seem like pushing a point too far, but next time you see a comedian on the TV, notice how his jokes lead into one another and link up to make a whole. This is the kind of thing that you must aim to do. You don't want your audience wondering about the relevance of your cannibal joke to *them* while you gamely try to get back onto the track of astronomy.

If you have been asked to speak at a function where you don't know the audience, it's advisable to find out as much as you can about the people who will be attending and the organization behind the function. Do some home-work and find out about any recent projects or achievements that the organization — be it company, charity or social club — has been involved in. Are there any famous or interesting names connected with it? Who is the chairman and who is on the committee, and are there any amusing stories to be told? Audiences love 'in' jokes, and if you can prove how well you've done your research they'll appreciate you all the more.

Different occasions require different kinds of speeches, and you'll find details about what kind of speech you'll need to make for most major social occasions in the last part of this section of the book. But it isn't just the formal requirements of an occasion that matter when it comes to preparing your speech.

The tone of the occasion is all-important too. A presentation at a rugby club when the team has just topped the league will be very different in tone to a presentation at a school speech day. Try to assess what the mood of your audience will be and what kind of role you will be expected to play. Will they want belly-laughs and funny stories about the captain, or will a more wry and gentle humour best suit the occasion? Make up your mind and choose your material accordingly.

12

It's also worth bearing in mind that if you've been asked to speak it's probably for a purpose. Whatever that purpose — whether it's to present a trophy or propose a toast — you should never get so carried away with your own words that you forget what you're there to do. There's many a speaker who's sat down after half an hour, still holding the award he was meant to present. The best way to avoid this kind of embarrassment is to plan your speech carefully and then stick to it. Try to resist the temptation, no matter how well you're being received, to improvise. It's improvisation that is likely to throw you off your stride.

Here's a simple check list of 10 Do's and Don't's which you should bear in mind as you sit down to prepare your speech.

Do's

1 Do check the age range and sex ratio of the audience.
2 Do find out what your particular function is to be and make sure that you prepare the right kind of speech.
3 Do find out how long you will be expected to speak.
4 Do some homework on the organization and any of the guests if you don't already know them.
5 Do adapt your material to suit the occasion.

Don't's

1 Don't try to revamp an old speech for a new occasion.
2 Don't risk offending anyone.
3 Don't speak for too long or try to improvise.

13

4   Don't include irrelevant material.
5   Don't forget to fulfil your function. If you've been
     asked to propose a toast or make a presentation
     then remember to do so.

Perfect Preparation

Once you know the kind of speech you're going to make and the sort of audience you'll be entertaining, you can begin to prepare your material. Preparation is absolutely vital if you're going to give a polished performance, and the longer you work on your speech the funnier it will be. If you have weeks to go before the event, so much the better!

Start by reading through this book and marking all the jokes, quotes, anecdotes and so on that you like and that you feel would be suitable for the occasion and the audience. Be ruthless and cut out anything that isn't related in some way to your subject or can't be adapted to fit. On a separate sheet, put down all the things that you *have* to say in the speech — the toast, the congratulations, the thanks — and all the points or thoughts that you would like to express.

With any luck you'll soon begin to see the material falling into place, with the quotes leading into your observations and the anecdotes illustrating them. This is exactly what you're aiming for: a seamless effect which allows you to move on through the speech without any apparent effort. You'll probably have to adapt some of the material if it's going to fit perfectly, so change the details of the jokes. Give the characters new names and occupations. If you're from Newcastle and you're going to be speaking in Newcastle, add some local Geordie colour —

and likewise wherever you're from. Most importantly of all, put everything into your own words. You'll feel more comfortable when you come to use the material if it's written in the kind of language you're used to, and it will make your speech seem that much more personal to the audience.

Sir Thomas Beecham once said of his orchestra that the important thing was 'to begin and end together, what happens in between doesn't matter very much.' Pretty much the same can be said of making a comic speech. If you can capture the attention of the audience with your first line, you're likely to have their attention for the rest of the speech. And if they're going to remember a single thing you said it's likely to be the final line — so make sure that it's worth remembering.

Some speakers like to work on the opening and closing lines of their speech together, linking them so that the last line finishes what the first line started. Whatever you decide to do, make sure that both the beginning and the end of your speech are absolutely relevant — both to the occasion and the central part of the speech. Stick to this and you won't run the risk of rambling.

Opening and closing a speech are the two most difficult things of all. If a brilliant opening occurs to you then use it — but if nothing original springs to mind, try using one of these opening gambits.

Quotations

You'll find nearly a hundred useful quotations in this book and one of them should be ideal for opening your speech. Some are very specific, some of them deliberately vague so that you can use them to suit a number of different subjects. When you're looking for the right one, bear in mind that it should allow you to move straight into the main part of your speech without any stress. If you have to force a quotation to fit your theme then forget it, it will look laboured and that's precisely what you're trying to avoid.

Don't use a quotation for the opening *and* closing of your speech; that would look too much like taking a short cut. But a quote can finish off a speech as well as it can start it. At the risk of being boring, do make absolutely sure that it's relevant to your main theme.

If you find something brilliantly funny you may be tempted to pretend that the words are your own. *Don't.* Someone in the audience is *bound* to have heard it before and it won't do your credibility much good. Always credit your quotations; it proves that you've done your home-work for the occasion.

Questions

A question can be a very effective way of getting your speech off the ground. Try asking an apparently serious question and following it up with an unexpected answer. Or ask a ridiculous question which will make the audience laugh — and laugh again when they discover the answer. You'll find suitable material in the *It's a Weird World* section of this book. This material can also be used for the 'Did You Know?' gambit. Find a relevant amazing fact and ask your audience if they know it. It will break the ice immediately and make your job as a speaker easier.

Jokes

A joke may seem the obvious way of starting a speech, but in fact jokes can backfire. If they work you'll have the audience eating out of your hand — but if they fall flat you'll have everyone in an agony of embarrassment and praying that you finish your speech quickly.

17

The best kind of joke to start with is one that has something to do with a member of the audience, or the function, or with something else relevant to the occasion. You may find that simply by changing a few details in one of the jokes in this book you've got the ideal opening gag — in which case use it. But try not to use an irrelevant joke simply because it's funny. It may get a laugh but it won't lead you into your speech and you'll still be left with the problem of getting yourself underway. And once you do get into the swing of things the audience may wonder why you prefaced the speech with an irrelevant gag.

Exactly the same advice can be applied to ending a speech. Looking for a new screenplay, Sam Goldwyn once remarked, 'What we want is a story that begins with an earthquake and builds up to a climax.' That's what you have to aim for too!

Never end your speech with an apologetic, 'Well, that's it, thank you for having me,' line. That only suggests that you've run out of ideas or that you couldn't be bothered to finish off the job properly. Even if you can't find the kind of climax that Goldwyn was looking for, you *can* end your speech in a funny and tidy way.

Anecdotes

If you can find an anecdote — and there are plenty in the section entitled 'A Funny Thing Happened ...' — that finishes off your theme perfectly then use it. The only type to avoid are the longer, rambling anecdotes because you don't want to lose your audience's attention during the final few moments of your speech. If you're speaking about friends, family or colleagues at work, try to remember an amusing incident involving them; nothing embarrassing or hurtful, of course, just something to show what nice people they are. If you judge it correctly,

18

this is *guaranteed* to bring your speech to a successful conclusion.

Jokes

In a way, ending a speech with a joke is even more risky than opening with one. After all, even if your opening joke falls flat you have the rest of your speech to regain the audience's interest. If you end with a bad joke, however, you'll only be remembered for one thing — your failure to pull it off. Only finish with a joke if you really can't think of anything better and if you're absolutely sure that it will work. When you're preparing your speech, take an occasional look at this checklist of 10 Do's and Don't's just to keep your aims in mind.

Do's

1   Do check your material to ensure that it's suitable for the audience you assessed in the last section.
2   Do make sure that you have included all the things you *have* to say — your vote of thanks or the toast, for example.
3   Do adapt all the material to ensure that it's relevant.
4   Do aim to start and finish your speech on a high note.
5   Do credit any quotations you use.

Don't's

1   Don't use any material that isn't relevant to the occasion or will cause offence.

2   Don't start your speech with a joke unless you feel confident that it will work.
3   Don't tail off at the end of the speech; finish properly.
4   Don't use too many quotes or anecdotes from the lives of other people.
5   Don't speak too long; make sure that your speech is the right length.

Now all you need to know is how to deliver the speech you've written!

Successful Delivery

Preparing your speech is one thing — and the most important of all — but delivering it is something else. Even the best-planned speech can be ruined by nerves, and by the same token a cool head can make a mediocre speech seem impressive. Fortunately just a few simple measures will ensure that your delivery does your speech justice.

Rehearsal

You don't need to learn your speech like an actor, but rehearsal will help you to become familiar with it and iron out any problems that weren't apparent on paper. For example, you may find that a particular sequence of words turns out to be difficult to say — in which case rewrite them. Try to learn half a dozen key lines which will take you smoothly from one part of your speech to the next so that you don't keep having to refer to your notes, and make sure that you know all the punchlines to your jokes. Even professional speakers sometimes forget their material, but knowing the key points allows them to get back on track with the minimum of fuss.

While you are rehearsing, experiment by using your voice to emphasize different points of the speech. If you have a tape recorder, use it to tape the various versions of

21

your speech, then play them back and decide which sounds the most interesting. Don't over-enunciate your words or make your speech sound too theatrical, though. The idea is to be as natural and relaxed as possible, and the best way of telling your jokes is to do it casually, without labouring them too hard. You want to appear confident, and to do that you must have done all your homework.

Body language

No matter how nervous you feel about speaking in front of an audience, you should try not to let them know it. It's body language which most often gives the secret away, so take some precautions to cope with your nerves. Begin by standing easily with your weight on both feet so that you feel balanced. This way you'll look steady, even if you don't feel it. Your main problem will be what to do with your hands. If you have notes, hold them in front of you at about waist-level with one hand. With your free hand, lightly grasp the note-holding wrist. If you're lucky there will be a lectern of some sort at which you can stand. Rest your hands on either side of it and you'll look perfectly at ease. Only royalty can get away with holding their hands behind their backs, and you'll look sloppy if you put your hands in your pockets, so don't adopt either of these postures. If you've no notes and no lectern, just stand with your left hand lightly holding your right wrist in front of you. It looks surprisingly natural. Next time you switch on the TV you'll probably notice how many presenters and comedians use the position!

Notes

The very worst thing you can do is *read* your speech.

Comic speeches need a touch of spontaneity, even if they've been prepared weeks in advance and you've been rehearsing for days. Reading a speech kills the chance of audience interaction. It makes the material seem dull, even if it isn't; it prevents eye contact, which is very important in breaking down the barrier between speaker and audience; and it destroys that important sense of a shared occasion, with speaker and audience responding to each other. On top of all that, the very fact that you are reading will indicate a lack of confidence — and your audience will be alerted to your discomfort and share in it.

That said, it's equally inadvisable to stand up and speak without the aid of any notes at all. Nerves can affect the memories of even professional speakers, so don't take any risks. Many people like to write their notes on postcards, using a single main heading and a couple of key phrases to prompt them. If you decide to do this, make sure that you number the cards clearly. You are bound to drop them if you don't, and reassembling them in the wrong order could create all kinds of chaos! Make sure, too, that you write your headings in large capital letters. When you're standing up and holding the cards at waist level you need to take in all the information at a single glance.

If cards seem too fiddly, write the main headings of your speech on a single sheet of paper, again using a few key words underneath to jog your memory. You'll know, from your rehearsals, those things you find difficult to remember and those which come easily. Jot down the points you get stuck on.

If you're going to use quotations then write them clearly on postcards and read them when the time comes. This ensures that you get them absolutely right and, far from doubting your competence, your audience will be impressed by your thoroughness.

There's no point in trying to hide your notes. Simply

use them as inconspicuously as possible. They prove that you have prepared a speech specially for the occasion and that you care about getting it right — and there's no need to be concerned about that.

On the day

On the day of the speech there are a number of simple precautions you can take to ensure that everything goes smoothly. Some of them may seem quite painfully obvious, but it's the most obvious things that tend to get overlooked, particularly when you're nervous.

The most basic precaution of all is to ensure that you arrive at the right place at the right time. If you can get there a little early you'll be able to check out the acoustics and the arrangements. For example, will you be speaking from a podium or simply standing up at the table? Is there a microphone — and if so, do you know how to work it? If you've had time to think these things through you're less likely to be flustered by them.

Wear the right kind of clothes. You'll feel very uncomfortable if you turn up at a black-tie dinner in your second-best suit, so make sure that you're correctly dressed for the occasion and that everything about you is neat and tidy. You don't have to look like a fashion plate; you simply have to avoid anything distracting. It's a good idea to slip off to the cloakroom before your time comes and check your appearance. There's nothing like a tuft of hair sticking up from the top of your head to take the audience's mind off what you're saying.

While you're in the cloakroom, use the chance to go to the loo. Nerves affect different people in different ways, but it's better to be safe than sorry!

If you know that you tend to put your hands in your pockets while you're speaking, remove all your loose change and keys so that you're not tempted to jangle them. And make sure that you have a clean handkerchief somewhere about you. A scrap of well-used tissue isn't going to impress the audience when you need to blow your nose.

If you've worked hard to make the opening words of your speech interesting and funny, it would be a great shame to waste them by starting to speak while the audience is still talking and settling down in their seats. So wait for silence, even if it seems to take an age, and when you've obtained it start confidently and loudly so that everyone can hear what you have to say. Whatever you do, don't be hurried. Public speakers talk quite slowly and allow plenty of pauses so that the audience can respond. Take it at a leisurely pace, making sure that you're heard throughout the room, and you'll win the audience's attention immediately.

Some people, but only a very few, are at their best after a few drinks. Unless you know for certain that alcohol will improve your performance, it's probably best not to drink before you speak. Drinking tends to dull reactions and instil a false sense of confidence — and you need to be completely in control of yourself and your material if you're going to make a success of the occasion. Naturally, once you've made your speech and it has been greeted with applause and laughter, you can reward yourself!

Whether you've been drinking or not, accidents do happen, and the best way of coping with them is by acknowledging them and turning them to your advantage. For example, the speaker who knocked a glass of water all over himself brought the house down with the throwaway line: 'Whoops! For a moment there I thought my trousers were on fire!' If someone in the audience drops a plate or falls off their chair, acknowledge it and pause for laughter rather than ploughing on as if nothing has happened. Although you have prepared your speech in advance, you should be aware of things happening around you and flexible enough to add a topical remark if necessary. And the better-rehearsed and more at ease you are with your material, the more confident you'll be about including the odd spontaneous line.

If you follow these guidelines you really can't go far wrong. But here, as a last-minute reminder, is a checklist of Do's and Don'ts that will ensure that your delivery will do justice to all the work you've put into your speech.

Do's

1 Do rehearse your material.
2 Do work on your posture so that you look relaxed and comfortable.
3 Do prepare your notes and quotations carefully.
4 Do take simple precautions — like dressing correctly and checking your appearance.
5 Do anticipate any accidents and interruptions and be prepared for them.

Don't's

1 Don't read your speech.
2 Don't make any last-minute attempts to change your accent or your appearance.
3 Don't arrive late or unprepared.
4 Don't start your speech before everyone is ready.
5 Don't drink before you make your speech.

The Right Speech for the Right Occasion

Most people are, quite understandably, nervous at the prospect of standing up and speaking in front of an audience. So it's quite comforting to know that for most social occasions there are tried-and-trusted guidelines which are guaranteed to keep you out of trouble. It's best, unless you have a great deal of public speaking experience, to observe them rather than risk giving the wrong kind of speech for the occasion.

After-dinner speeches

The after-dinner speaker doesn't have to propose toasts or give votes of thanks. He or she has only one job to perform, and that's to entertain the audience with an amusing speech for fifteen minutes or so after dinner. After-dinner speeches are difficult because the speaker has to rely entirely on his or her own wits — but they can also be very rewarding, giving you a chance to show off your skill and wit in front of a willing audience.

Preparation is the most important ingredient of an after-dinner speech, because if you can't speak confidently and amusingly for the prescribed time you're stuck. And the moment a speaker begins to ramble or becomes boring, he has failed in his task — which is to entertain. So for the after-dinner speaker above all others, the section on preparation which you'll find earlier in this book is vital reading.

The second most important ingredient is wit. Although most after-dinner speakers can include a serious moment in their material, no one will want to listen to anything too downbeat. Keep it funny — and you'll find no shortage of suitable jokes and anecdotes in this book.

The final ingredient is brevity. However well your speech seems to be going, don't be tempted to extend it. A short but wickedly amusing speech that keeps the audience spellbound is far better than a longer but only sporadically funny performance. If you should find that your speech doesn't seem to be going down as well as you'd hoped, and if after ten minutes or so things haven't picked up, then cut it short, conclude properly, and sit down. Fortunately, if you follow the guidelines in this book you should have no reason to fear a cool reception!

Presentations

There are a number of social occasions when a knowledge of the formula of a presentation speech will come in useful. Retirement presentations at work, presentations to people who have won awards, school speech days — you'll be relieved to discover that there's one simple formula that covers the lot!

Here's the basic formula being used for a retirement presentation:

1   Name the company (or the award) and its origins:
    Gloss and Matt Brothers have been manufacturing paint in Puddleton for more than fifty years.
2   State the reason for the presentation:
    It's been a long-established custom in this company that

when a valued employee retires we make them a special presentation of a golden paintbrush.

3 State what the recipient has done to deserve the honour:

Gordon Vinyl has represented this company for the past thirty years. His efforts, first as a salesman and now as a sales controller, have made Gloss and Matt Brothers' paint the most widely sold paint in the south-west of England. His reputation, both in sales and in the company generally, is second to none, and we are all very sad to be saying good-bye to him this evening.

4 Make the presentation.

Gordon, I'd like you to accept this golden paintbrush as a token of our thanks and esteem on the occasion of your retirement from this company.

If the person making the presentation has an amusing anecdote about the recipient it can be included, but don't speak for too long and don't hog the limelight. If you are the person to whom the presentation is being made you can reply following this formula:

1 Say thank you:

Thank you, Mr Matt, for this lovely paintbrush.

2 Acknowledge the company or the organization:

When I first joined the company it was operating out of a small warehouse in Puddleton. Now that I see its factories all over the country and its adverts on television I take great pride in knowing that I have helped it grow and flourish. Naturally I'm very sad to be leaving, but I'm most honoured by this award.

3 Say what you intend to do with the award:

I shall hang this paintbrush in my sitting-room so that as I sit relaxing and enjoying my retirement I am reminded of all of you still here. Thank you.

Don't be modest about your award. If you say that you

can't think what you've done to merit it you'll find that some people in the audience agree while others don't believe a word of it. Accept it with grace and don't speak for too long.

Introductions

If you ever have to present a speaker at a meeting, just follow these guidelines. They're simple but they will ensure that you include all the important details that your audience need to know.

1 Introduce the subject and make it sound interesting.
2 Stress the importance and topicality of the matter under discussion. No one wants to believe that they're about to hear a speech on something trivial.
3 Introduce the speaker and outline his or her qualifications and expertise.

If the speaker is already known to you and the audience, waive the rules and introduce them with an anecdote. Remember, though, not to steal their thunder. It's always best to double-check a speaker's name, qualifications and if there's anything about the subject that they would prefer you not to mention in your introduction. Mistakes can happen — as the chairman who finished his introduction and sat down, only to learn that he had introduced the wrong subject, blown the speaker's main argument and pronounced his name wrong, discovered.

Toasts

A toast, as Lord Butler once remarked, should be like a woman's skirt — long enough to cover everything but short enough to be interesting. Follow his advice if you're asked to propose a toast and allow yourself a couple of minutes at most for your introductory remarks.

As with all speeches, make your comments brief, relevant and witty. If you know the people to whom you are proposing the toast then include a personal anecdote about them — but resist all temptation to turn it into a full-blooded speech. You'll find a whole section of toasts for various social occasions in this book, but if none of them seems ideal a simple and sincere tribute along the lines of, 'I'd like you to join me in a toast wishing our friends another twenty-five years of happy marriage. Ladies and gentlemen, George and Caroline,' will do perfectly. Simplicity and sincerity can't, in the long run, be beaten.

Opening functions

Everything, from supermarkets and bridges to the local fête, needs to be opened. If you're invited to open a function the one rule to remember is to be brief and to the point. Your audience will be waiting to get on with whatever it is you're opening, so don't hold them up. Speak for five minutes at the very most, and be prepared to cut your material and finish gracefully if you find you're losing the battle. Be sure, however, to cover these five main points.

1   Thank the person who introduced you. (Before you can do this you'll have to find out who they are and what position they hold.)
2   If there is a reason why you in particular have been asked to open the function, say what it is.
3   If it's a charity function give some details about the charity. If it's a new facility, say how the local community will benefit.

4   Thank the people who organized the function for their hard work and encourage everyone to spend money.
5   Declare it open.

There's really nothing more to it than that.

Votes of thanks

If you have organized a function or you're on a committee you will one day have to propose a vote of thanks to a guest speaker. It's difficult to prepare a vote of thanks in advance because it has to be spontaneous to be effective, and by writing it in advance you'll ruin any chance of it sounding fresh.

Prove to the speaker that you've listened intently to his remarks by commenting lightly on some of the points made in the speech — but remember not to turn it into an action-replay of what has gone before. Don't, even if you disagree with what's been said, feel tempted to turn it into a debate, either. Simply say how much you enjoyed the speech and why, and thank the speaker as generously as honesty permits and as briefly as courtesy allows.

Weddings

Before you begin to write your wedding speech give a few minutes' thought to the kind of wedding it's going to be. If it's an informal affair with a buffet reception and no bridesmaids then you can afford to relax the rules. But if it's a grand gathering your speech should observe the formalities.

Remember, too, that if the guests are on their feet they won't give you their attention for long — so make your speech as brief and amusing as possible. One final tip.

Make sure that everyone has something in their glass before you make a toast. Furtive groping for the nearest bottle is enough to distract from the funniest speech.

Most weddings are family affairs, so be careful that your material won't offend anyone, not even your grandmother. Try to avoid anything cynical, too. This may sound painfully obvious, but a great number of jokes wheeled out at weddings manage to imply that the groom has been trapped into marriage or that every blushing bride turns into a harridan the moment the ring is placed on her finger.

The order and content of the speeches has become fixed by tradition and for the sake of continuity it's probably best if all concerned observe the guidelines.

The father of the bride

The father of the bride is the first to speak. He rises when the best man has obtained silence for him and after a speech that lasts five minutes at the most, he proposes the toast to the bride and groom. In the section of this book entitled 'Drink to Me Only' you'll find a variety of toasts suitable for weddings, but if none of them seem exactly right for the occasion it's difficult to beat a classically simple one along the lines of, 'I'm sure, ladies and gentlemen, that you will raise your glasses and join me in a toast of good health and great happiness to the bride and groom.'

The bridegroom

The bridegroom follows his father-in-law with a speech of thanks to the guests, to his new family and, finally, a toast to the bridesmaids. As before, you'll find a suitable toast in the relevant section of this book.

33

If anyone at a wedding is expected to give a comic speech, it's the best man — but he shouldn't be funny at the expense of his official duties, which are to reply on behalf of the bridesmaids and to read out the telegrams and telemessages. If the best man has some personal anecdotes about the bride and groom they're bound to go down well. He should never, however, be risqué or cynical. Weddings are special occasions and marring them with a dubious joke or thoughtless comment is unforgivable.

Family occasions

There are a great number of family occasions which can be enhanced by a good speech. Chistenings, birthdays, engagements and wedding anniversaries are obvious contenders, and for the speaker they can be particularly pleasant occasions because so many of the rules of speaking can be relaxed. When else will you be able to speak in front of an audience who will judge you so charitably?

Despite that, you'll have to put in just as much work on a speech for your family as you would for any other audience. You may be familiar with them (literally!) but don't let that breed contempt.

Prepare your material as thoroughly as you would for any other occasion so that you don't ramble, and check that nothing you intend to say will offend anyone. Remember that families can generate difficult undercurrents, so steer well away from anything touchy — like jokes about relatives who don't get on well, or problematic marriages.

If you can fill ten or fifteen minutes with amusing anecdotes and relevant comments then do so, but if you sense that your audience is getting restless then cut your material and end gracefully. It's particularly important when you're speaking in front of your family to be sincere. Don't be over-effusive or falsely modest; your family will know you well enough to sense whether you mean what you say, so you'd better believe it!

It's impossible to detail all the social functions at which you may be asked to speak, but the general guidelines offered in this part of the book will still apply, whatever the occasion. Remember that if you're in doubt it's better to check with the organizers of the function to find out what they want you to do than to prepare and deliver the wrong type of speech. Once you know what they want you should have no trouble giving it to them!

PART TWO

The Material

Only Joking

It's almost impossible to say what makes an ideal joke for a wedding or which is most appropriate for a retirement presentation — and that's why this section contains jokes about a wide variety of subjects. Reading through it you're guaranteed to find something that's just right for your purpose.

Whichever jokes you decide to use, remember to add as much personal detail as you can and rewrite them in your own words. That way you won't just have borrowed your material from a book, you will have made it your own.

A Mother Superior heard one of her nuns ask a pupil of the convent school to define the state of matrimony.

'It's a time of torment which some of us must experience before we are allowed to experience a better world,' the child replied.

'No,' the nun corrected. 'You have just defined Purgatory, not matrimony.'

'Don't bother the child,' said the Mother Superior. 'Perhaps she's been allowed to see the light.'

When a man in his eighties went to his solicitor to file for a divorce against his wife, who was in her seventies, the solicitor asked how long they had been married.

'Fifty-two years,' the old chap replied.

'And why do you want to get divorced after all this time?' the solicitor enquired.

'Enough is enough,' said his client.

A country girl who could neither read nor write was in the habit of signing for her wages with a cross in the farmer's account book. One Friday she came in and, instead of signing with the cross as usual, she drew a circle.

'Why don't you make your cross?' asked the farmer.

'I suppose you don't know,' she said, 'but I got married last week and I've changed my name.'

Many years ago a shy young man began courting an equally timid girl. He took her to the pictures, for walks in the country and did everything that a lover was supposed to do, but somehow he could never find the courage to ask her to marry him. And of course, she was far too bashful to take the initiative. So the years went by with the couple still courting. Eventually they both began to draw their pensions — and still he hadn't managed to pop the question.

One evening as they sat by the fire, Mary decided that she couldn't wait any longer. 'Jack,' she announced, 'isn't it about time that we thought about getting married?'

'Don't be silly,' said Jack. 'Who'd have us at our age?'

A recently married golfer was one day asked by his mother-in-law whether she could accompany him on a round, just to see what the game was about. Naturally the man was nervous and anxious to prove how good a player he was. As he stationed her near the green of the first hole, he confided to his partner, 'See that woman there? That's my mother-in-law. I want this drive to be especially good.'

'Don't be stupid,' said the partner, 'You'll never hit her from here.'

The family next door were most concerned when their uncle, who'd been a bachelor all his life, married a girl in her twenties shortly before his eightieth birthday. They were even more alarmed when, on his return from the honeymoon, he boasted that they had made love three times a day for the entire fortnight.

'But Uncle,' they said, 'a person can *die* from this amount of activity!'

'So what?' he replied. 'If she dies, she dies.'

A husband decided to take his wife out for a perfect romantic evening to celebrate their wedding anniversary. They went to the theatre, then for a candlelit dinner and finally for a walk down by the river in the moonlight. By the time they arrived home they were both in the mood, and to round off the evening perfectly the husband produced a bottle of champagne — and two small white pills.

'What are these?' asked the wife as she raised them to her lips. 'They're like aspirins.'

'They *are* aspirins,' he conceded.

'But I don't have a headache.'

'Great — let's go straight to bed!'

'Oh darling,' said the bridegroom, 'to think that you'll be putting up with my ugly old face for the rest of my life!'

The bride gazed at him fondly. 'Don't worry,' she assured him. 'You'll be out at work until it gets dark most days.'

A man was talking to his friend in the pub and the conversation came round to how difficult it was for a couple to share the same interests. 'Just the other night, for example,' he said, 'we were going out. I wanted to see the local theatre's production of *Hamlet* but my wife fancied going to see *The Sound of Music*. Eventually, though, we came to an arrangement.'

'Oh, really?' said his friend. 'And did you enjoy *The Sound of Music*?'

41

'I love you so much,' said the young man, 'but I'm only a teacher. Do you think you could live on a teacher's salary?'

'I'm sure I could,' replied the girlfriend. 'But darling, what will *you* live on?'

She was bossy, interfering and fussy, and Jane tolerated her around the house for as long as she could, but after two months she couldn't stand it a moment longer. She ran to her husband as he returned from work and cried, 'John, I simply can't stand your mother living here a day longer!'

John turned pale. '*My* mother? I thought she was *your* mother!'

The happy couple were nearing their honeymoon hotel when the bride was overcome with embarrassment. 'Oh,' she sighed, 'I don't want all those people to know that we're newly married. Isn't there something we could do? We could pretend to be an old married couple . . .'

The new husband pondered for a moment. 'What can we do to give the impression we've been married for years?'

'That's easy,' said the taxi driver. 'When we arrive you just have to give her all the suitcases to carry.'

The romantic young man turned to the beautiful young girl in his bed and asked, 'Am I the first man you ever made love to?'

She thought for a moment, then said, 'You could be — I have a terrible memory for faces.'

A man once married a woman who never stopped talking, and she served on numerous committees where she gave her opinions on a variety of subjects. Her long-suffering husband never gave a murmur about this until one evening when she returned from a council meeting. 'You won't believe it,' she told him 'but you should have heard me this evening. I was positively outspoken.'

At which the husband looked up wearily from his paper and said, 'But dear, who would dare outspeak you?'

In the middle of a furious row with her husband a wife stormed, 'I wish I'd listened to my mother! She told me we were incompatible.'

'Your mother said that?' asked the husband, looking suddenly distressed. 'How I've wronged that poor woman all these years!'

A girl went to the doctor to ask for some help in losing weight before her wedding, and he prescribed a course of pills for her. A few days later she returned to the surgery. 'These pills have terrible side effects, Doctor,' she said worriedly. 'They make me feel terribly passionate and I get carried away — the other night I actually bit off my boyfriend's ear!'

'Don't worry,' said the doctor. 'That would only be sixty calories or so.'

There was once a very ambitious businessman who was so determined to get to the top of his career that he decided to forsake marriage in the pursuit of success. And indeed he was successful, and such a workaholic that he never seemed to miss female company. Then at the age of seventy he retired — and amazed everyone who knew him by announcing that he was going to marry his secretary, a very shy girl of seventeen.

On their wedding night he joined his bride in bed. 'Tell me, my dear,' he said, 'did your mother ever explain the facts of life to you?'

The girl blushed. 'No, I'm afraid she didn't.'

'Hmmmm ... This is awkward — you see, I seem to have forgotten them.'

At a dinner party the guests were discussing the forth-coming marriage of someone known to all of them — a lady famed for her sex life.

'She's actually confessed to her new husband, told him everything about her past,' one said.

'*All* those affairs?' another commented. 'What courage she has!'

'Courage, yes,' agreed a third. 'And what a memory!'

A father was giving his son some advice on the evening before his wedding. 'Always remember,' he said, 'that there are two ingredients in a marriage — honesty and good sense.'

'What do you mean by honesty, Dad?' asked the young man.

'That's simple. Once you have given your word to your wife about something you must keep it.'

'And what do you mean by good sense?'

'Never give your word.'

The hotel manager was giving some advice to his staff about how to cope with embarrassing circumstances. 'Suppose one of you enters a room and finds a lady in a state of undress. Anything you do or say could make matters worse, but there is a simple way out,' he instructed, 'Just pretend that you're short-sighted and say something like, "Oh, I'm terribly sorry, *sir*. I'll come back in a minute." Then the woman will think that you didn't notice her properly and be spared her blushes.'

The very next morning a young waiter on duty taking breakfast to guests' rooms knocked at a bedroom door and, receiving no answer, poked his head around the door. There on the bed a naked young couple were indulging in an energetic bout of lovemaking. Suddenly they sensed his presence, and there was a ghastly silence — until the waiter remembered the lecture of the day before.

44

With complete confidence he asked, 'Would either of you gentlemen like breakfast?'

Shortly before Christmas one year the workers at a Post Office depot came across a letter addressed to Santa Claus. When they opened it, they found inside a heart-rending letter from an old age pensioner asking Santa to send five pounds to cover her gas bill. Feeling full of the Christmas spirit, the postmen clubbed together and raised the money without much trouble, and with a note saying 'Merry Christmas from Santa' they sent it to her.

The next week there came another letter from the same elderly lady, thanking Santa and asking if he would send the money to cover her electricity bill. There was another whip-round and the cash was sent to her. The next week a third letter arrived, full of thanks and with yet another plea for money — this time for thirty pounds. The postmen did their best but could only raise half the sum, which they duly sent off.

After Christmas a fourth note was received at the depot, and this time when they opened it, instead of a request for money, the postmen found a letter saying, 'Dear Santa, thanks very much for the money. You've been so good to me that I can't believe you let me down with the money I asked for. I reckon those bloody postmen opened the letter and nicked some of the notes ...'

All marriages look wonderful on the wedding day but the rot sets in soon after the honeymoon. A young man, two years married, sat slumped in front of the TV set watching the racing. The *Sporting Life* lay open on the floor in front of him. His wife, meanwhile, was trying to prepare a meal, sweep the floor and comfort their son, who was wailing in his playpen.

The husband, distracted from the racing, turned to look at the child. Did he get up to see what was wrong? He did not. He just shouted to his long-suffering wife,

'Darling, baby's nose is running again.'

At this the poor woman lost her temper. 'Don't you ever,' she shouted, 'think of *anything* except horses?'

The happy couple had laid out all their presents for the wedding guests to admire. In pride of place was a cheque from the bride's father for a thousand pounds. And standing in front of it was a man laughing hysterically. 'Who's that?' asked the groom.

'Just Daddy's bank manager,' explained the bride.

At an international summit meeting the English ambassador, the French ambassador and the Russian ambassador were occupying a break in negotiations by discussing the nationality of Adam and Eve.

'She must have been English,' said the English ambassador. 'Only an Englishwoman would be so selfless as to give away all her food to her husband.'

'Only the French would have been sitting naked in a garden enjoying a picnic,' said the French ambassador. 'They were without doubt French.'

'No, no, you're both wrong,' said the Russian. 'Here are two people who have no clothes to wear, very little food to eat, nothing to do and they think they're in paradise. They *have* to be Russians.'

A motorist who had broken down on a country road was staring hopelessly into the engine when, to his amazement, a cow ambled up. It took a long hard look under the bonnet, then said, 'It's the carburettor that's the problem.'

The motorist was so stunned that he ran down the road — and bumped straight into the cowman who was driving some more beasts into a field. He stood and listened while the motorist told him the amazing story of what had happened.

'Was she a white cow with a brown patch between her eyes?' he asked.

'Yes! Yes!' cried the motorist.

'I wouldn't take any notice if I were you,' said the cowman. 'That's Daisy and she doesn't know a thing about cars.'

There was only one minute to play in the jungle football match and the crowd was tense as the anteater passed the ball to the flea, who leaped down the pitch and prepared to take a shot at goal. Suddenly the defending elephant raced up and squashed the poor striker flat.

'You've killed a player,' cried the ref. 'Get off!'

'But ref,' sobbed the emotional elephant, 'I only meant to trip him!'

Two lunatics were allowed out of the asylum for a day trip to London. They went to the House of Commons and watched happily as the MPs hissed and booed and catcalled each other. Then suddenly a bell rang and everyone raced away into the lobbies ... 'Ah,' said one lunatic to the other, 'someone has escaped.'

A company chairman had to give a speech at a conference and asked his personal assistant to draft it for him. The following day he stormed into the office and confronted the PA. 'I asked for a twenty-minute speech,' he complained, 'but it lasted for an hour. And what's more, it was so boring it had everyone asleep.'

'I *did* write a twenty-minute speech,' replied the assistant. 'And I supplied you with two carbon copies ...'

A man who had been unemployed for a long time eventually found work in a china shop. At the end of his first week, he dropped a huge vase. His superior called him over. 'That was a Ming vase,' he said. 'It cost thousands — and we'll be deducting some money each week from

47

your pay until the cost is recovered.'

The man just smiled broadly and said, 'Wonderful! At last I know I've got a steady job!'

A novice went to Mother Superior and confessed that she was pregnant. 'Go to your room,' she was told, 'and drink a glass of vinegar and the juice of a dozen lemons.'

'But that won't get rid of the baby,' the young nun replied.

'It may not,' said the reverend mother, 'but at least it will take that smile off your face.'

Asked by his grandson why the ten commandments were written on two tablets of stone instead of one, a Jewish grandfather explained that at first God had approached the French to see if they would like the commandments. The French read them but declined the offer, saying that they could not accept 'Thou shalt not commit adultery' because it was part of their way of life.

God then went to Ireland to see if they'd like them. They gave one look at them and exclaimed, 'Never! How could we love our neighbours when we're just over the water from the English?'

Depressed, God took the commandments to Israel and offered them to the Jews. 'How much are they?' asked the Jews.

'They're free,' said God.

'In that case we'll take two.'

Two Russian defectors living in America were growing increasingly homesick — but because they weren't sure of the reception they'd get if they went back, they drew straws to decide who would return and test the water. They arranged that once he was back in Russia, the returning defector would write to the defector still in America. 'I'll write in black ink if everything's all right and red ink if it's not,' the Moscow-bound one arranged.

After a silence of several weeks, the man in America received a letter. It was written in black ink and read, 'I'm having a wonderful time in Russia. It's great to be back. There's only one problem — I couldn't buy any red ink.'

St Peter arrived at the Heavenly Gates one morning to find a huge queue of men behind the notice which read 'Queue here all men who are hen-pecked by their wives.' But behind the second notice, 'Queue here all men who are not hen-pecked by their wives,' there was only one weedy-looking little chap. 'Why are you queuing here to enter Heaven?' St Peter asked.

'I'm not sure,' said the little man. 'My wife just told me to stand here.'

'That's the tenth time you've been to the bar this evening,' an office manager's wife warned him at the company Christmas party. 'What will everyone think?'

'Don't worry,' he replied. 'Every time I order a drink I say it's for you.'

A doctor at a civic dinner was waylaid by another guest as he made his way to the table and quizzed about the woman's health problems. It took him ten minutes to escape from her, by which time he'd missed his first course.

'Do you think I should send her a bill?' he asked the solicitor sitting next to him.

'Why not? After all, you've rendered her a personal service by giving her advice.'

The doctor forgot all about it until he arrived at his surgery the next morning to find a letter from the solicitor. It read: 'To legal services, twenty pounds.'

As she climbed onto a bus one afternoon a young teacher thought she recognised a man sitting across the aisle. She gave him a smile but he looked blankly at her and she realised that she had made a mistake. 'Excuse me,' she said. 'I thought for a moment that you were the father of two of my children.'

A zoo keeper was sent to the airport to collect a consignment of penguins one hot summer's day. Unfortunately on his way back the van broke down, so he got out and tried to find the fault. The penguins were getting very fidgety, so he was pleased when another van driver pulled up to help.

'Do me a favour,' he said. 'The penguins are very uncomfortable in the back in this heat. Would you take them to the zoo for me? Here's a tenner for your trouble.'

So together the two men unloaded the penguins into the other van and off they went. After a couple of hours the AA turned up to fix the engine, and with relief the zoo keeper drove back to the zoo to make sure that the penguins were okay after their troubled journey. Imagine his shock when he got there to find that there was no sign of them. Where could they be? He jumped back into the van and set off for the police station — but halfway there he saw the penguins all waddling down the pavement, following the man who had helped him out earlier.

'Hey,' he yelled. 'What do you think you're doing with my penguins? I gave you ten pounds to take them to the zoo!'

'I know that,' said the other man. 'I took them to the zoo, and they seemed to like it. But I've still got some money left over so I thought I'd take them to the pictures.'

A famous professor had been studying insects and their behaviour for years, and during a symposium at one of the country's top universities he had decided that the time had come to demonstrate his findings to the scientific community. Knowing how long he had been working on his project, and suspecting some brilliant new developments, all the nation's insect experts were there.

The professor placed a spider on the table. 'Take five steps forward,' he told it. The other scientists held their breath as the insect obeyed the instruction. 'Now take two steps back,' came the command. Again the spider obeyed. A ripple of astonishment went round the assembled experts. A spider with intelligence!

Then the professor pulled all the legs off the spider and placed it back on the table. 'Take five steps forward,' he commanded. Nothing happened.

'There, gentlemen,' the professor said proudly. 'That just goes to prove that when you pull a spider's legs off it goes deaf.'

A very respectable lady was holding a smart dinner party with a number of extremely staid guests. So she was horrified when, halfway through the soup, the door of the dining-room opened and her two small children, aged four and six, came in — completely naked.

There was a moment's pause and then, to cover their confusion, all the guests started speaking very loudly at once. Meanwhile the children tiptoed silently around the room and, having completed a circuit, went out the way they had come in. Silence fell again, just as one child said to the other, 'See, I told you the jar said Vanishing Cream!'

Two babies had been parked side by side in their push-chairs while their mothers talked. One baby asked the other, 'Are you a boy or a girl?'

'I don't know.'

'Just a minute,' said the first, 'I'll have a look for you.' And he dived beneath the covers and came up giggling a few moments later. 'You're a girl and I'm a boy,' he announced.

'How can you tell the difference?' the first asked.

'It's easy. You're wearing pink bootees and I'm wearing blue ones.'

A visiting speaker was addressing a group of sixth-formers on the problems of overpopulation. 'Do you realise,' he announced, 'that somewhere in the world a woman is giving birth to a child every ninety seconds?'

A hand shot up in the audience. 'Hadn't we better find this woman and stop her?'

Simon's rich auntie was coming to tea and his mother warned him before she arrived that he must be on his best behaviour and speak only when spoken to. And he did in fact behave very well, except for staring at the aunt throughout the meal. At last she could bear it no longer.

'Goodness, Simon,' she asked, 'why are you staring at me like that?'

'I was waiting for you to do your trick,' he said.

'What trick might that be?'

'Daddy says you drink like a fish and I wanted to see you do it.'

A little girl was chatting to her mother who was trying to get a nappy onto her screaming baby son. 'Mum, where did our baby come from?' the child asked.

'He came from Heaven,' replied the mother.

The girl listened to the baby's screams before commenting, 'You can't blame them for kicking him out, can you?'

A visitor sat aghast in his friend's house and watched their three-year-old son knock two-inch nails into an antique rosewood dining-table. The doting parents, who had a reputation for being totally indulgent, just went on talking as if nothing was happening. Finally the visitor summoned up the courage to comment on it.

'Have you seen what Damien's doing?' he asked.

The mother smiled fondly. 'He's well coordinated for his age, don't you think? It's his favourite game. Sorry about the noise.'

'Does he do it regularly?'

'Yes, mostly with the Chippendale chairs in the hall. They seem to be his favourite.'

'But doesn't it work out very expensive?' asked the visitor.

The mother looked suprised. 'Not really,' she shrugged. 'The nails only cost twenty-five pence a dozen.'

Flicking through a photo album with his son, a father came across some photos of his wedding day. The little boy looked at them and, pointing to his mother in her wedding dress, asked, 'Was that the day Mum came to work for us?'

On a trip to a country park a little boy saw a peacock for the first time. 'Over here quick,' he yelled to his parents. 'There's a hen in full bloom!'

'It's a great sin to profit from someone else's mistake,' said the vicar.

'In that case,' said the harassed-looking parishioner, 'I wonder if you'd care to refund the fee you took when you married me to my wife.'

When two people were married before the Second World War they weren't encouraged to express their built-up irritation with each other as young people are today. Instead they were told that, if either of them was tempted to say anything angry or unkind, he or she should leave the house and go for a walk until the bad feeling had worn off. This goes some way to explaining why the most difficult of the older generation seem to live longest — they're incredibly fit!

Each Friday night on his way home from work a middle-aged husband treated himself to a large Scotch. Knowing how much his wife hated him drinking, he would take care to conceal the smell by sucking an extra-strong peppermint on the way home. This went on for years, until one Friday night, as he left the pub on his way home, the man realised that he didn't have any mints on him. The sweetshop was shut, so he hastily went back into the pub and ate two pickled onions. As he walked in the front door his wife took one look at him and said, 'That's enough — I'm leaving you!'

The husband was thunderstruck. 'What do you mean?' he asked.

'For ten whole years I've put up with you coming home every Friday night smelling of whisky and pepper-mints,' she told him, 'but if it's going to be whisky and pickled onions I'm going back to mother!'

'What have you ever achieved in your life, except to fritter your time away?' the elderly lady asked her equally elderly husband.

The husband replied, 'Don't worry, dear. All our family are late developers.'

Mr Brown, who was due to retire the following morning, tossed and turned all night. Eventually his wife turned on the light and asked him, 'What's the matter? Are you worried about saying goodbye to all your friends at work?'

'It's not that,' he said worriedly. 'I keep wondering how we're going to manage on my pension. We've got nothing in the way of savings and we've still got the HP payments to pay off ...'

'I've got a secret,' said Mrs Brown. 'When we got married I knew you weren't likely to earn a great deal and so I decided that every time we made love I'd put aside some money in the bank. And do you know,' she smiled, 'over the years it's added up to a tidy sum. Wasn't that clever of me?'

Mr Brown merely looked more distressed than ever. 'If

only you'd told me! At that rate I wouldn't have spread my deposits around so much.'

A man approaching retirement went along to see the company doctor for one final check-up. To his horror the doctor said, 'I don't know quite how to put this — but your heart is on its last legs and you've only got six months to live.'

'Is there nothing I can do?' asked the shocked man.

'Well,' said the doctor, 'you can give up alcohol and cut out smoking. Don't eat any fried food or sugar and don't even *think* about sex.'

'And this will make me live longer?' the man asked hopefully.

'No,' replied the doctor, 'it'll just seem like longer.'

A local reporter went to interview a man who had just reached the ripe old age of ninety and had entered a marathon. 'Tell me, to what do you attribute your amazing energy and fitness?' he asked.

'Well, I don't drink and I don't smoke and I've never bothered much with women,' the old gent answered.

At this point there was a tremendous crash from upstairs. 'That'll be my father,' the old man said. 'He always gets fresh with the nurse when he's had a few.'

An employee who had successfully taken his company to court over an alleged industrial injury hobbled out on his crutches — only to be met by the company lawyer. 'I'm sure you've faked this whole thing,' the lawyer said, 'and you have conned my client out of thousands of pounds. So just be warned that I intend to have you followed day and night until I uncover your fraud. Why don't you give me details of your movements so that it will be easier for both of us?'

'Very well,' said the invalid with a smile. 'Tonight I'm staying at the Dorchester. Tomorrow I fly to Paris for a week. And the week after that I'm going to Lourdes where I might, if I'm lucky, experience a miracle cure!'

A very elegant lady was walking through Mayfair after a charity ball when a tramp approached her and begged the price of a cup of coffee. She looked him up and down with distaste as her companion opened the door of the Rolls Royce.

'Honestly, you people have a nerve,' she exclaimed. 'I've been dancing my feet off all night long in aid of charity, and here you are asking for *more.*'

A young British aristocrat decided that there must be more to life than champagne, fast cars and country houses and so went to India to look for a guru. Before long he found one, and went to join the ashram. 'Do you realise that we believe that the only way to spiritual perfection is through silence?' asked the guru. The young man nodded. 'At the end of your first year with us you will be allowed to say one sentence,' said the guru. 'In this way you will learn that most speech is unnecessary.'

Life at the ashram was hard; devotees spent most of their time listening to the teachings of the guru and living a very basic existence. Nevertheless, the aristo stuck it out, and at the end of his first year he was called in and asked what his one sentence was.

'I'm afraid I'm not getting enough to eat,' he blurted out before being dismissed. Things improved slightly for him, and at the end of his second year he was called back again. 'I get terribly cold at night,' he said, 'and I'd be grateful for another blanket.' Once again he was dismissed. For a third year he put up with the privations in the hope of attaining spiritual enlightenment, but this time when he was called in to speak he admitted, 'I'm awfully sorry but I'm not happy here and I'd like to leave.'

'I'm not surprised,' said the guru. 'Ever since you arrived you've done nothing but moan!'

A Funny Thing Happened . . .

*Real life is infinitely stranger and more amusing than fiction —
and that's why a real-life anecdote can form the high-point of a
speech. But no matter how funny a story, it won't work for you
unless you can weave it firmly into your speech and make it relevant to what you have to say. The very best anecdotes of all are
those related to the occasion or to someone present at the function; if you can do some research beforehand and discover a
pertinent story you'll delight your audience.*

A Hastings housewife wrote to a national newspaper
saying that she knew her husband was having an affair
when he climbed out of the bed in the early hours of the
morning and went to get dressed.

'What are you doing?' she asked.

'I've got to go home now,' he replied.

A young couple set off for their honeymoon in Devon
recently. Unfortunately they were so absorbed in each
other that after pulling off the motorway for a tea break
they took the wrong slip road onto the M6 and, after
driving all night, found themselves in Scotland.

The congregation at a wedding service in Chesterfield had
to stifle their giggles when the vicar, who naturally
enough had not an impure thought in his head, gave a

sermon which included the observation that, 'Sometimes in a marriage the couple have been known to get on top of one another . . .'

A young woman wrote to a magazine's agony aunt with the following question. 'My boyfriend is very good looking and we get on well except that he's a bit of a square. I like going to discos and pop concerts and he doesn't. He says I'm a case of arrested development, but I measure 36-23-36. What do you think he means?'

At a wedding in Pennsylvania the ceremony was almost over and the bride and groom had almost finished saying their vows. As the groom uttered the words 'I do' he collapsed and fell to the floor. The clergyman bending over him heard him whisper 'My God — I do,' again before he died. The wife asked to be declared an 'official widow.'

At a recent wedding in Berkshire the bride's father, determined to show off, planned a wedding with all the trimmings. It went well and looked very impressive until the end of the service, when the bride and groom processed out of the church with choir and clergy behind them. As they came to the door the bride caught her heel in the wrought-iron heating vent. For a few seconds she tried to wrench it out, but realising she was stuck she pulled her foot free of the shoe and limped out. The chief chorister, showing presence of mind, bent down and picked up the shoe — only to find that the grating came up with it. He stepped neatly over the hole but was too late to warn the vicar, who fell straight into it!

After a very busy day, the best man at a west London wedding was becoming steadily more drunk — and more and more bitter about women. When conversation at the bar turned to holidays and the best place for them, one of his fellow drinkers began to extol the virtues of Wales. The best man couldn't prevent himself from adding a cynical comment. 'Wales! There are only two worthwhile things that come from Wales, and that's prostitutes and rugby players.'

Silence fell over the place as the bridegroom's brother-in-law approached. 'I heard that,' he said, 'and I thought you ought to know that my wife was born and bred in Wales.'

'Really?' said the best man. 'What position did she play?'

An article in the *Daily Mirror* tells the sad story of an unfortunate girl arriving alone in London. 'She was picked up by two men as she got off the bus at Victoria coach station. Within minutes she was drinking coffee with them. Within hours she was no longer a virgin. Within a week she was being sold to rich Americans and Arabs in a luxury hotel. She realised too late what was happening to her.'

An anxious hostess who was to entertain the Aga Khan wrote to the Heralds of the Colleges of Arms about a matter of etiquette. This is the reply she received. 'The Aga Khan is held by his followers to be the direct descendant of God. An English Duke takes precedence.'

In 1980 an Australian businessman, who'd had his eye on his secretary for a long time, was thrilled when she invited him back to her home on the evening of his birthday. On their way there she chatted to him animatedly, determined to put him at his ease, and he felt sure that she was giving him the come-on. At her flat she gave him a large whisky and suggested that he take off his jacket and tie while she popped into the bedroom for a moment. He needed no urging, and convinced that he was in for a delightful evening, he took the opportunity to remove more than his jacket. In fact he was stark naked when his young son, his wife and his work colleagues emerged from the bedroom carrying a birthday cake and everything else needed for the party ...

In 1971 a raid on a South Carolina brothel resulted in the arrest of 800 men. In the days that followed the Sheriff responsible for the case received dozens of calls from men asking that he remove their name from the list — and one from an elderly man who offered him $100 to have his name *added*.

After his divorce, a London man joined a dating agency in search of a new partner. The computer sorted through its list to find him the perfect mate and came up with one woman who seemed to satisfy all his requirements and who was looking for someone just like him. It turned out to be his former wife, who was making use of the same service. They met again and decided that, as they seemed suited for each other in every way, they might as well remarry.

Katherine Hepburn and Spencer Tracy had a long and very successful partnership in films, but at their first meeting an observer might be forgiven for wondering if they could work together. On being introduced to her new leading man Miss Hepburn is reported to have observed, 'I see I'm a little tall for you, Mr Tracy.'

To which Spencer Tracy replied, 'Never mind, Miss Hepburn. I'll soon cut you down to size.'

Forbidden to marry by her eighty-six-year-old brother, a seventy-six-year-old Greek woman persuaded her eighty-four-year-old suitor to elope with her. Their plans went wrong, however, when the brother pounced on the runaway couple as they descended from her bedroom. The fiancé fell off the bottom rung and broke his ankle and the brother tripped over in the scuffle and broke his leg. They ended up in adjoining beds in the hospital, with the sister holding both their hands!

A Yugoslavian man arranged to elope with his young girl-friend and, as they'd planned, spirited her away from her home wrapped in a blanket. He put her in his car and drove speedily away. Only after he was some miles away did he stop to greet his beloved — but when he pulled the blanket back he discovered that he'd abducted her seventy-three-year-old grandmother. What's more the old lady took advantage of his state of shock to beat him up!

In 1973 a newspaper reported an unusual disturbance at a Pakistani wedding. The bride turned on the guests in the wedding party and felled her father-in-law with a bottle of whisky, fracturing his skull. She then set about her father and locked her mother in the toilet before running into the street, stealing the bridegroom's car and crashing it. All he could say, as she disappeared into the crowd, was, 'This is the first time she has expressed any emotion towards me.'

Lots of things can stand in the way of love, and in the past class was a vital ingredient in a relationship — as a steward on board a ship bound for India discovered when he fell for Lady Veronica Maitland, a beautiful nineteen-year-old who was to grow up into a woman famous for her style and wit. After a night of bliss spent in her cabin, the steward made so bold as to approach her the next day. She reproved him coldly, saying, 'In the circles in which I move, sleeping with a woman does not constitute an introduction.'

No matter how hard people try, there is always someone who manages to put their foot in it. At a presentation lunch only a few months ago the speaker who had been engaged for the occasion was forced to withdraw. His reason was hazy but it was widely understood that he had had a mild nervous breakdown. A substitute was arranged, but at the eleventh hour the original speaker telephoned to say that he was available to speak after all. Unfortunately the chairman wasn't able to inform everyone of this change of plan, and when he arrived at the function he found the speaker in conversation with the wife of the Treasurer.

'Here you are at last,' she greeted the chairman. 'I was just explaining to Mr Jones that our original speaker had gone completely round the bend ...'

An English diplomat at the Moscow embassy was called on to speak to a Russian trade mission in Russia. He worked hard at his speech and practised his pronunciation until it was perfect, but unfortunately as he rose to speak the words for 'Ladies and gentlemen' went clean out of his head. He hadn't bothered to jot them down on his notes, so he gazed around desperately, seeking inspiration. On the far side of the room he spotted two doors which must be labelled Ladies and Gentlemen, he reasoned — and so he began by quoting from the doors. His audience looked confused but clapped politely at the end of the speech, and he sat down reasonably pleased with himself.

'You made a good speech,' said a Russian, leaning towards him, 'But tell me, why did you choose to open it by addressing us as male and female toilets?'

James Whistler, the celebrated Victorian artist, owned a pet poodle on which he doted. One day when the dog appeared to be suffering from some kind of throat infection he took it to see the country's leading ear, nose and throat specialist — who was less than delighted at being asked to treat an animal but nevertheless carried out an examination and prescribed treatment. The very next day Whistler received an urgent call from the specialist and hurried round to see him, worried that it was something to do with the poodle's illness. The doctor greeted him with the words, 'Thank you for coming so promptly, Whistler. I want to consult you about having my front door painted.'

An American senator had been asked to speak to the graduating class of an American university, and despite some thought, failed to come up with a suitable ending to the speech he had prepared. In fact it wasn't until he actually entered the hall where he was to make his address, via two doors marked PUSH, that his inspiration came. He would, he decided, conclude with some thoughts about pushing forward in the world, about thrusting ahead and opening doors ...

The ceremony began, and at the appointed moment he rose to speak. As he came to the end he slipped in his tailor-made conclusion. 'There's only one thing anyone needs to get ahead in this great country of ours. What is it? I hear you ask. It's nothing magical. It's nothing impossible. In fact it's written on the very doors of this hall ...' He pointed dramatically. Hundreds of heads turned in unison — and found inscribed on the doors a single word. PULL.

Sir Malcolm Sargent, the famous conductor, was asked, in his seventies, to what he attributed his great age.

'Well,' he said, 'I suppose I must attribute it to the fact that I haven't died yet.'

Dr Johnson was a guest at a dinner party in his later years when he was subjected to some rude questioning by an impolite young man at the table.

'Tell me, Doctor,' he said, 'what would you give to be as young and sprightly as I am?'

'Why, sir,' responded Dr Johnson, 'I should almost be content to be as foolish and conceited.'

Sir Thomas Beecham committed a gaffe when, feeling weary after conducting the Halle in a concert in Manchester, he headed straight for his hotel room. Entering the lobby he saw a lady whom he recognised waiting for the lift, but he couldn't put a name to her face. He tried to conceal his ignorance by being very general in his remarks, and just as he was about to go he remembered in a blinding flash that she had a brother. He asked politely how he was.

'He is very well, thank you, Sir Thomas.'

'And what is he doing at the moment?' the conductor asked.

'He is still king.'

President Reagan found himself in an embarrassing situation during the state visit of President Mitterand of France to Washington. Mr Reagan, who speaks no French, was leading Mme Mitterand into a formal banquet when, for no apparent reason, she stopped and would proceed no further. She tried to explain something in French, but Mr Reagan did not understand. Nor did a nearby butler who did his best to move them on. Finally an interpreter was summoned. He was able to explain that Mme Mitterand was unable to move because the President was standing on her dress.

During a Palm Springs golf tournament Bob Hope was entertaining the cameras with some joking repartee to his very attractive young scorekeeper.

'How old are you?' he asked.

'Twenty-four,' she replied.

'Why, I've got balls older than you,' he joked before realising what he'd said.

64

During an Easter service in Stockholm Cathedral the city's mayor dozed off in his pew. Noticing this, and anxious not to attract too much attention, a verger crept up to the sleeping mayor and whispered the number of the next hymn into his ear. His action did not have the desired effect. The mayor sprang to his feet and surprised the rest of the congregation with his cry of 'Bingo!'

Halfway through the premiere of *Heaven's Gate* Michael Cimino's mega-disaster western, an hysterical member of the audience ran from the auditorium. 'This is the most disgusting, degrading and horrible film I've ever seen,' she cried to a man passing her in the lobby. He was Michael Cimino.

The late Diana Dors started life with one disadvantage — her name. She was born Diana Fluck! Legend has it that not long after her rise to stardom in British films, she was invited to a garden party in her home town. The vicar who was to open it made an address from the platform welcoming her, and to prove that he'd known her before she had become famous he decided to use her real name. Anxious not to allow an unfortunate slip of the tongue to mar a happy occasion, he concentrated hard when the time came to introduce her.

'Ladies and gentlemen,' he announced, 'I'm going to ask you to welcome a very special guest this afternoon. The world knows her as Diana Dors. We, of course, know her as Diana Clunt.'

Mr George Lawrence must have felt equally as embarrassed when, working as a parking attendant at the Horse of the Year Show, he told one young woman who tried to drive her car into the VIP area to park it 'and walk, just like everyone else.' The lady in question was Princess Anne.

For the Record

There's no disgrace in using a witty quote to open or illustrate your speech — in fact a well-researched quote can really lift the material. In this section you'll find some quotations that are obviously suitable for certain social occasions, others that are just plain funny and some which probably seem a bit off-beat. We guarantee you'll find a use for all three kinds!

Remember when using a quote to credit its source. If you don't, someone in the audience is bound to recognise it and mark you down as a cheat. Giving a credit proves that you've done your homework properly.

Men, women and marriage

An archeologist is the best husband any woman can have — the older she gets the more interested he is in her.

Agatha Christie

Marriage is the result of the longing for the deep, deep peace of the double bed after the hurly-burly of the chaise longue.

Mrs Patrick Campbell

We'll be together for ever. We are like twins.

Britt Ekland, talking about Rod Stewart

The average girl would rather have beauty than brains because she knows that the average man can see much better than he can think.

Ladies Home Journal, 1947

In my view he is too old for her.

*Earl Spencer trying to play down
rumours of his daughter's engagement to Prince Charles*

A man would often be the lover of his wife — if he were married to someone else.

Elinor Glyn

Men are like wine — some turn to vinegar but the rest improve with age.

Pope John XXII

Behind every successful man stands a surprised mother-in-law.

Hubert Humphrey

Behind every successful woman there's a man trying to stop her.

Anon

Outside every thin girl there's a fat man trying to get in.

Katherine Whitehorn

Mae West is famous for her wonderful maxims. Here are just a few of her best:

It's not the men in my life that count's — it's the life in my men.

Give me a sixteen-year-old and I'll return him at twenty-one.

Marriage is a great institution but I'm not ready for an institution yet.

Mae went to a reception covered in diamonds, which provoked a female guest to say admiringly:
    'Goodness, what lovely diamonds!'
    To which came the reply: 'Goodness had nothing to do with it.'

A woman's guess is much more accurate than a man's certainty.

Rudyard Kipling

Chumps always make the best husbands. When you marry, Sally, grab a chump. Tap his forehead first, and if it rings solid, don't hesitate. All the unhappy marriages come from the husband having brains. What good are brains to a man? They only unsettle him.

P.G. Wodehouse

The hardest task in a girl's life is to prove to a man that his intentions are serious.

Helen Rowland

Woman begins by resisting a man's advances and ends by blocking his retreat.

Oscar Wilde

Hell, if I'd jumped on all the dames I'm supposed to have jumped on — I'd never have had time to go fishing.

Clark Gable

When a man who had been very unhappily married promptly married again after the death of his first wife, *Dr Johnson* declared, 'It is the triumph of Hope over Experience.'

What I don't like about politics is the disruption to one's family life.

Cecil Parkinson, before his fall from favour

The best part of married life is the fights.

Thornton Wilder

Anyone who says he can see through women is missing a lot.

Groucho Marx

When you're bored with yourself, marry and be bored with someone else.

David Pryce-Jones

One doesn't have to get anywhere in a marriage. It's not a public conveyance.

Iris Murdoch

It's the good girls who keep the diaries; the bad girls never have time.

Tallulah Bankhead

A diplomat is a man who remembers a woman's birthday but never remembers her age.

Robert Frost

A successful man is one who makes more money than his wife can spend. A successful woman is one who can find such a man.

Lana Turner

Nudity on stage? I think it's disgusting. But if I were 22 with a great body, it would be artistic, tasteful, patriotic and a progressive religious experience.

Shelley Winters

There's a broad with a future behind her.

Constance Bennett on Marilyn Monroe

Bigamy is having one husband too many. Monogamy is the same.

Anon

I have learned that only two things are necessary to keep one's wife happy. First, let her think she is having her own way. Second, let her have it.

Lord Snowdon

Marriage is popular because it contains the maximum of temptation with the maximum of opportunity.

George Bernard Shaw

A girl must marry for love, and keep on marrying until she finds it.

Zsa Zsa Gabor

Happy the man with a wife to tell him what to do, and a secretary to do it for him.

Lord Mancroft

Keep your eyes open before marriage — and half-shut afterwards.

Benjamin Franklin

All Herbert's affairs start with a compliment and end with a confinement.

Maud Beerbohm Tree, wife of actor
Herbert Beerbohm Tree

Marriage is an attempt to turn a night-owl into a homing pigeon.

Anon

A man is incomplete until he is married. Then he is finished.

Zsa Zsa Gabor.

Youth and Age

As a graduate of the Zsa Zsa Gabor School of Creative Mathematics, I honestly do not know how old I am.

Erma Bombeck

I refuse to admit that I'm more than fifty-two, even if that does make my sons illegitimate.

Lady Astor

It's not that I'm afraid to die, I just don't want to be there when it happens.

Woody Allen

What most impresses me about America is the way the parents obey the children.

The Duke of Windsor

Youth is a wonderful thing; what a crime to waste it on children.

George Bernard Shaw

Children aren't happy with nothing to ignore, and that's what parents were created for.

Ogden Nash

Asked how he liked children, *W.C. Fields* replied, 'Lightly grilled on toast.'

Setting a good example for your children takes all the fun out of middle age.

William Feather.

71

A grandmother is someone who spent all her time telling your mother what not to do when she was young, and now spends her time criticising your mother for giving you the same advice.

Calvin Giles, aged 12

Old age isn't so bad when you consider the alternative.

Maurice Chevalier

It is better to wear out than to rust out.

George Horne

It has been said that there is no fool like an old fool, except a young fool. But the young fool has first to grow up to be an old fool to realise what a damn fool he was when he was a young fool.

Harold Macmillan

Life is like playing the violin solo and learning the instrument as one goes on.

Samuel Butler

There are times when parenthood seems nothing but feeding the mouth that bites you.

Peter de Vries

Baby: A loud noise at one end and no sense of responsibility at the other.

Father Ronald Knox

Parents are the very last people who should be allowed to have children.

H.E. Bell

To be a successful father, there's one absolute rule: when you have a kid, don't look at it for the first two years.

Ernest Hemingway

Life is rather like a tin or sardines, we're all of us looking for the key.

Alan Bennett

Work and success

Work fascinates me. I could sit and watch others doing it for hours.

Jerome K. Jerome

The brain is a wonderful organ. It starts working the moment you get up in the morning and does not stop until you get into the office.

Robert Frost

Success is just a matter of luck. Ask any failure.

Earl Wilson

If lawyers are debarred and clergymen defrocked, doesn't it follow that electricians can be delighted; musicians denoted; cowboys deranged; models deposed; tree surgeons debarked and dry cleaners depressed?

Virginia Ostman

As one door closes another slams in your face.

Rachel Heyhoe Flint

Be polite to everyone until you've made your first million. After that everyone will be polite to you.

John Douglas

Work is the curse of the drinking classes.

Oscar Wilde

What is worth doing is worth the trouble of asking some-body to do it.

Ambrose Bierce

Anyone who works is a fool. I don't work — I merely inflict myself on the public.

Robert Morley

It is impossible to enjoy idling thoroughly unless one has plenty of work to do.

Jerome K. Jerome

Getting things done in this office is like mating elephants. It's done at a high level, it's accomplished with a great deal of roaring and screaming and it takes two years to produce a result.

Anonymous office graffiti

The Executive's Expense Account
　In Frankfurt she was Helga,
　She was Polly in New York.
　In Cannes she was Francesca
　With a very sexy walk.
　In Stockholm she was Eva,
　The best of all the bunch,
　But down on his expense account
　She was taxi fares and lunch.

Bill Locke

Miscellaneous

Cough and the world coughs with you. Fart and you fart alone.

Trevor Griffiths, The Comedians

Experience is a good teacher, but she sends in terrific bills.

Minna Antrim

Never keep up with the Joneses. Drag them down to your level. It's cheaper.

Quentin Crisp

Never trust a man with short legs — brains too near their bottoms.

Noel Coward

Try everything once except incest and folk-dancing.

Sir Thomas Beecham

If the grass is greener in the other fellow's yard, let *him* worry about cutting it.

Fred Allen

The Pope's got charisma. I'd like to sign him up.

Lord Grade

A metallurgist is an expert who can look at a platinum blonde and tell whether she is virgin metal or a common ore.

Anonymous

If there's a pile-up in there, they'll have to give some of the players artificial insemination.

Curt Cowdry, US sports commentator
on American Football game

If voting changed anything they'd make it illegal.

Anonymous

Not only is there no God, but try getting a plumber at weekends.

Woody Allen

I tell you flat, Elvis can't last.

Jackie Gleason

UNPRECEDENTED EVENT — UNDERGRADUATES SCRATCH BALLS.

Oxford Mail

In the fight between you and the world, back the world.
Frank Zappa

The two most beautiful words in the English language are
'Cheque Enclosed.'
Dorothy Parker

In a report last week of the court case involving Mr---- of
Dagenham, we wrongly stated that Mr---- had previously
been found guilty of buggery. The charge referred to was,
in fact, one of burglary.
Dagenham Post

First things first, second things never.
Shirley Conran

The weak shall inherit the earth, but *not* its mineral rights.
John Paul Getty

He has had seven craps as scrum half for England.
Jimmy Hill, BBC sports presenter

You're not the acting type.
Alec Guinness's headmaster

I love Mickey Mouse more than any woman I've ever
known.
Walt Disney

Being a thief is a terrific life, but the trouble is they do put
you in the nick for it.
John McVicar

In Brief

When you prepare your speech, make sure that you include a couple of quick one-liners early on. They'll help you break the ice and give you confidence before going on to a longer or more complicated joke. Use them later in your speech to provide variety and keep your audience on their toes.

The secret of delivering these witticisms is to drop them casually into your speech as if they were off-the-cuff observations. Don't labour them hard and don't pause for a laugh. Let them catch the audience out at first. This might sound like throwing good material away, but in fact the audience will appreciate your relaxed presentation and they'll be flattered that you trust them to think for themselves.

Did you hear about the chap who blamed mathematics for his divorce? His wife put two and two together.

A manucurist once went out with a dentist, but they decided not to get married on the grounds that if they did they'd be sure to end up fighting tooth and nail.

My wife is like an angel, always up in the air and forever harping on about things.

My husband is a very versatile man. He can do anything wrong.

Women are entirely to blame for men's lies. They keep insisting on asking the most awkward questions.

I was thrilled to discover that my daughter had split up with one of her boyfriends in particular — the one she called 'tall, dark and hands ...'

A good husband is one who will wash up when asked and dry up when told.

Overheard in church the other day, a lady praising the new vicar. 'I know very little about sin until he came — and he does make it so enjoyable.'

My daughter has always liked bringing out the animal in men — you know, the fox, the mink, the racoon ...

You know you're getting old when a girl says 'no' and all you feel is relief.

At a recent wedding one of the guests noticed a number of the bride's ex-boyfriends among the party and asked how they felt about being invited. 'Well,' said one, 'you don't feel bitter about the winner when you've been eliminated in the semi-finals.'

Would you say that marriage was the difference between painting the town and painting the living-room?

Married couples have a lot to learn from fish. Keep your mouth shut and you'll manage to stay out of the worst trouble.

In the old days, if a bridegroom jilted a girl then the best man was expected to marry her. Then he was known as the second best man.

78

The first time John went back to Sue's flat for a drink he was hoping for a whisky and sofa. What he got was a gin and platonic.

Many a romance begins when a girl sinks into his arms — and ends up with her arms in his sink.

Men say that women have no sense of humour — but that's just because they spend so much of their time laughing at men.

Would you say that when Adam met Eve he turned over a new leaf?

When God created woman, She was only practising.

I've got a brilliant head for money. Have you noticed the slot in the top?

There's no point in trying to make a fool of me — I'm doing very well on my own, thank you.

As Sam Goldwyn once said, 'A bachelor's life is no life for a single man.'

If incest is a relative bore and necrophilia is a dead bore, would you say that celibacy is never boring?

Two can live as cheaply as one for about half as long.

When a man asks for advice what he really wants is approval.

To be a success, a woman has to be twice as good at everything as a man. Fortunately, this is not difficult.

Don't try making love in a field of wheat. That really is going against the grain.

At a recent wedding in Dundee the bride's father was so mean that even the confetti was on elastic.

Someone once remarked to Sam Goldwyn on the beauty of his wife's hands. 'Yes,' he replied. 'They're so beautiful I was thinking of having a bust made of them.'

Bill's mother always said he could marry any girl he pleased. Unfortunately he didn't please any of them.

A boss is a man who's early when you're late and late when you're early.

Nothing is impossible for people who don't have to do it themselves.

A committee is a group of men who, individually, can do nothing, but collectively can meet to decide that nothing can be done.

Early to bed, early to rise, makes a man boring.

I never repeat gossip, so please listen carefully the first time.

I used to be indecisive, but now I'm not so sure.

Doing a really good job on something is like wetting yourself in dark trousers. You get a warm feeling where it counts but no one else notices.

People who work for the factory up the road are known as mushrooms — because they're crowded together, kept in the dark, and every so often someone shovels manure over them.

Men who put women on pedestals seldom knock them off.

A board meeting is something that keeps minutes and wastes hours.

All's well that ends well — and vice versa.

Did you hear about the Irish entrepreneur who made a million selling one-piece jigsaw puzzles?

Would you say that Adam was the world's first book-keeper? After all, he turned over a leaf and made an entry.

When a man tells you he got rich through hard work, just try asking him *whose*.

Show me a man who smiles at defeat and I'll show you a happy chiropodist.

More women train drivers, please. A woman's right to choo-choose.

To err is human, but to make a real mess of things you need a computer.

A girl's best friends may be her legs, but sometimes even best friends have to part.

Whenever you feel the urge to exercise, just lie down and wait until it passes.

The world is divided into two sorts of people. Those who are willing to work and those who are willing to let them.

Underneath every successful man there's usually a woman.

Money may be the root of all evil, but a man needs his roots.

A man must do something to relieve the monogamy.

Let him who is stoned cast the first sin.

The devil finds work for idle glands.

Never put off until tomorrow what you can avoid altogether.

You can fool some of the people all of the time, and all of the people some of the time, but you can make a fool of yourself anytime.

Coming home, a stationery tree jumped into the road and hit me.
    I knocked over a man, but he admitted it was his fault as he'd been knocked down before.
    To avoid a collision I ran into another car.

Quotes from motor insurance claims

It's a Weird World

A snippet of amazing information is a perfect way of making your audience prick up their ears, and once they've done that they'll listen attentively for the rest of your speech. You'll find some very strange stories and facts in this section. Use them either as they stand, to illustrate your point, or turn them into questions which will flummox your listeners and break the ice. And just think how clever such information makes you look!

'Thou shalt commit adultery,' was one of the Ten Commandments in a 1631 edition of the Bible. And it went on to say 'Sin on more.' The printers were fined for the errors.

Women in ancient Greece used to calculate their age from the date they were married, not when they were born. So spinsters didn't, technically, exist!

Women in northern Siberia show their love for their menfolk by bombarding them with the largest slugs they can find.

In 1956 a French man was gaoled for seven years for manslaughter after breaking his wife's neck because she had undercooked the roast. Ten years later he was back in court, this time because his second wife had overcooked the roast and he had knocked her down and killed her. He got another eight years, even though the judge sympathized, agreeing that badly cooked food *was* a terrible provocation.

Attila the Hun, the scourge of Europe, was so small that he was more or less a dwarf, which perhaps explains his aggressive outlook. He can't have been too unattractive, however, because he died making love to a blonde.

In 1983 a geography test was held for the geography students of the University of Miami. It revealed that 8% of them couldn't even find Miami on a map of the world.

Among the presents given to Queen Victoria on her wedding day was a cheese nine feet in diameter and weighing half a ton.

Aiyavuk, a thirteenth-century Tartar princess, laid down an unusual condition for her suitors. They had to have a wrestling match with her. If they won, they kept her; if not, they had to give her a hundred horses. By the time someone finally managed to win her hand, she possessed ten thousand horses.

A resident of Chatham Island, New Zealand, married his grandfather's second wife. When the baby was born the mother was also its great-grandmother.

The two highest IQs both belong to women.

Nero's wife Poppaea was the originator of the tradition of bathing in asses' milk. She needed five hundred she-asses to be sure of filling her bath.

No one's perfect, not even famous film stars. Grace Kelly nearly married Clark Gable but was put off by the way in which his dentures clicked together. And Vivien Leigh didn't like kissing him in *Gone With The Wind* because she said his breath smelled.

Talent doesn't necessarily show at an early age. Fred Astaire's first screen test notes read: 'Can't sing, can't act. Can dance a little.'

A small ad. in a Nairobi newspaper: 'Young farm worker wishes to marry beautiful girl with tractor. Please send photo of tractor.'

Another small ad. in a Wisconsin paper: 'Young man would like to meet young lady with two boxes of twelve-gauge shotgun shells, object matrimony'

There's no safety in numbers. A seventeenth-century Turkish sultan got bored with his harem of more than a hundred wives and ordered them all to be drowned.

A hippopotamus can run faster than a man.

When Princess Anne was married to Mark Phillips in 1973, the hovercraft *Princess Anne* trailed two old boots behind it as it crossed the Channel.

Peter the Great of Russia loved one of his mistresses even though she had been unfaithful to him. After he had had her executed for her infidelity he kept her head in a jar of alcohol by his bed.

At a recent Turkish wedding a clause was inserted to the effect that the wife, who was to be her husband's second bride, should not let a single grain of rice enter the house. Apparently the first wife had served her husband with rice twice a day, every day, for twenty-two years.

A high court judge has ruled that a woman who murders her husband is not eligible for a widow's pension because she 'has brought the condition on herself.' Hard luck.

It's an ancient Red Indian custom to name a baby after the first thing the parent sees on leaving the tent where the child has been delivered. That explains names like Running Water and Sitting Bull. What we don't know is whether modern American Indians are called Fire Hydrant and Lincoln Continental.

Winston Churchill was born in a ladies' cloakroom. The Duke of Edinburgh was born on a dining-table.

Some parents believe that the more unusual a child's name, the better it will be remembered in later life. For example, a set of American children were named Bugless, Energetic, Euphrates, and Goliath Smith. Other fond parents in the United States at the end of the nineteenth century managed to call their children Bunyon Snipes Womble and Calder Wellington Womble, while in the register of a New Orleans hospital are Luscious Pea and Halloween Buggage.

In 1963 the *Times* reported a wedding between a Mr Cock and his bride, whose maiden name was Prick.

In 1978 a Saudi Arabian father saved some money by holding a double wedding. Unfortunately he managed to confuse his two heavily-veiled daughters and married them off to the wrong men. The girls pronounced themselves so happy with their respective husbands that they decided not to swap.

In 1969 a Mexican couple finally tied the knot. Nothing strange about that, you may think. Except that they had been engaged since 1902.

A husband took his wife to the divorce court on the grounds that she was always throwing things at him and this constituted cruelty. However, the judge ruled in her favour because she almost invariably missed him.

Even that legendary couple Napoleon and Josephine had problems on their honeymoon. Josephine's dog, which always slept in her room, attacked Napoleon as he climbed into bed on their wedding night.

One of Picasso's mistresses left him because of his regular infidelities. Nothing odd about that? He was in his eighties at the time.

Sigmund Freud could never understand a railway time-table and so never travelled alone.

Sir Isaac Newton was a member of Parliament, but his only recorded speech was a request that the windows be opened as it was getting hot.

William Buckland, nineteenth-century Dean of Westminster, ate the embalmed heart of Louis XIV for dinner one evening!

Drink to Me Only

The best toasts are the simplest and the most sincere. If you're in any doubt about the kind of toast to make, go for the classic kind described in Part One of this book. For weddings and other occasions when everyone is feeling suitably sentimental, you'll find some more elaborate toasts here. And you can always adapt a one-liner to make an appropriate toast.

A final tip. Before you raise your glass, be sure that you know the name of the person you're toasting. Who could possibly forget that?, you're asking. In 1981 a Scottish businessman got it wrong when he proposed a toast to Prince Charles and his bride-to-be, 'Lady Jane.' And four years later President Reagan was still having trouble; he gave a speech of thanks to 'Princess David.'

Ladies and gentlemen, please raise your glasses to the match of the day — and may they score all the goals they want.

Ladies and gentlemen, here's to a fool in love, and the woman who will keep reminding him.

Let's celebrate this day when two people have become one by drinking to the future — when they will gradually discover which one of them they have become.

To the happy couple. May familiarity breed contentment.

Ladies and gentlemen, the bride and groom; if she is his sugar plum, and he is the apple of her eye, I give you best wishes for a long and happy fruit salad.

Here's to God's first thought, man. And to His second thought, woman. And don't forget that second thoughts are usually the best.

Ladies and gentlemen, in the law the term 'man' always embraces 'woman'. Now that the happy pair are legally married I wish them much happy embracing.

Let's drink to a couple with such good taste that they chose each other.

To the happy couple. May they remember that they should not be afraid to be different, just like the black notes and the white notes on a piano — and may they have many long and happy years playing in harmony.

To the happy couple. You won't necessarily share the same friends, but as long as you have the same enemies you'll get along fine.

To the bride and groom; may they have the patience to accept those things they cannot change, the strength to change those they can, and the wisdom to know the difference.

To the bride and groom. Remember that if you want to keep ringing each other's bells you'll have to work like the clappers.

Raise your glasses, first to the miss that was, then to the mister that is — and finally to the mystery that is to come.

People sometimes wonder whether there is life after death. My advice to you is not to worry about that but to make sure that there is life *before* death by making the most of it.

May every man become what he thinks himself to be.

May Dame Fortune always smile upon you — but never her daughter, Miss Fortune.

To your good health. May you live for a thousand years and I be there to count them.

Here's champagne to our real friends and real pain to our sham friends.

The Ladies — we admire them for their beauty, respect them for their intelligence, adore them for their virtue and love them because we simply can't help it.

Let's drink to the kind of troubles which last only as long as our New Year's Resolutions.

Here's to children. They're not only a comfort in old age but they help us reach it faster, too.

Ladies and gentlemen, may we always get ourselves into hot water. It's the only way to keep clean.

May you live as long as you like to, and like to as long as you live.

May we never have friends like shadows, who keep close to us in sunshine but desert us on rainy days.

Here's to our sweethearts and wives. May our sweethearts soon become our wives and our wives ever remain our sweethearts.

Comic Speeches for the Legal Profession

● ● ● ● ●

Contents

PART ONE

How to make a comic speech

Ground Rules

With the exception of a few lucky extroverts, most people contemplate the idea of having to make an amusing and witty public speech with trepidation and rapidly weakening knees. And if you're involved in the law, whether as a policeman, a lawyer, a local councillor, civil servant or even as an aspiring politician, you'll have discovered that public speaking is all part of the job. That doesn't make it any easier, of course, but fortunately the art of making a public speech is rather like that of cooking. Given a recipe, the right ingredients, some basic instruction and a little application, almost anyone can produce something fit for public enjoyment. And that's what this book sets out to do. It provides all the information you'll need to prepare and deliver an amusing and entertaining speech, from the ground rules — like how to assess your audience and what kind of speech to make on a particular occasion — through to ways of coping with your nerves on the day. And because this is the *complete* guide to comic speech-making, you'll also find hundreds of jokes, anecdotes and quotations suitable for all kinds of occasions and guaranteed to ensure that you're never at a loss for a witty word.

Know your Audience

Even experienced public speakers admit to feeling nervous when they stand up in front of an audience, but they cope by putting some of that nervous energy into preparing their material, rather than trying to ignore the impending occasion. The best way of pleasing an audience is by giving them what they want — a speech specially designed for them and the occasion, full of apparently effortless, amusing stories and ideas that are of direct interest and relevance.

Some speakers like to think that they have perfected a kind of general-purpose speech which, with a few additions and alterations, will go down well with any audience and on any occasion. It's certainly true that if you suspect that you're going to be asked to make an impromptu speech a few ready phrases and jokes can come in useful, but this kind of general-purpose material won't really interest anyone for long.

The key word for anyone asked to speak in public is *preparation*. How many times have you suffered an after-dinner speaker who has mumbled and faltered his way through some feeble and irrelevant jokes, leaving you wondering what he was on about? Or cringed as a work colleague has told a string of off-colour gags at a company conference? The very worst speakers of all are those who imagine themselves to be such gifted natural orators that they don't bother to prepare any material. Instead they drone on for as long as the fancy takes them — usually until their audience are nodding off in their seats!

To ensure that you avoid these pitfalls, you'll have to create a specially tailored speech for every occasion. And before you can sit down and write it, you'll have to give a few seconds' thought to work out just what's required.

The Audience

You may think that your sporting jokes are hilarious, and they may, indeed, have gone down well at the police rugby club. But are they as likely to have the same appeal for the local Rotarians or Neighbourhood Watch committee? If you've been invited to speak as a representative of your organisation or profession you'll be expected to tell topical anecdotes and jokes. What's more, you'll have to prepare different material for different audiences. The ladies of the Townswomen's Guild and the gentlemen of the local tradesmen's federation will respond to quite different sorts of material. That may seem obvious, but it doesn't seem to occur to a great number of speakers that it's the audience who decide whether the material is funny or not. If the audience don't like your jokes you might as well give up. So before you do anything else, assess your audience and decide on the right kind of material for them.

Age is one of the most important factors. If you know that the audience is going to be young and sophisticated choose some of the sharper material in section two of this book and, if necessary, add some up-to-the-minute detail. If your audience is past retiring age adapt some of the stories to suit them, likewise.

An all-male gathering will probably enjoy more robust material than an all-female one, but as a general rule it's wise to avoid dirty jokes altogether — particularly if you're present as a representative of your profession. If any of your jokes embarrasses or concerns you, then cut

11

it. Your unease will communicate itself to your audience and they won't be able to relax while you're speaking.

Find out as much as you can about the group of people to whom you'll be speaking and the subject they're expecting you to talk on. In this way you can make sure that everything you have to say is relevant to the occasion. They may have had other speakers in the past who have covered topics that encroach on your own. Try to ensure that you don't cover old ground.

Speaking at a formal function where you don't know the audience has its problems as well as its advantages. If you make a mess of the occasion you won't have to meet any of the guests the next day, which will spare your blushes, certainly. But you'll have to work that much harder to discover details of the people expected to attend the function, particularly, if it's appropriate, the names and titles of the organising committee. Do some homework and see if you can come up with any interesting or amusing stories about them or the other guests, and include these in your speech. This may sound like unnecessarily hard work, but some topical and personal references can make all the difference between a good and a brilliant speech. They prove that you care enough to have done some special research, and there's nothing an audience responds to more warmly than personal interest.

The occasion

Different occasions require different kinds of speeches, and you'll find information about the right speech for most legal and political occasions in the last part of this section of the book. But remember that it isn't just the formal requirements of a function that matter when it comes to preparing your speech.

Bear in mind the tone of the occasion. What kind of mood will your audience be in? What sort of entertainment will they expect? A boozy evening function will require a different kind of approach to a lunchtime gathering. Should you be witty and sophisticated or go for the belly-laugh? Use your judgement and bear the tone of the occasion in mind when you select your material.

If you have been asked to propose a toast or present a prize, make sure that you do so — don't get so carried away that you forget what you're there for. Many a speaker has risen to make a five-minute presentation speech and sat down half an hour later still holding the trophy! The best way of avoiding this kind of embarrassment is to plan your speech well in advance and then stick to it. Try to resist the temptation to improvise, no matter how well you're being received. It's improvisation that is likely to throw you off your stride.

Here's a simple check list of 10 Do's and Don't's which you should bear in mind as you sit down to prepare your speech.

Do's

1   Do check the age and sex ratio of the audience.
2   Do find out what your particular function is to be. Have you been asked to propose a toast or make an after-dinner speech? Make sure that you prepare the right kind of speech.
3   Do find out how long you will be expected to speak.
4   Do some homework on any special guests or members of the audience.
5   Do adapt your material to suit the occasion.

Don't's

1   Don't use old material
2   Don't risk offending anyone with blue jokes.

3　Don't speak for too long and don't try to improvise.
4　Don't include irrelevant material.
5　Don't forget to fulfil your function. If you've been asked to make a toast or offer a vote of thanks then remember to do so.

Perfect Preparation

Once you know the kind of speech you're going to make and the sort of audience you'll be entertaining, you can begin to prepare your material. Preparation is absolutely vital if you're going to give a polished performance, so allow as much time as possible to work on the speech.

Start by reading through this book and jotting down all the jokes, quotes, anecdotes and so on that you like and that you feel are directly relevant to your audience. Be ruthless and cut out anything that isn't related in some way to your subject and anything that can't be adapted to fit. On a separate sheet, put down all the things that you *have* to say in the speech and all the points that you particularly want to make.

With any luck you'll begin to see the material falling into place, with the quotes leading into the points you want to make and the stories illustrating the theme. This is exactly what you're aiming for — a seamless speech with one idea moving into the next without any effort. You'll probably have to adapt some of the material if it's to fit in perfectly, so change the names and locations and details to suit the occasion. For example, if you're going to be speaking in Newcastle and you're using a joke set in London, change the location and add some · Geordie colour. Most importantly of all, put everything into your own words. You'll feel more comfortable when you come to use the material if it's written in the kind of language and the style you're used to, and it will make your speech seem that much more personal to the audience.

Sir Thomas Beecham once said of his orchestra that the important thing was 'to begin and end together, what happens in between doesn't matter very much.' Pretty much the same can be said of making a speech. If you can capture the attention of the audience with your first line, you're likely to have them with you for the rest of the speech. And if they're going to remember anything when they get home it's likely to be your final line — so make sure that it's worth remembering.

Some speakers like to work on the opening and closing lines of their speech together, linking them so that the last line finishes what the first line started. Whatever you decide to do, make sure that both the beginning and the end of your speech are absolutely relevant — both to the occasion and the central part of the speech. Nothing irrelevant should be allowed in at all or you'll begin to look as if you're rambling.

Opening and closing a speech are the two most difficult things of all. If a brilliant opening occurs to you then use it — but if nothing original springs to mind, try using one of these opening gambits.

Quotations

You'll find dozens of useful quotations in this book and one of them should be ideal for opening your speech. When you're looking for it, bear in mind that it should allow you to move straight into the main part of your speech without any stress. If you have to force a quotation to fit your theme then forget it. Always inform your audience that it *is* a quote and not your own words. It's quite likely that someone in the audience will have heard it before and they might think you a fraud if you don't name the person who said it first.

Don't use a quotation for the opening *and* closing of your speech because that would look too much like cheating, but a quote can round off a speech perfectly. Again, you'll find something suitable in the relevant section of this book — and again, make sure that it ties in completely with the main subject of your speech.

Questions

A question can be a very effective way of getting your speech off the ground. Try asking an apparently serious one and following it up with a ridiculous answer. Or ask a ridiculous question to which there's no answer. Whichever kind you choose, aim to raise a laugh from the audience and break the ice.

The 'Did you know?' gambit is also a useful one. Find an amazing fact in the relevant section of this book and ask your audience if they knew it. It's bound to start your speech off with a bang!

Jokes

A joke may seem the obvious way of starting a speech, but in fact jokes can go badly wrong. If they work you'll have the audience eating out of your hand — but if they fall flat you'll have everyone in an agony of embarrassment and praying that you finish quickly.

The best kind of joke to look out for is one that has something to do with a member of the audience or with something directly relevant to the occasion. You may find that simply by changing a few details in one of the jokes in this book you've got the ideal opening — in which case use it. But never use a joke simply because you think it's funny.

Exactly the same advice can be applied to ending a speech. No speech, no matter how well-received, can be counted a great success unless it ends on a high note. Looking for a new screenplay, Sam Goldwyn once remarked, 'What we want is a story that begins with an earthquake and builds up to a climax.' That's what you have to aim for too!

Never end with an apologetic, 'Well, folks, that's about it,' line. That only suggests that you've run out of ideas or that you couldn't be bothered to finish the job off properly, and there's really no excuse for that. Even if you can't find the kind of climax that Goldwyn was looking for, you can end your speech in an amusing and tidy way.

Ending a speech with a joke is even more risky than opening with one. After all, even if your opening joke falls flat you have the rest of your speech to regain the audience's interest. If you end with a damp squib, no matter how good the speech the audience will remember you for only one thing — your failure to pull it off. Only finish with a joke if you can think of nothing better and if you're absolutely certain that it will work.

Anecdotes

There's bound to be an anecdote in this book that will encapsulate and illustrate your theme perfectly. You can use it to finish your speech in classic style, but beware of using anything too long or rambling. You don't want to lose your audience's attention in the last few moments. If you're speaking about friends, family or colleagues at work, try to uncover an amusing story about them; nothing embarrassing, of course, just something to show what nice people they are. This is *guaranteed* to bring your speech to a successful conclusion.

When you're preparing your speech, take an occasional look at this checklist of 10 Do's and Don't's just to keep your aims in mind.

Do's

1   Do check your material to ensure that it's suitable for the audience you assessed in the last section.
2   Do make sure that you have included all the things

you *have* to say — your vote of thanks or the toast, for example.

3   Do adapt all the material to ensure that it's relevant.

4   Do aim to start and finish your speech on a high note.

5   Do credit any quotations you use.

Don't's

1   Don't use any material that isn't relevant to the occasion or will cause offence.

2   Don't start your speech with a joke unless you feel confident that it will work.

3   Don't tail off at the end of the speech; finish properly.

4   Don't use too many quotes or anecdotes from the lives of other people.

5   Don't speak too long; make sure that your speech is the right length.

If, when you finish preparing your speech, you feel confident that you've observed these guidelines, you can be sure that you're halfway towards success. Now all you need to know is how to deliver the speech you've written!

Successful Delivery

Preparing your speech is one thing — and the most important of all — but delivering it is something else. The best speech can be ruined by poor delivery and the thoroughly mediocre made to pass muster by good technique. Fortunately just a few simple measures will ensure that your delivery does your speech justice.

Rehearsal

You don't need to learn your material like an actor, but rehearsal will help you to become familiar with it and iron out any problems that weren't apparent on paper. For example, you may find that a particular sequence of words turn out to be difficult to say, or you might have problems pronouncing certain words — in which case rewrite them. Try to learn half a dozen key phrases which will take you smoothly from one part of your speech to the next so that you don't keep having to refer to your notes; no matter how nervous you're feeling, this will make your speech seem smooth and practised.

While you're rehearsing, experiment by using your voice to emphasise different points of the speech. Try changing your tone and volume, too, for effect. If you have a tape recorder then use it to tape the various versions of your speech — then you can play them back and decide which sounds the most interesting and lively. Don't, by the way, worry about your accent. Lots of speakers try to iron out their natural accent, but they forget that the way they speak is all part of their personality. Without it they seem very dull. As you listen to yourself speaking you'll begin to recognise the most successful ways of delivering certain parts of your speech. For example, the best way of telling your jokes is to do it casually, without labouring them too much. If you feel that there's a rather dull patch in the speech try animating it by changing your tone or emphasis, or even just speeding it up a bit. It's this kind of preparation that will give you polish on the day.

Body Language

No matter how nervous you feel about speaking in front of an audience, you should try not to let them know — and it's the body which most often gives the secret away.

Begin by standing easily with your weight on both feet so that you feel balanced. This way you'll look steady, even if you don't feel it. Your main problem will be what to do with your hands. If you have notes, hold them in front of you at about waist level with one hand. With your free hand, lightly grasp the note-holding wrist. If you're lucky, there will be a lectern of some sort at which you can stand. Rest your hands on either side of it and you'll look very much at ease. Only royalty can get away with holding their hands behind their backs, and you'll look sloppy if you put your hands in your pockets, so don't adopt either of these postures. If you've no notes and no lectern, just stand with your left hand lightly holding your right wrist in front of you. It looks surprisingly natural and relaxed. Next time you switch on the TV you'll notice how many presenters and comedians use the position!

Notes

The very worst thing you can do is *read* your speech. Comic speeches need a touch of spontaneity, even if they've been prepared weeks in advance and you've been rehearsing for days. Reading a speech kills it dead. It makes the material seem dull, even if it isn't; it prevents eye contact, which is very important in breaking down the barrier between speaker and audience; and it destroys that important sense of a shared occasion, with speaker and audience responding to each other. On top of all that, the very fact that you are reading will indicate a lack of confidence — and your audience will be alerted to your discomfort and share in it.

That said, it's equally inadvisable to stand up and speak without the aid of any notes at all. Nerves can affect the memories of even professional speakers, so don't take any risks. Many people like to write their notes on postcards, using a single main heading and a couple of key phrases to prompt them. If you decide to do this, make sure that you number the cards clearly. You are bound to drop them if you don't, and reassembling them in the wrong order could create all kinds of chaos! Make sure, too, that you write your headings in large capital letters. When you're standing up and holding the cards at waist level you need to take in all the information at a single glance.

If cards seem too fiddly, write the main headings of your speech on a single sheet of paper, again using a few key words underneath to jog your memory. You'll know, from your rehearsals, those things you find difficult to remember and those which come easily. Jot down the points you get stuck on.

If you're going to use quotations then write them clearly on postcards and read them when the time comes. This ensures that you get them absolutely right and, far from doubting your competence, your audience will be impressed by your thoroughness.

Don't try to hide your notes. Simply use them as

inconspicuously as possible. They prove that you have prepared a speech specially for the occasion and that you care about getting it right — and there's no need to be concerned about that.

On the day

On the day of your speech there are a number of simple precautions you can take to ensure that everything goes smoothly. Some of them may seem quite painfully obvious, but it's the most obvious things that are over-looked, particularly when you're nervous.

Electronic assistance — in the form of microphones and public address systems — needs handling with care. When you accept an invitation to speak, enquire if a microphone is to be provided. If it is, test it before the other guests arrive so that you don't have the embarrassing experience of opening your speech to find that it's not working. Make a point of checking how to raise or lower it, so that if the previous speaker was a giant or a midget you can readjust it without fuss, and try it out, so that you know how far away from it you need to stand. Microphones have a life of their own. You will have to speak directly into some, while others pick up sounds from several feet away. Find out which variety yours is *before* you get to your feet.

If the microphone squeals at you, or despite your preparation, booms too loudly or not at all, get it adjusted during your preliminary remarks, and wait, if necessary, until the fault has been corrected. If may seem amusing to begin with, but the audience will soon tire of it and you won't have a chance to communicate your humour and ideas if they are unable to hear what you have to say or are in constant danger of being deafened.

If you know that you tend to put your hands in your pockets while you're speaking, remove all your loose change and keys so that you're not tempted to jangle them. And make sure that you have a clean handkerchief somewhere about you. A scrap of well-used tissue isn't going to impress the audience when you need to blow your nose.

If you've worked hard to make the opening words of your speech interesting and funny, it would be a great shame to waste them by starting to speak while the audience is still talking and settling down in their seats. So wait for silence, even if it seems to take an age, and when you've obtained it start confidently and loudly so that everyone can hear what you have to say. Whatever you do, don't be hurried. Public speakers talk quite slowly and allow plenty of pauses so that the audience can respond. Take it at a leisurely pace, making sure that you're heard throughout the room, and you'll win the audience's attention immediately.

Some people, but only a very few, are at their best after a few drinks. Unless you know for certain that alcohol will improve your performance, it's probably best not to drink before you speak. Drinking tends to dull reactions and instil a false sense of confidence — and you need to be completely in control of yourself and your material if you're going to make a success of the occasion. Naturally, once you've made your speech and it's been greeted with applause and laughter, you can reward yourself!

Whether you've been drinking or not, accidents do happen. Cope with them by acknowledging them and turning them to your advantage. For example, the speaker who knocked a glass of water over himself brought the house down with the throwaway line, 'Whoops! For a moment there I thought my trousers were on fire!' If someone in the audience drops a glass or falls off their chair, acknowledge it and pause for laughter rather than ploughing on as if nothing has happened. Although you have prepared your speech in advance, you should be aware of things happening around you and flexible enough to add a topical observation or funny remark if necessary. And the better-rehearsed and more at ease you are with your material, the more confident you'll be about including the odd spontaneous line.

If you follow these guidelines you really can't go far wrong. But here, as a last-minute reminder, is a checklist of Do's and Don't's that will ensure that your delivery will do justice to all the work you've put into your speech.

Do's

1   Do rehearse your material.
2   Do work on your posture so that you look relaxed and comfortable.
3   Do prepare your notes and quotations carefully.
4   Do take simple precautions — like dressing correctly, checking microphones and checking your appearance.
5   Do anticipate any accidents and interruptions and be prepared for them.

Don't's

1   Don't read your speech.
2   Don't make any last-minute attempts to change your accent or your appearance.
3   Don't arrive late or unprepared.
4   Don't start your speech before everyone is ready.
5   Don't drink before you make your speech.

The Right Speech for the Right Occasion

Every speech you make should be created for the occasion, and every occasion requires a particular sort of speech. For example, the kind of speech that will go down successfully at a conference will be quite different from a presentation speech.

Here are brief guidelines covering the kind of speeches required for most business and social occasions.

After-dinner speeches

It's both an honour and an ordeal to be invited to make an after-dinner speech. An honour, because it indicates that the people who have extended the invitation have confidence in your ability to entertain them, and an ordeal because of all types of speaking engagement, after-dinner speeches require the most work and preparation.

Preparation is absolutely essential. Most wise after-dinner speakers talk for between ten and twenty minutes, and if you're not well prepared it's impossible to speak confidently and amusingly for that length of time. Preparation will also give you the advantage of seeming spontaneous and relaxed, no matter how you feel, and this in itself is important. A tense, nervous speaker can't expect to win the confidence of those listening to him.

Some very successful public speakers are renowned for composing their speeches on the back of a menu ten minutes before they are introduced to their audience. Don't be tempted to copy them. Others have tried — which is why in so many circles the audience dread the after-dinner speech even more than the speaker!

After-dinner speakers have a single purpose, and that is to amuse the guests after a good meal and round the evening off perfectly. To that end, ensure that all your material is suitable for the occasion. Embarrassing people with a string of off-colour stories won't help your cause, and neither will moralising or lecturing. Keep it witty and lighthearted — and you'll find plenty of material in the second section of this book to enable you to do so.

Remember also to be brief. When you are first asked to speak, make a point of finding out how long you will be expected to talk for. Twenty minutes should be the absolute limit, and don't exceed it by a single minute. It's always better to be brief and wickedly amusing than to speak for forty minutes and generate only the occasional laugh. No one ever complained that a speech was too short, only that it was too long.

Sometimes, no matter how good a speaker and his material, circumstances combine to ruin all the preparation. Bad acoustics, a fractious audience and poor introductions and early speeches can make it impossible for you to make your mark. In this case, the best thing to do is give in gracefully. Don't just stop in mid-sentence; condense your argument, get to the conclusion and sit down with your head held high. There is no point in prolonging your agony.

Conferences and conventions

Humour is a vital ingredient for conferences and conventions, particularly if you're one of the last speakers at an all-day or even days-long gathering. No matter how serious your topic, a joke or amusing quotation will help to capture your audience's attention, and once you have their interest it will be easier to keep it.

If you know that you're going to be one of the last people to speak, bend one of the major guidelines of the earlier section of this book and *don't* prepare your material too thoroughly. If you're very unlucky you may find that the earlier speeches have effectively covered all that you had planned to say in your own address. It's better, in this situation, to be prepared with a good general outline — one with plenty of relevant humour and wit (because that's what will be required at the end of a long day's speeches) — and build on it as the conference progresses. Listen to the other speakers making a note of their argument and the things you disagree with or strongly approve of. Insert all these points in your outline to prove that you've been listening, and in this way you'll ensure that your speech is completely integrated and relevant.

Energy and enthusiasm are both important on these kinds of occasion. Be positive and amusing; give people what they want to hear but also give them some food for thought. Above all, try not to look on it too much as an ordeal. After all, it's not often that you get the chance to sell yourself in front of an audience from your own field — an audience who will be able to appreciate an excellent and entertaining specialised speech.

Appeals and fundraising

Fundraising functions and appeals require some speaking skill. Before you can ask people to donate money you will have to put them in a frame of mind in which they'll be happy to give — and an amusing and sincere speech can do this. Obviously you will have to tailor the humour to fit the cause or appeal that you want to make. An appeal speech shouldn't be too humorous, and there are bound to be some serious moments in it as you explain the need for the donations. But if you can make the audience warm to you and your cause you will have a better chance of raising funds.

An appeal for a police benevolent fund might begin with an amusing anecdote before moving on to stress the valuable contribution to society of that force, the serious side of law and order, and the necessity for the fund. It might then end with a wryly amusing observation, though not one so funny as to entirely disperse the seriousness of the appeal.

If your audience can sense your sincerity, and if they like you, you'll have more chance of raising money than if you simply bludgeon them with hard facts.

Presentations

Presentations follow a simple formula that can be adapted for all kinds of occasions, from retirements to formal award ceremonies. The most important point to remember is to give the audience all the basic information they need to understand what is going on and appreciate the significance of the occasion. Speak for five minutes at the most and try not to steal the limelight from the person who is being honoured. By all means tell an anecdote about the recipient if you know him or her, but don't take too long about it.

This is the basic formula:
1 Name the award and give some details about its background and donor, if there is one.
2 State the reason for the presentation.
3 State what the recipient has done to deserve the award.
4 Present the award.

If you're to be the recipient at a presentation you'll need to do a little homework before you can prepare your speech. This is the pattern your reply should follow:

1   Say thank you to the person making the presentation and, if relevant, to the organisation he or she represents. (You'll have to find out their names and details in advance.)

2   Acknowledge the donor of the prize if different from those already mentioned above.

3   Say what the award means to you and what you will do with it if it's something like a trophy. If you have a relevant anecdote to tell, use it at this stage, integrating it with the other information.

If you have watched the Oscar ceremony on television you may feel tempted to elaborate on all the behind-the-scenes effort that went into your achievement. Don't, it's usually boring. Neither should you be unduly modest and say that you can't think what you've done to deserve it. Accept the award with good grace and be brief and amusing in your speech.

Toasts

The speech accompanying a toast on a light-hearted occasion should be amusing and perhaps a little longer than a formal toast. It's not the time to start telling jokes, however, and it shouldn't last more than five minutes at the very most — in fact two minutes is about the optimum length. As with all comic speeches, everything you say should be relevant to the occasion and should lead directly up to the toast at the end. Don't tell an irrelevant story and then tack the toast on.

Other things best avoided are those cliched, overblown and often sentimental toasts so beloved of many speakers. This is particularly true in a business or professional function. Far better on such occasions to use a witty and apt quotation or one-liner, followed up by a simple 'To absent friends' or 'To Bill.'

The guidelines in this section should see you through most of the functions at which you could be required to make a comic speech. If, however, you are invited to speak on an occasion that isn't specifically covered here, find out from the organisers exactly what they require of you and make sure that you give it to them. Just bear in mind the three golden rules of successful comic speech-making — wit, brevity and preparation — and you can't go wrong.

Here is a final checklist of Do's and Don't's to be considered when you're working out what kind of speech to make for a particular occasion.

Do's

1 Do assess the audience and the formal require-ments and tone of the occasion.
2 Find out how long you will be required to speak for and on which subject.
3 What kind of function will you be fulfilling? Are you to make an after-dinner speech, propose a toast or present an award?
4 Research all necessary information, including names and titles.
5 Do start work on it *now*!

Don't's

1 Don't plan to speak for any longer than necessary.
2 Don't leave it to the last moment to find out details of the function and the people expected to attend.
3 Don't be over-effusive or falsely modest.
4 Don't use an old speech and try to revamp it at the last moment.
5 Don't forget to include your thanks and acknow-ledgements.

PART TWO

The material

Only Joking

In this section you'll find all the material you need to create your comic speech. There are jokes, anecdotes, quotes, one-liners and funny facts about all aspects of the law, so that whether you're a policeman, a solicitor or a politician you need never be at a loss for a few entertaining words.

Whichever branch of the law you are involved with, you'll find plenty of suitable jokes here. When you've chosen those you want to use, adapt them so that they are completely relevant to your theme and add your personal touch with topical and local details. By the time you've finished you won't simply have borrowed them from this book — you'll have made them your own.

A young couple, newly-married, set off on their honeymoon in Cornwall in the groom's van. As they left the London suburbs behind on their long journey west, their thoughts turned more and more to the pleasures ahead of them — a whole week alone together, safe from prying eyes. Finally their impatience became too much to cope with, so they pulled the van onto a grass verge on the edge of a small village and, to ensure total privacy as well as shelter from the drizzle, crawled underneath the vehicle and set to with a will. After some time the young man became aware of the presence of a third person, and looked up to find a pair of heavy boots, unmistakably those of a policeman, positioned by his head. As he gazed up some six feet, the police constable asked what he thought he was doing.

'I'm just fixing the van,' the young man replied.

'I'll give you three reasons why I do not believe you,' said the policeman. 'Number one, you are the wrong way up. Number two, a small crowd which has just turned out of the local pub is cheering you on. And number three, someone has stolen your van.'

A chief constable was invited to make an after-dinner speech to a gathering of local Round Tablers. After the occasion he approached the reporter from the local paper, who had been present, and asked him not to repeat any of the amusing anecdotes he had told as he wished to use them again for other functions. Much to his chagrin, when he read the account of the evening's proceedings in the next issue of the paper, he came across the words, 'The chief constable made an excellent speech, but unfortunately some of the tales he told cannot be repeated here.'

A policeman stood and watched while a lady reversed her car very slowly into a parking space. When she'd switched off the ignition he went up to speak to her.

'Haven't you seen the notice, madam? You shouldn't be parking here.'

'But officer,' she protested, 'it says FINE FOR PARKING.'

It was New Year's Eve and the young policeman stopped to ask a man what he was doing, lying in the gutter.

'I'm not drunk,' the man hastened to assure him. 'I'm from the Water Board. The lady's pipe has burst and I've got my arm through this grating to free the stopcock.'

The policeman was in the witness box. 'I was in plain clothes when the defendant came up and tried to pass me this twenty pound note.'

'Counterfeit?' asked the prosecuting counsel.

'Yes, sir. She had two.'

A police constable flagged down a car one night and breathalysed the young woman driving it. 'My goodness,' he commented when he saw the results. 'You've had a stiff one tonight.'

'Gosh!' said the girl. 'Does that show too?'

A certain Chief Inspector Watkins was a bit of a name-dropper. This annoyed one of his police colleagues so much that he bet Watkins £500 that he couldn't claim to know the Prime Minister, the President of the United States or the Pope. 'I know all three, and I'll prove it,' said Watkins, so the two of them set off for Downing Street. Watkins had a word with the policeman on the door of Number 10, went inside and, an hour or two later, re-appeared with the Prime Minister, who seemed to be a close friend of his. Next they flew to Washington, and the scene was repeated with President Reagan. Finally they arrived at St Peter's Square in Rome. Chief Inspector Watkins left his baffled companion down below, dis-appeared into St Peter's and moments later appeared on the balcony in the company of his Holiness, the Pope.

His stunned colleague watched in disbelief before reaching in his pocket for his chequebook. Just as he was about to sign the cheque he was even more flabbergasted to hear a voice behind him asking, 'Who's that up there with Chief Inspector Watkins?'

There were roadworks at Hyde Park Corner and a single young constable was trying to control the traffic as it sped about him. On the far pavement a little old lady kept beckoning to him. He ignored her for as long as he could, but finally decided that she might be in trouble, so hold-ing up most of London's rush-hour traffic, he went over to her and asked if he could be of assistance.

'How kind of you, young man,' she said shyly. 'I just wanted to tell you that your number is the same as the number of my favourite hymn.'

Did you hear about the police constable who was drunk

on Christmas Eve? He flagged down a car and asked the driver if it was licensed. When the driver replied that it was, he said, 'Great! I'll have a Scotch and soda.'

A policeman was walking through a graveyard late one night when he noticed a hole in one of the graves. Suspecting vandals, he at once went to fetch the vicar and brought him along to see it. 'Oh, yes,' said the vicar, unconcerned. 'That's just old Mozart. He's decomposing, you know.'

A policeman stopped a drunk one night and asked him why he was walking with one foot on the kerb and the other in the gutter. 'Is that what I'm doing?' asked the drunk. 'Thank heavens for that, I thought I was a cripple.'

During the days of Prohibition the police were tipped off that a certain man was selling liquor illegally from his premises. The police accordingly raided the house and found several hundred empty whisky bottles in the cellar. 'How did these get here?' they asked the householder. 'I'm sure I don't know,' the man replied, 'I've never bought an empty whisky bottle in my life.'

A man came into a pub with an exceptionally ugly dog on a lead. The barman remarked on the dog's odd looks as he served his customer, and was astonished to be told, 'He's a fine dog — a first-class police dog.' When the barman expressed his surprise that such a creature could be a genuine police dog, he was told, 'He's in plain clothes at the moment.'

A drunk was walking home along the roadside late one night with a bottle of whisky in each coat pocket when he was knocked down by a hit-and-run driver. A police constable arrived on the scene and shone his torch on the man, who was lying groaning in the gutter, to reveal a pool of blood. 'Thank God for that,' exclaimed the drunk. 'I thought it was my whisky.'

'You've been travelling at seventy miles an hour,' said the police patrolman to the speeding motorist.

'Impossible,' replied the driver. 'I haven't even been out an hour.'

A police cadet of the Royal Ulster Constabulary was sitting the oral part of an examination and was asked what he would do if he were driving along a dark country lane late at night at a speed of forty miles per hour and suddenly found himself being followed by a car full of hooded men.

'Eighty!' he replied without hesitation.

The driver of a car towing a horsebox was stopped on the motorway for speeding. 'Actually, I'm amazed that you can do ninety miles an hour with a horse in the back,' the policeman said amiably, 'What've you got in there, a Shetland pony?'

The driver got out of the car and opened the back of the horsebox. There was nothing inside. 'Well,' he shrugged, 'someone's got to transport the non-runners!'

A young constable was escorting a drunken driver down to the cells at the police station. 'You're going to have to be locked up for the night,' he explained.

'What's the charge?' demanded the prisoner.

'There's no charge, it's all part of the service.'

A police officer stopped a car one night and informed the driver that he believed the latter had pornographic literature hidden in the boot.

'Nothing of the sort!' protested the driver.

'I don't even have a pornograph.'

A young policeman spotted an old man pulling a cardboard box on a lead down the street. Not wishing to upset the old gent, as he assumed he was a little dotty, he approached him with the remark, 'Nice-looking dog you've got there, sir.'

Much to his surprise the old man rounded on him and explained indignantly, 'It isn't a dog, it's a box.'

Feeling a proper fool, the policeman apologised for his mistake and moved on. Turning to the box the old man winked and said gleefully, 'Fooled him that time, didn't we, boy?'

A policeman was cycling down a country lane one bitterly cold winter morning when he stopped to look at a blackbird lying in the road. The bird was obviously suffering from the cold but was not yet dead. A herd of cows passed by and with a flash of inspiration the PC dropped the bird into a steaming cowpat, realising that the creature had to be warmed up quickly. Sure enough, after a while the bird was seen to struggle free, whereupon it began to chirp and sing loudly. All at once a cat leapt from the undergrowth, seized the bird and made off with it.

The PC reflected on these events as he cycled on down the road, and he drew the following conclusions. First, it's not just your friends who drop you in it; secondly, it's not just your friends who pull you out of it; and thirdly, never make a song and dance about it.

A police constable was playing rugby one Saturday when he fell badly and put one of his shoulders out. He was hurried to the hospital casualty unit, in great pain, where the doctor seized hold of him and wrenched the joint back into position with some force. The policeman, quite understandably, gave an almighty yell.

'Honestly,' said the doctor, 'you tough chaps are such cissies. I've seen women give birth without a murmur, and that can be terribly painful.'

'Just try putting a few of the babies back and see how they react,' said the policeman.

A police constable nearing retirement was asked to keep an eye on the local factory, where there had been a lot of pilfering in the last few months. Accordingly the PC did some spot checks on some of the employees as they left work, and he soon became suspicious of one man in particular, who left work every day with a large haversack attached to his bike. However, although the policeman checked through the contents of the bag on several occasions, he never found anything.

Eventually his retirement came around, and he held a small party in the local pub to celebrate. One of the guests was the man whose haversack he'd searched. 'You know,' the ex-copper said to the worker, 'I owe you an apology. I was convinced for a long time that you were pilfering from the factory.'

'Don't worry,' the man smiled. 'As a matter of fact, you weren't wrong. Every night for the last six months I've been taking a brand new bicycle home . . .'

The motorist pulled up a few yards down the road, got out of the car and ran back to the scene of the accident.

'What's the matter with you? Are you blind?' asked the pedestrian, picking himself up from the road.

'Blind, what do you mean, blind?' asked the motorist. 'I hit you, didn't I?'

'All right, yes, I did kill my wife,' the man confessed. 'But she was driving me crazy. She kept a pig in our bedroom and the mess and smell were terrible.'

The detective constable looked at him curiously. 'Couldn't you simply have opened the window?'

The murderer was aghast. 'And let all my pigeons out?'

A nurse was threatened by a would-be mugger as she walked home from the hospital late one night. Not one whit disturbed, she rounded on him with the words, 'Don't even think about it! You don't scare me — why, I've *washed* bigger men than you!'

'And why did you break into the shop three nights in a row?' asked the policeman.

'The dress was for my wife,' explained the thief, 'and she made me change it three times.'

A policeman went to call on a lady. 'I'm afraid we've had a complaint from the Post Office that your dog is chasing the postman on his bicycle.'

She seemed surprised. 'I can't believe that, officer. You see, my dog can't ride a bike.'

'You must take things quietly,' said the doctor, finishing his examination.

'Oh, I do!' said the burglar.

A coach-load of Americans were being shown around St Paul's Cathedral. The guide was pointing out various things of interest and, stopping at a monument, pointed to it and said, 'Here are the remains of one of this country's most admired men and a famous lawyer ...'

An American lady turned in surprise to her husband. 'Gosh,' she said, 'I didn't know the English buried two people in their graves.'

'Well,' said the doctor as he finished examining the barrister, 'I don't know what's wrong with you but you must have Alice.'

'What on earth is Alice?' asked the barrister.

'I don't know that,' replied the doctor, 'but Christopher Robin went down with it.'

A doctor and a lawyer were trading friendly insults. 'Well,' said the doctor, 'I'm not saying all you fellows are crooks, but your profession doesn't exactly make angels of men, does it?'

'No, I have to admit that's where your profession has the advantage over ours,' the lawyer replied swiftly.

Three survivors of a shipwreck sat on a life raft. They were a doctor, a priest and a solicitor. At last they spotted land but realised that they could not make it without help so, as the solicitor was the best swimmer of the three, he volunteered to swim to shore and summon aid. He accordingly dived into the sea and set off for land. Almost at once a shark appeared and began circling around him, but after a moment or two it swam off without touching him. The two in the boat were vastly relieved, and the priest burst out, 'What a great thing is the power of prayer!'

'Prayer my foot!' retorted the doctor. 'What we have just seen is a case of professional respect.'

A lawyer had his photo taken by a well-known society photographer. He was portrayed in his usual pose, hands in his jacket pockets. Admiring the finished portrait at an exhibition of the photographer's work one day, the lawyer heard one of his clients say, 'It would have been even more lifelike if he'd had his hands in someone else's pockets!'

Finding himself short of time, a famous barrister asked his assistant to draft a speech for him to make at a law school that evening. The assistant did as instructed, but the following morning the barrister stormed into the chambers in a foul mood.

'That speech you wrote for me yesterday was so boring that half the audience fell asleep and the other half crawled out under the tables,' he protested. 'And what's more, I asked you to make it half an hour long and it lasted for an hour.'

'I did write you a half-hour speech,' replied the implacable assistant. 'And I supplied a carbon copy.'

The solicitor was feeling rather under the weather so he went to see his doctor. The doctor examined him and, finding nothing wrong, started to question him about his lifestyle in case it yielded any clues. Had he perhaps been drinking a little too much? Smoking too much? Had he been getting enough sleep? And so on. After a pause he asked tentatively, 'Sex?'

'Infrequently,' replied the solicitor.

There was a short pause. 'One word or two?' asked the doctor.

A solicitor's small son asked his mother, 'Mummy, why do all fairy tales begin with "Once upon a time"?'

'Not all of them do,' his mother replied. 'The ones your father tells start with, "Sorry I'm late, dear, I was held up at the office".'

A lawyer was present at the funeral of a wealthy but stingy man. A fellow guest arrived late at the funeral when the clergyman had almost finished extolling the deceased's virtue from the pulpit. He slipped into the seat next to the lawyer and whispered, 'How far has he got?'

'Just opened for the defence,' came the reply.

A young law student was taking an oral examination, and doing very badly. He seemed to be unable to remember a single thing he'd learned at university.

'Okay,' said the examiner, 'here's one more chance for you. What is justice?'

The student thought a bit, then muttered hopelessly, 'It's no good. I knew all about it before I came into this room, but now my mind's a complete blank.'

'Young man,' said the examiner, 'this is a very serious matter. It seems that ten minutes ago only two people were sure what justice is — you and God. And now *you* have forgotten.'

A solicitor was reading a man's will to his assembled family. 'I have always promised to mention my wife in my will,' it read. 'So hello, Doris.'

Sloane Ranger secretary to barrister in kilt: 'I've always been curious to know what, if anything, is worn under the kilt.'

'It's simple,' said the barrister with a smirk. 'Nothing's worn — everything's in first-class condition.'

A glamorous redhead waved at a barrister as he was walking down the Strand with his wife. The wife, somewhat peeved, demanded to know who the woman was. 'Oh, just someone I met yesterday,' replied the barrister, adding as an afterthought, 'professionally, of course.'

'Whose profession — yours or hers?' asked his wife.

A young solicitor was asked by a colleague how he felt about his forthcoming marriage to a rather older woman. 'Well,' he replied thoughtfully, 'it's a question of knowing what is to be done but wondering how to make it more interesting.'

A solicitor's wife rang her husband's office from the airport just before catching a plane, and spoke to his secretary. 'I'm in a hurry,' she said. 'Would you tell Mr Hargreaves that I forgot to switch off the electric blanket when I left this morning.'

'Certainly,' said the secretary. 'May I ask who is speaking?'

A successful young barrister was invited back to his old university college to address some of the students. After the meeting, he decided to visit his old rooms for nostalgia's sake. He knocked at the door and after a few minutes' wait it was opened by a flustered young man. The barrister explained why he had come, and the student reluctantly invited him in. The older man looked around, exclaiming, 'The same old bed! The same old bookshelves! The same view from the windows!' At that moment the wardrobe door swung silently open, revealing a girl hidden among the hanging clothes.

'Oh, that's my sister,' blurted out the young man.

'Same old story,' added the barrister.

The barrister and his new wife were honeymooning in a hotel which the barrister knew well from his bachelor days. At breakfast on the first morning he beckoned to one of the waiters and said, 'I say, where's my honey?'

The waiter looked somewhat taken aback, glanced at the young bride and murmured in a low voice, 'I'm sorry, sir, but she doesn't work here any more.'

A barrister got married to a schoolteacher during term-time and one of her colleagues took over her class while she was away on honeymoon. On their return, the couple went to a party where the hostess, not realising that the barrister had met his wife's colleague, attempted to introduce them. 'We've already met,' smiled the barrister. 'Caroline took my wife's place during our honeymoon.'

A witness claimed during a recent court case that the defendant had been drunk as a judge when the crime was committed. 'You mean drunk as a lord,' interposed the judge.
'Yes, my lord,' the witness agreed.

The jury had listened carefully while the rules of insanity were explained to them. Their verdict on the case was unanimous or, as the foreman put it, 'We are all of one mind — insane.'

An Irishman was convicted of bigamy and the judge expressed his disgust that the accused could have tricked so many women. 'But I was only trying to find a good one,' the Irishman protested.

The scene was a divorce court. 'Would you please tell the court whether your husband drinks,' said the lawyer.
'He does take an occasional drink to steady himself,' admitted the wife.
'And does this have any harmful effects?' asked the lawyer.
'Only when he gets so steady he can't move.'

A young man was on trial for the savage murder of both his parents. It seemed an open-and-shut case and obvious to all that the man was guilty. Nevertheless the jury was out for several hours deliberating, and eventually to everyone's surprise they emerged to announce a verdict of 'Not guilty.'

The judge was so astounded that he asked the foreman how they had come to such a decision. 'It's like this, your lordship,' the foreman explained. 'What with him having had two such 'orrible deaths in the family so recently we thought we'd give him the benefit of the doubt.'

A judge was sentencing a burglar with several previous convictions. 'I shall be obliged to give you the maximum sentence laid down by the law,' he warned.

'Maximum?' the burglar retorted. 'Don't regular customers get a discount?'

A man being tried in court on a murder charge managed to speak to one of the jurors and bribe him with a promise of £2,000 if he could get his fellows jurors to reduce the charge to manslaughter. A verdict of manslaughter was brought in, and the accused, vastly relieved, rushed straight across the courtroom to thank the man he had bribed. 'It was terribly difficult,' the latter exclaimed as he counted the cash. 'All the others wanted to acquit you!'

In an Irish courtroom the accused had just been found guilty of fraud. 'Ten days in prison or a £500 fine,' declared the magistrate.

The prisoner thought about it for a while, then decided, 'I'll take the £500.'

Judge and barrister had disagreed violently during a court case, and the judge was now summing up at the end of proceedings. As he spoke the barrister made his feelings pretty obvious by fidgeting continuously, sighing, raising his eyes to the ceiling and so on, until eventually the judge turned to him and asked, 'Am I right in thinking that you are expressing your contempt of this court?'

'No, my lord,' returned the barrister, 'I am attempting to conceal it.'

An Irish jury were sent out to consider their verdict. 'It's a very simple case, so it shouldn't take you long,' were the judge's final remarks as they left. Two hours later they were still deliberating so the judge called them back.

'What's taking so long?' he asked.

'Well, it only took us ten minutes to reach our verdict,' he was told, 'but we're having a bit of trouble trying to elect a foreman.'

The defendant was unable to attend the closing stages of the court case owing to illness, so his solicitor sent him a telegram reading, 'Justice has been done.'

'Appeal at once,' came the reply.

There's no helping some people. Take the case of the man who went before the court requesting damages for injuries to his arm, which he claimed were the result of industrial negligence. 'Would you show me how far you can raise you arm now?' asked the prosecuting counsel.

With a great deal of effort the man raised his arm six inches. 'And could you raise it higher before the accident?' asked the counsel.

'Oh yes,' said the witness. 'I could raise it *this* high ...' (Ilustrate this joke by raising your arm high in the air.)

Three elderly judges were discussing how they'd like to die. 'I'd like to be killed outright in a car accident,' said the first.

'I'd prefer an aeroplane accident, myself,' said the second.

'You two have absolutely no ambition,' said the third. '*I* want to be shot by a jealous husband.'

The judge suddenly noticed that there were only eleven jurors in court and stopped proceedings to ask where the twelfth was. 'It's all right,' one of the others explained. 'He had to go on urgent business, but he left his verdict with me.'

During an altercation in the divorce courts a wife complained that her husband was leaving her without any reason. 'In that case I'm leaving you exactly as I found you,' the husband exclaimed.

A man was acquitted on a charge of stealing a pair of trousers. At the conclusion of the case, as the courtroom began to empty, his barrister (whose first case it was) came over to congratulate him. 'You can go now, you're a free man,' he said with a glow of pride.

His client looked shifty. 'I'd rather not, if you don't mind,' he said, watching the prosecuting barrister. 'You see, I've got them on.'

The judge smiled gently at the elderly lady who stood trembling in the dock. 'Tell us, why did you steal the purse?'

'I wasn't feeling well and I thought the change might do me good.'

After the trial the barrister went down to the cells. 'I wish I could have done more for you,' he said to his client, who was waiting to be taken away.

'Thank you, but ten years is *quite* enough,' said the prisoner.

During a trial for attempted rape, the victim was asked to tell the court what the assailant had said to her. As she was too distressed to do so, she was given pen and paper and asked to write the words instead, so that they could be handed round the courtroom. This she did, and the piece of paper made its way along the jurors. There was a slight pause when it reached an elderly woman who had nodded off to sleep, but her neighbour, a young man, roused her and placed the paper in her hand. She read it, looked at him — and slapped him hard across the face.

A judge was discussing a case with a colleague of his and finished by saying, 'Well, I really can't understand it. All those people sleeping together before they were married! I certainly never slept with my wife before we were married. Did you?'

The other judge shrugged. 'Don't know. What was her maiden name?'

The magistrate looked wearily at the defendant in the dock, who seemed vaguely familiar. 'Have you ever been up before me before?' he asked.

'I don't know, your honour. What time do you normally get up?' replied the man in the dock.

The accused had just been sentenced and was asked if he had anything to say.

'Bugger all!' came the reply. The judge, who had not been able to catch this remark, leaned forward and asked counsel for the defence what the man had said.

'Bugger all,' he was told.

'No, no,' insisted the judge. 'He must have said something, I saw his lips move.'

During the last days of capital punishment, a beautiful young woman was sentenced to death. As a last request she asked if she might leave this world naked, as she had entered it. The request was granted and as the moment for her hanging approached she walked towards the hangman, who couldn't take his eyes off her body. 'And it's all yours, if you keep your trap shut,' she murmured.

Ronald Reagan, President Mitterand and Mrs Thatcher found themselves sitting alone together at a conference.

'I have a problem and I need your help,' admitted President Reagan. 'I have eighteen personal bodyguards, and I know for certain that one of them is a Russian spy. But which one?'

Mrs Thatcher nodded sympathetically and Mr Mitterand said, 'I have a similar sort of problem. You see I have eighteen mistresses and I know for certain that one of them is being unfaithful — but I cannot tell which one.'

'That's nothing,' snapped Mrs Thatcher, 'I have eighteen people in my cabinet. One of them, I know for certain, is intelligent. But *which* one?'

It was just before Christmas and the British ambassador to Washington received a phone call from a newspaper tycoon, asking what he would like for Christmas. The ambassador thought it would be wrong to accept any kind of gift, and refused as politely as he could, but the friendly American insisted that he name his wish for Christmas. Finally the ambassador said, 'Well, if you insist, a box of candy would be nice for the family.'

Imagine his astonishment when he came across a lead article in the tycoon's newspaper, which read, 'At this season of goodwill, we have been asking official representatives of other nations about their wishes for Christmas. The German ambassador hopes for the relief of world poverty, the French ambassador hopes for progress in the SALT talks, and the British ambassador hopes for a box of candy to share with his family.'

A politician was addressing a public meeting, and reading his speech from notes. He hadn't had time to go over it with his speech-writer before delivering it, but all went well until he reached the final words. 'And what, ladies and gentlemen, is the answer to these burning questions which confront us today?'

He turned the page and read the words, 'Now you tell them.'

A man went to his doctor for a brain transplant and was offered two to choose from — a bus driver's for £1,000 and a politician's for £100,000.

'Does that mean that the politician's is better than the bus driver's?' he asked.

'Not exactly,' said the surgeon. 'It's just that the politician's has never been used.'

A British politician of senior rank was paying an official

visit to a small, recently independent African country. On his arrival he was heartened by the enthusiastic welcome he received from the crowd of locals who listened to his first public speech. After every few words he was interrupted by hearty cries of 'Ambongo! Ambongo!' He went to bed that night feeling that things had got off to a good start. Imagine his surprise, however, when during the course of a visit to a dairy farm the following day he was warned by the farmer, 'Mind where you tread. There's a lot of *ambongo* lying about!'

A man was on his way to the polling station to vote in the General Election when he was approached by the Tory candidate, who offered him £20 if he would vote for him. He agreed to do so, took the money and went on his way. A little further down the road he met the local Labour man who offered him £10 for his vote. The man took the £10, agreed to vote Labour and went on his way. When he got to the polling station he voted for the Labour candidate, reckoning that if both men were crooked, at least the Labour chap was 50% less crooked than the Tory . . .

During the run-up to the General Election a poster outside the village hall announced a forthcoming talk entitled 'How the Tories can do it.' Someone had scrawled underneath, 'Next week: How to hang blancmange on your living-room walls.'

A famous Labour politician died and went to heaven. After a few hours there he realised that most people seemed to be walking around in pairs, and when he saw Tony Benn in the arms of Joan Collins he went straight to St Peter and asked to be introduced to his partner.

'I'm sorry, I've been so busy I forgot,' said St Peter. 'Here she is.' And he ushered forward Mrs Thatcher.

The Labour man recoiled. 'This is terrible!' he cried. 'After all I've done for the poor and downtrodden of the world! How can you do this to me when you've paired up

Tony Benn with Joan Collins?'

'Now look here,' said St Peter sternly, 'how I punish Joan Collins is my own affair!'

While on a visit to Liverpool Mrs Thatcher fell in the Mersey. A boy passing by jumped in and pulled her out, not realising who she was. As they stood dripping on the bank, Mrs Thatcher shook him firmly by the hand. 'Thank you so much,' she said. 'As a reward for your bravery I'll give you anything you want. All you have to do is name it.'

'I'd like a state funeral,' said the lad.

'A state funeral? Don't be a silly boy! You can have a Rolls Royce or a holiday in the Bahamas! Why on earth should you want a state funeral?' she asked.

'Because when my dad finds out about what I've done, he'll kill me,' replied the lad.

A politician was visiting a local mental hospital and came across a group of inmates sitting around a table passing sheets of paper to and fro. He asked the governor of the hospital, who was showing him round, what sort of therapy this was, and received the reply, 'Oh, it's not therapy. They're all ex-civil servants, and they're imagining themselves back at work.'

Two road-sweepers were cleaning up all the rubbish in Downing Street one morning. Suddenly a gust of wind blew a sweet-wrapper into the open doorway of Number 10. One of the road-sweepers rushed in to retrieve it and apologise. A minute later he came out and announced ruefully to his companion. 'I was too late. She'd already signed it.'

A politician was invited to talk to the inmates of the local lunatic asylum. He accepted the invitation, but was pestered continually during his speech by comments of 'Rubbish!' 'Baloney!' and so on from one of the inmates. When he had finished, the governor thanked him and apologised for the man's bad manners.

'However, one good thing has come of it,' he added. 'He's been here for five years and it's the first time I've heard him say anything sensible.'

A politician was making a bad job of addressing a meeting, and one by one his audience got up and left, until at last only one man remained. The politician stammered to a halt and thanked the man for staying to the end. 'That's all right,' the latter replied. 'Had to, you see I'm the next speaker.'

A Tory party canvasser was knocking on doors the night before the General Election. At one house he had a great deal of difficulty in opening the front gate because it was wired up and tied with rope, but at last he managed to unfasten it. He set off up the garden path, but realised after only a few footsteps that he was treading on wet concrete.

At that moment the front door opened and a burly-looking chap came out. The candidate sprinted back down the path as fast as he could, in the circumstances, shouting over his shoulder, 'I'm from the Labour party and I'll be back in the next day or two!'

The Prime Minister was on a visit to a mental hospital where she was introduced to some of the patients. She shook hands with one elderly lady, who asked her who she was. Upon hearing that she was the Prime Minister, the old lady patted her sympathetically on the shoulder and murmured, 'Don't worry, they'll help you get over that. When I first came here I was sure I was Doris Day.'

A local politician and his wife had gone to a dinner party and were unfortunate enough to find themselves seated next to a very bitter business man who had just gone bankrupt. Throughout the meal he criticised the local council for rising rates, lack of support for small businesses and the state of the town. Then he went on to lambast the government, the Prime Minister and, finally, politics and politicians of all colours.

Embarrassed, the politician remained silent, but his wife finally asked, 'Surely you'd agree that there's *some* difference between the parties?'

'No, no,' shouted the man. 'You're all just as bad as each other. A plague on all your houses, that's what I say.'

The wife smiled coolly at him. 'When the plague comes to our house,' she said, 'you *must* come and visit us.'

When the elderly MP of a Yorkshire constituency died a thrusting young man phoned the national agent.

'I don't want to seem too keen,' he said, 'but I wonder whether I might take the place of our late MP . . .'

The agent thought for a while before replying, 'If the undertaker will agree to it then I won't object.'

An actress with five marriages behind her was asked by a journalist why she was divorcing husband number six.

'Well,' she said, 'he turned out to be not at all the kind of husband I was used to.'

Deep in the dungeons of an east European castle three political prisoners were sitting shackled together. The first one said gloomily, 'I was arrested because I voted for Shlobovitz.'

'That's odd,' said the second. 'I'm here because I was overheard saying that I hated Shlobovitz and would never vote from him.'

'You're not going to believe this,' said the third, 'but I *am* Shlobovitz.'

An Englishman, an Irishman and a Scotsman had been sentenced to death by firing squad in a remote South American capital. First the Englishman was taken out of his cell and put up against the wall. As the soldiers raised their rifles he shouted at the top of his voice 'Avalanche!'

The soldiers dropped their rifles in panic and ran, and the Englishman made good his escape. When the Scotsman's turn came to be shot, he decided to follow his friend's example. He shouted 'Flood!' at the crucial moment and made his escape in the same fashion.

Last came the Irishman. He had watched the others and felt confident that he could escape in the same manner. The soldiers raised their rifles and the Irishman shouted at the top of his voice 'Fire!'

Did you hear about the dumb blonde who visited her boyfriend in prison? He whispered to her to get hold of some wire-cutters and hide them in a cake which she was to bake for him. On the next visit she appeared empty-handed. 'What's gone wrong?' asked the boyfriend.

'Well, I got the wirecutters,' she said. 'But tell me, how do I bake a cake?'

The occupants of a crowded commuter train from Sevenoaks were discussing why British Rail was going bankrupt.

'It's bad management,' said the bank manager.

'It's the dirt and squalor,' said the secretary.

'It's the bad time-keeping,' said the computer whizz-kid.

Just at that moment they saw the ticket collector coming and all hid under their seats.

Sherlock Holmes and Dr Watson were having breakfast together. 'Ah, Watson, you're wearing your red thermal underwear,' announced Holmes as he passed the corn-flakes.

'That's absolutely amazing, Holmes. How did you deduce that?' exclaimed his friend.

'Elementary, my dear Watson. You've forgotten to put on your trousers.'

Three Russians were having a glass of vodka in a Moscow bar. One of them pulled out a copy of Pravda and began reading it. 'Tut, tut,' he said as he read the article by one of the Kremlin's leading men.

'What's that?' asked the second. He leaned over and read the same article, then shook his head. 'Tut, tut. Tut, tut.'

'Now look here,' said the third man, looking nervously over his shoulder. 'If you two are going to start discussing politics I'll have to leave.'

The boss stormed into his secretary's office. 'Now look,' he said, 'you've just had the morning off to go to the hairdresser and now I find a note from you asking for a rise. And all because you came to help out at the Birmingham sales conference last week. Who put you up to it?'

She smiled sweetly. 'My solicitor.'

Did you hear about the couple who bought a fierce dog to guard their property? The husband spent ages training it to scare off all possible intruders and the wife, figuring she might as well teach him a few tricks too, taught him to carry a shopping bag and fetch the newspaper. When they were burgled the poor dog was so confused that he held the torch for the thieves.

A man from the Ministry of Agriculture called at a farm and told the farmer, who was very elderly and rather confused by the latest EEC directives that he had to brand all his livestock. 'All right, I'll try,' the old chap agreed.

Several weeks later the civil servant called back to see how things were going. 'Not bad,' said the farmer. 'I've just finished the chickens but I'm having the devil of a job with the bees.'

In the days of Ancient Rome a Christian was thrown to the lions. The Emperor, who was watching, was astonished when he saw the man whisper a few words in the ears of all the lions which approached him, after which they turned and slunk away. Summoning the Christian before him, the Emperor begged to know what he had said to the animals, and told him he could go free if he revealed his secret.

'Simple,' said the Christian, 'I told them that if they ate me they'd have to make an after-dinner speech.'

A Funny Thing Happened

Real life can be far funnier than any joke, which is why this section is packed with true anecdotes about the law and law-breakers. No matter how much you enjoy them, don't include any of these anecdotes in your speech without ensuring that they're absolutely relevant to the rest of your material. It's not that your audience won't enjoy them — they will — just that they'll be confused about why you dropped an irrelevant story into the middle of your performance.

A Nottinghamshire traffic warden was too zealous at his job, according to the police force. In his fifteen years pounding the pavements he handed out some 17,000 tickets, which choked the files and the administrative machinery. In the end he was dismissed.

Owing to an unfortunate misprint, a newspaper made a reference by name to a certain 'defective' rather than 'detective' in the local police force. The man in question rang the newspaper offices at once and demanded an apology in the next issue of the paper. This duly appeared, and read, 'Constable X is not of course a defective in the police force. He is a detective in the police farce.'

A police raid on a brothel in the USA a few years ago resulted in the arrest of more than 700 clients. In the next few days hundreds of these men rang police headquarters pleading to have their names taken off the charge sheet, because of the damage to their reputations. However, one of the callers had a somewhat original request. He was a retired dentist, aged eighty, offering a considerable sum to have his name *added* to the list.

The policeman of St Arnaud, a tiny town in Australia, were more than delighted when they were told about plans to build a modern police station with offices, accommodation for twenty-seven constables, showers and parking space for fifty cars. The problem was that there were only three policemen at St Arnaud! The building was designated for a bustling Melbourne suburb 200 miles away, St Albans, and a clerk had made an administrative error.

In 1982 a would-be bank robber found himself trapped in the bank he'd broken into. He had to dial 999 and tell the police, 'I'm in Lloyds, by the safe.'

If you can't find a parking meter in a restricted parking zone, you might choose, like Lady Diana Cooper, to park on double yellow lines and leave a note under the windscreen wiper for the traffic warden. Lady Diana's son used to collect some of the notes his mother wrote — and here are a few examples of her style.
   'Dear Warden, Taken sad child to cinema. Please forgive.'
   'Dear Warden. Only a minute. Horribly old (80) and frightfully lame.'
   'Beware of the DOG.' (The dog was a chihuahua.)
   'Dearest Warden. Front tooth broken off; look like an 81-year-old Pirate, so at dentist 19a. Very old, very lame. No meters. Have mercy!'
   She was usually let off, and several of the notes have 'forgiven' pencilled at the bottom.

In 1978 a bank robber sent a letter threatening to blow up a branch of Barclay's Bank if the manager did not leave £15,000 in cash in a bag outside an AA call box on the

Staines bypass. Unfortunately, despite a first-class stamp, the letter arrived late. In fact it arrived twelve hours after the threatened 'bomb' was supposed to have gone off.

An unemployed Midlands man had a bright idea for obtaining free groceries. All he had to do was tear coupons off tins of baby food and send them away for free shopping vouchers. He was finally caught in the act, ripping off labels in a supermarket, and was fined £100 by magistrates. The evidence at the hearing revealed that though he had obtained £15 worth of free food, his bus fares to a number of supermarkets had cost him £16.

When the public take law and order into their own hands the results can be alarming, as a hijacker on an internal American flight discovered when he held a knife to a stewardess's throat and ordered the captain to take him to Cuba. He needed hospital treatment after being kicked, punched, hung upside down and strapped in a seat and sat on by two weighty passengers.

American poet Robert Lowell was once given a five month prison sentence for refusing to serve in the army. Before he was transferred to a Connecticut jail to serve his stretch he spent some time in a New York prison, where his cell was next to that of a convicted murderer.

'I'm in for killing,' his neighbour told Lowell. 'How about you?'

'Oh, I'm in for refusing to kill,' responded Lowell.

An American motorist was stunned to return to his car, which he'd left for only twenty minutes, and find the wing dented and the paintwork scraped. Fortunately there was a note tucked under his windscreen wiper. It read, 'I have just run into your car. People have seen me and now they're watching me write this note. They think I am leaving my name and address, but they are wrong.'

When powers to censor pornography were returned to

local authorities in the USA some years ago, a small town set up its own 'obscenity committee'. As chairman the somewhat surprising choice was a blind ex-businessman. He was delighted with his new role, and when interviewed for the local paper admitted that his phone hadn't stopped ringing since his appointment. The reporter, with all the tact he could muster, then asked the old gentleman how he managed to pass judgement on films which he could not see for himself. 'That's easy,' the chairman replied. 'The other committee members sit with me and fill me in on the action when the screen goes silent.'

The general public require a certain standard of hold-up notes, as a would-be American robber discovered when he passed his note to a cashier. 'I got a bum,' it read. 'I can blow you sky height. This is a held up.' The cashier read it, passed it on to another cashier, and another — and then they all fell about laughing. The raider was so distressed that he sped off into the night.

In 1959 an Italian criminal, Giovanni Nardi, escaped from Genoa to South America, fleeing fraud charges. In his absence he was sentenced to imprisonment. Eleven years later he returned to Italy, feeling certain that by now he would be safe. Hailing a cab, he asked to be taken to a destination that the driver didn't know. They stopped to ask for directions — and the man they apprehended turned out to be the policeman who had led the Nardi case all those years ago.

A Canadian gentleman who became the victim of a mugger found himself better off after the attack than before it. His attacker seized his wallet, removed $30 in cash and transferred it to his own. Unfortunately he got confused, and as he ran off he threw his victim the wrong wallet, which contained instant compensation of $300.

Admitting that he had given a false name to the policeman who arrested him, a student named Smith said, 'I

didn't think they would believe my name was Smith
because I had no identification on me, so I told them it
was Jones.'

There are a great many amusing anecdotes about F.E.
Smith (1872-1930), the great British barrister and politician. Margot Asquith once said of him, 'Very clever, but
his brains go to his head.' Here are just two of the more
famous stories involving him.

Smith was questioning a nervous witness. 'Have you
ever been married?' he asked.
'Yes, sir,' replied the witness.
'And whom did you marry?'
'A ... a woman, sir.'
'Of course, of course,' snapped Smith. 'Did you ever
hear of anyone marrying a man?'
'Well, yes, sir,' said the witness bravely. 'My sister
did.'

On another occasion F.E. Smith had to conduct a long
and complex case in front of a judge who experienced
some difficulty in understanding the train of events. At
the end of the hearing Smith summed up his case with a
rapid account of the issues and implications of what they
had heard.
'I'm afraid, Mr Smith, that I am none the wiser,' said
the judge.
Smith smiled wearily. 'Possibly, my lord, but you are
better informed.'

A former Lord Chief Justice was asked to define the
difference between whisky and water. His reply was, 'If
you make the former in private, that is a felony; if you
make the latter in public, that is a misdemeanour.'

Croydon magistrates were bewildered by some of the
evidence being given by a defendant, and so was the
prosecuting counsel. 'Are you making up your evidence

as you go along?' he asked.

'Do you think I could make up these lies?' the accused replied.

A judge in California dismissed a woman juror before the case opened, explaining, 'This woman is my wife. She never pays any attention to what I say at home and I have no reason to believe that her behaviour in court would be any different.'

A farm labourer called Kilty appeared in court charged with not paying a cab fare.

'Are you guilty or not guilty?' the judge asked.

'Kilty,' said the accused, mishearing the question. He was immediately jailed, and despite all requests the judge ruled that, having pleaded guilty, he should serve his sentence.

A jewel thief up for trial at Preston Crown Court in 1983 was about to plead not guilty to a charge of handling stolen gems when one of the victims pointed out that the accused's wife was wearing some of the loot. The defendant hurriedly changed his plea.

A man acquitted of rape was told by Mr Justice Melford Stevenson, 'I see you come from Slough. It's a horrible place. You can go back there!'

A most interesting case of breach of contract came before the courts in Holland some years ago, brought by a young man against his somewhat older next-door neighbour. The young man and his wife wanted a child and had been trying for four years without any success. At last, in desperation, they came to an agreement with their neighbour, a father of six, that he would help the wife conceive. However, after ten months and no results, all parties became very concerned. The neighbour took himself off for a medical checkup, only to be told that he was sterile. At this point his wife was forced to confess that their large family had all been fathered by another man and, to crown it all, he was sued for breach of contract by his young neighbour.

A man who had already been convicted a number of times for indecent exposure was arrested for baring his buttocks to a group of girls. When he appeared in court he said, 'It was a stupid compromise.'

The notorious Judge Jeffreys, of Bloody Assizes fame, is said to have pointed his cane at the accused man in the witness box during a certain trial, remarking, 'There is a rogue at the end of my cane!'

To which the man replied, 'Which end, my lord?'

When Lord Bacon was Chancellor of England, he presided over the trial of a man named Hogg. Appealing for mercy, the latter had a sudden flash of inspiration and pointed out that, after all, as Hogg and Bacon they were related. 'Not until the Hogg's been hung,' replied Lord Bacon.

James Whistler, the American artist of the last century, was once asked in court if it was true that he had asked two hundred guineas for a picture which had taken him 'only two days' work.'

'Oh no,' he replied. 'I ask that for the knowledge of a lifetime.'

Sir Oswald Mosley once got up to address a meeting and, to thunderous applause intermingled with jeers and boos, gave a Fascist salute. When the noise died down a voice from the back of the hall was heard to say, 'All right, Oswald. You may leave the room.'

An American senator, Barry Goldwater, was a keen amateur photographer, and when one of his pictures of President Kennedy turned out particularly well he sent the statesman a copy and asked him to autograph it.

When it was returned it bore the inscription, 'For Barry Goldwater, whom I urge to follow the career for which he has shown so much talent — photography . . .'

A former governor of New York stood up to address the inmates of Sing Sing prison, and without thinking launched into his speech with the words 'My fellow citizens'. Suddenly realising that this was an incorrect form of speech, as the prisoners had forfeited their citizenship, he began again with 'My fellow convicts,' before deciding to start on a completely different tack with, 'Well, in any case, I'm glad to see so many of you here.'

During the war years a man was knocked down and killed by an army motor-cyclist. The Secretary of State for War sent a message to the coroner expressing his regrets, adding, 'The Secretary is deeply disturbed that his department should be concerned in any way with the shortening of human life.'

In 1961 President John Kennedy made his brother Robert attorney general. There was immediate uproar, with much talk of undue influence and nepotism.

'I can't see that it's wrong to give him a little legal experience before he goes out to practise law,' the president replied.

A former MP for the Isle of Wight was speaking to a gathering of WI members and began with the unfortunate remark, 'How pleasant it is to see so many old Cowes faces!'

During the 1922 election Lady Astor was contesting the Sutton division of Plymouth. While out canvassing she was accompanied by Admiral of the Fleet Earl Beatty, in full dress uniform. One evening they knocked at the door of a small house in a down-at-heel neighbourhood. The door was opened a crack and an elderly lady peeped out. Before Lady Astor could say anything the woman beckoned them in, saying 'Up the stairs, and second door on the left.'

'I don't think you understand,' Lady Astor murmured, and proceeded to explain who she was, but she was interrupted.

'I don't know about that. My husband said that when the lady comes with the sailor, show 'em both upstairs.'

Lord John Russell is said to have once asked David Hume the philosopher what, in his opinion, was the object of legislation. Hume replied, 'The greatest good to the greatest number.'

'What do you consider the greatest number?' Russell asked.

'Number one,' Hume replied.

The first woman MP, Lady Astor, was speaking in public and was constantly interrupted by a heckler, who at last commented in a loud voice, 'Your husband's a millionaire, isn't he?'

'I hope so,' Lady Astor retorted. 'That's why I married him.'

There are so many brilliant anecdotes involving Winston Churchill that they would fill a book. Here are just a few.

The elderly Winston Churchill had just finished giving an interview to a young reporter. The latter fumbled his thanks and expressed his hopes that they might be able to talk again the following year.

'I don't see why not,' Churchill replied. 'You look a healthy young man to me.'

During the war Churchill kept his two shorthand-typists very busy and occasionally one of them had to stay on late to finish some work for him. One evening he apparently announced, 'Tonight I want both of you to stay late. I am feeling fertile.'

A newspaper reporter was once seated next to Churchill while the latter was making a speech at a function. The reporter noticed that the piece of paper Churchill was holding in his hand while he spoke was not his notes but an old shopping list. Afterwards he remarked on this to Churchill, who replied that *he* knew it was only a shopping list but it gave his audience confidence.

The playwright George Bernard Shaw sent Winston Churchill two tickets for the opening night of one of his plays with a cheeky note attached, which instructed him to come and bring a friend, 'If you have one'. Churchill replied by saying that he was busy that night but would like two tickets for the second night, 'If they have one'.

Winston Churchill to MP Bessie Braddock, after she had accused him of being drunk: 'Bessie, you're ugly but tomorrow I'll be sober.'

Will Paling once called Winston Churchill a 'dirty dog' in the House. Ignoring the chorus of protest from fellow Tories, Churchill turned to Mr Paling and said to him, 'The honourable Member need not withdraw. Indeed, I would invite him to repeat what he has said outside this chamber, and I will then show him what a dirty dog does to a paling!'

When Abraham Lincoln was a lawyer he was approached by a man who wanted his help to press for a claim of $600. Lincoln investigated the case and discovered that if the money were to be regained it would entail the ruin of a widow and her family of six children. He therefore wrote as follows to his would-be client.

'We shall not take your case, though we can doubtless gain it for you. Some things that are right legally are not right morally. But we will give you some advice for which we will charge nothing. We advise a sprightly, energetic man like you to try your hand at making six hundred dollars in some other way.'

Lloyd George was addressing an audience when a woman stood up and shouted, 'If I were your wife I'd give you poison!'

His reply was swift. 'Madam, if I were your husband I'd take it!'

Calvin Coolidge, one-time President of the USA, was known to be a man of few words. A story is told of how his wife once asked him what the sermon had been about when he returned from church. 'Sin,' he replied. His wife, seeking to find out a little more, then asked what had been the preacher's opinion of sin. 'He's against it,' Coolidge replied.

Harold Macmillan, commenting on a story told by Harold Wilson that when he was young he was so poor that he had had to go to school without boots on, said that he supposed it was because the boots were too small for him.

Lloyd George was addressing a meeting when a heckler threw a cabbage at him. Deftly he caught it and announced to the crowd, 'I fear one of my opponents has just lost his head.'

Jack Benny's wife was very fond of jewelry, and in 1963 she was robbed of her most lavish item, a large diamond ring. Benny was away from home at the time and only learned of the incident from a reporter. He called his wife several times, only to be told on each occasion that she was out. Finally he found her in.

'Where have you been?' he asked.

'At the jeweler's, looking for another ring,' she told him.

'At a time like this you go shopping for jewelry?' he exclaimed.

'Yes,' she explained. 'It's like when you fall off a horse. If you don't get right back on you'll never ride again.'

The French love the works of Sir Arthur Conan Doyle as much as the British, as Sir Arthur himself discovered when he took a cab from a station to his hotel in Paris. When he got out, the cab driver acknowledged him by name.

'How do you know who I am?' Doyle asked.

The cab driver explained, 'I read in the paper that you were coming to Paris from the South of France. It was evident that your hair was last cut by a barber of the South of France and I could tell from your appearance that you were English. From these signs I deduced your identity.'

'This is extraordinary. You had no other evidence?' asked the great writer.

'Nothing,' said the driver, 'except the fact that your name is on your luggage.'

A young Arab girl was flown to a London hospital in a seriously ill condition in 1977. She was semiconscious and her condition deteriorated as doctors tried to find out what was wrong with her. The prognosis looked very bleak, when suddenly the nurse who was caring for her realised that all the symptoms the child was exhibiting corresponded with a case of poisoning in Agatha Christie's *The Pale Horse*, which she was reading in her spare time.

A glance through to the end of the plot revealed that Dame Agatha's victim had died of thallium poisoning. Tests on the girl indicated that she, too, was suffering from the same poisoning. It took just three weeks to cure her, and when the case was written up in a medical journal Dame Agatha received her proper thanks.

Quote — Unquote

Policemen, lawyers, politicians, judges, criminals — they're all here, and all with a few amusing words. There are witty quotes from great thinkers, slips of the tongue that people have been hoping we'd forget and words of surprising wisdom from unexpected sources!

He is no more dangerous than any other murderer.
> *Irish detective announcing the escape of a prisoner.*

An unfortunate misprint in a police journal read: 'Suggestions for stuffing the Inspectorate will be passed on immediately.' The correction in the next issue of the paper read: 'Suggestions for staffing the Inspectorate will be pissed on immediately.'

Clue: what the police find when they fail to arrest a criminal.
> *J.B. Morton*

If soldiers were asked to do in battle what the average motorist does at weekends for fun, the officer in charge would be court-martialled for brutality.
> *Malcolm Muggeridge.*

I am Prince Philip and I'm on my way to see the Archbishop of Canterbury. I'm a bit late and I didn't want to keep His Grace waiting.
> *Prince Philip on the eve of his wedding, having been stopped for speeding.*

The only thing I really mind about going to prison is the thought of Lord Longford coming to visit me.

Richard Ingrams.

You can get much further with a kind word and a gun than you can with a kind word alone.

Al Capone.

A kleptomaniac can't help helping himself.

Henry Morgan.

A third-rate burglary attempt not worthy of further White House comment.

Ron Ziegler, press spokesman, on the Watergate break-in.

He was completely lovable to every individual while working for me. Never was there any deviation from the highest proper sense of things.

The ex-employer of the Boston Strangler.

These are just a few insurance claims put in by motorists after accidents:

I thought the window was down, but I found it was up when I put my head out.

I struck a pedestrian in order to avoid hitting the bumper of the car in front.

I thought I wasn't injured, but when I took my hat off I found I had a fractured skull.

The man had no idea which way to run so I ran over him.

I've come about my overdraft.

Unemployed man found in a Kent bank after closing time.

Being a thief is a terrific life, but the trouble is they do put you in the nick for it.

John McVicar.

I was brought up to open doors for ladies.

John Gotti, alleged Mafia boss.

It ain't no sin if you crack a few laws now and then, just so long as you don't break any.

Mae West.

No brilliance is required in the law. Just common sense and relatively clean fingernails.

John Mortimer.

Justice is too good for some people and not good enough for the rest.

Norman Douglas.

When lawyers talk about the law, the normal human being begins to think about something else.

Richard Ingrams.

Innocence: The state or condition of a criminal whose counsel has fixed the jury
Accuser: One's former friend; particularly the person for whom one has performed some friendly service
Truthful: Dumb and illiterate.

Ambrose Bierce.

Do not unto others as you would that they should do unto you. Their tastes may not be the same.

George Bernard Shaw.

The long and distressing controversy over capital punishment is very unfair to anyone meditating murder.

Lord Fisher, British clergyman.

A verbal contract isn't worth the paper it's written on.

Samuel Goldwyn.

Battledore and shuttlecock's a very good game when you ain't the shuttlecock and two lawyers the battledores, in which case it gets too excitin' to be pleasant.

Charles Dickens.

Biggs, it is my unpleasant duty to inform you that your earliest possible release date is 12 January 1984.
Governor of Lincoln jail to Ronald Biggs.

When you have to kill a man it costs nothing to be polite.
Winston Churchill.

I am much obliged, my lord.
Anthony Collingwood, British butler jailed for theft,
to the judge who sentenced him.

We lawyers frequently ask ourselves questions because in that way we know that we will get prompt and intelligent answers.
Lord Denning.

A jury consists of twelve persons chosen to decide who has the better lawyer.
Robert Frost.

Wise men plead causes, but fools decide them.
Plutarch.

Well, he would, wouldn't he?
Mandy Rice-Davies during the Profumo affair.

The government is the only known vessel that leaks from the top.
James Reston.

'*Blackburn Times* reporter Valerie will not forget the night she danced with Prime Minister Edward Heath at a Young Conservatives Ball — and ended up in the maternity ward of the local hospital.'
Extract from UK Press Gazette.

I used to say that politics was the second oldest profession, and I have come to know that it bears a gross similarity to the first.
Ronald Reagan.

A politician is a fellow who will lay down your life for his country.

Texas Guinan.

Politics is a funny game. One day you're a rooster, the next you're a feather duster.

Fred Daley, Australian politician.

We're going to move to the right and left at the same time.

Governor Jerry Brown.

Politics are very much like war. We may even have to use poison gas at times.

Sir Winston Churchill.

I don't know a lot about politics, but I know a good party man when I see one.

Mae West.

Politics is a thing that only the unsophisticated can really go for.

Kingsley Amis.

In politics, if you want anything said, ask a man; if you want anything done, ask a woman.

Margaret Thatcher.

I've always had a weakness for foreign affairs.

Mae West.

The fate of a nation has often depended on the good or bad digestion of a prime minister.

Voltaire.

Power is the ultimate aphrodisiac.

Henry Kissinger.

All power tends to be an aphrodisiac and absolute power leaves you feeling rotten by Wednesday.

Lord Acton.

Being in politics is like being a football coach. You have to be smart enough to understand the game ... and dumb enough to think it's important.

Eugene McCarthy.

How nice to see you all here.

Roy Jenkins, opening a speech to jail inmates.

Shoplifters will be killed and eaten.

Sign in an Essex toyshop.

Seeing that my daughter Anne has not availed herself of my advice touching the objectionable practice of going about with her arms bare up to the elbows, my will is that, should she continue after my death this violation of the modesty of her sex, all the goods, chattels, moneys, land, and other that I have devised to her for the maintenance of her future life shall pass to the oldest of the sons of my sister Caroline.

Should anyone take exception to this my wish as being too severe, I answer that license in dress in a woman is a mark of a depraved mind.

Nineteenth-century Yorkshire vicar's will.

For the love of Kirk, I would have skied down Everest in the nude with a carnation up my nose.

Joyce McKinney, found guilty of abducting a Mormon missionary.

No man has a good enough memory to make a successful liar.

Abraham Lincoln.

It is forbidden to steal towels, please. If you are not person to do such is please not to read notice.

Sign in Tokyo hotel room.

76

Mass murderers are simply people who have had *enough*.
Quentin Crisp.

There is one way to find out if a man is honest — ask him. If he says 'Yes', you know he is crooked.
Groucho Marx.

A politician is someone who approaches every subject with an open mouth.
Oscar Wilde.

It's not the people in prison who worry me. It's the people who aren't.
The Earl of Arran.

A man cannot be too careful in the choice of his enemies.
Oscar Wilde.

In the Nuts (unground), (other than ground nuts) Order, the expression nuts shall have reference to such nuts, other than ground nuts, as would but for this amending Order not qualify as nuts (unground) (other than ground nuts) by reason of their being nuts (unground).
A nutty piece of British law.

It is regretted that it was not possible to send the enclosed forms to you before the date by which, had you received them, you would be required to forward copies to this office.
Government form sent to employers.

Winston has devoted the best years of his life to preparing his impromptu speeches.
F.E. Smith.

Billings' Law: Live within your income, even if you have to borrow to do so.
Josh Billings.

Gates' Law: If there isn't a law, there will be.

W.I.E. Gates.

Roos' Law: If there's a harder way of doing something, someone will find it.

Ralph E. Roos.

Truman's Law: If you can't convince them, confuse them.

Harry S. Truman.

Believe It Or Not

Who is the heaviest MP currently sitting in the House of Commons? What do Oscar Wilde and John Bunyan have in common? Find out in this section of strange facts and bizarre legal stories. They're guaranteed to make your audience laugh and, believe it or not, they're all true!

SAS men were brought in to test the defences of a newly-completed Northern Ireland security complex. Unfortunately they discovered that they could break in and out of the place with ease. The most devastating security problem of all was the fact that some of the doors had been put on the wrong way round, allowing the 'prisoners' out but keeping staff locked in.

Police were called in by a Midlands mother to have a word with her son, who was becoming awkward, had started smoking and was going out with a girl. On investigation the police were surprised to discover that the man was 36 years old.

Police alerted to the fact that a 'safe' had been dumped by a road in Halesowen in 1983 mounted guard over it until winching equipment arrived to retrieve it. After a lot of fruitless tugging one of the officers noticed that the 'safe' was in fact an electricity junction box, firmly cemented to the ground ...

Statistics show that more murderers have come from Yorkshire than from any other county.

A driver charged with knocking down a pedestrian admitted that he had done so, but added in his defence, 'He agreed that it was his fault as he'd been knocked down before.'

In 1972 a French medical student at the University of Marseilles shot dead one of his tutors. When he was asked why he'd done it, he replied that the man had been a hindrance to his medical career.

On a flight from New York to Miami a passenger found himself sitting next to a young man who kept muttering phrases about slavery, freedom and overthrowing bad government. Fearing that they had a hijacker aboard, he alerted the stewardess, and when they touched down the young man was pounced upon by armed personnel. Fortunately, as he was later able to explain, he was an actor and he'd been rehearsing his lines for a play. The lines? They came from the American Declaration of Independence!

A Viennese man who had spent twenty-two years in prison for various thefts decided to solve his kleptomania by chopping his hands off in a machine. He was sentenced to four years for doing so.

A London man who was arrested for urinating in public protested that, before commencing the offence, he had stuck a notice saying GENTLEMEN to a tree nearby. 'I always carry the sign with me in case of need,' he explained.

A Kenyan forger was tracked down after someone noticed that he'd put his own portrait on the banknotes he was counterfeiting.

A bank robber who thought he'd got clean away with his hold-up found the police waiting for him when he returned to his home. The note he'd handed to the bank cashier had been written on the back of an envelope. On the other side was his name and address.

Hooliganism isn't a new development in the world of sport. In AD 392 the Emperor Theodosius cancelled future Olympic Games after the 293rd Olympiad had ended in riots and arson.

In 1976 a Pakistani cricket umpire was beaten to death by the fielding team after making a number of controversial decisions.

Al Capone, Sophia Loren and Chuck Berry all have something in common. What is it? They've all been prosecuted for tax evasion.

Three chatty Texas burglars were caught because a parrot in the house they'd burgled and robbed memorised their names.

Oscar Wilde and John Bunyan both wrote major works (*The Ballad of Reading Goal* and *Pilgrim's Progress*) while they were in prison.

A solicitor once sent a bill to one of his clients, which read as follows: 'To crossing the Strand after seeing you on the other side to discuss your case with you — 6s 8d. To recrossing the Strand after discovering the person was not you, 6s 8d.'

The longest will on record was that of Mrs Frederica

Cook, who died in the USA in the early 1900s. It ran to 95,940 words in four bound volumes. The shortest was the will left by Karl Tausch in 1967. It consisted of two words, in Czech, meaning 'All to wife.'

In ancient Ireland it was a capital offence to fell a sacred hazel or apple tree.

The Queen does not have to pay income tax. Nor does she need numberplates for her cars, dog licences for her corgis or stamps for her letters.

The game of bowls once had to be banned in England because it was distracting the peasants from their archery practice.

Oliver Cromwell was once publicly denounced for taking part in the 'disreputable' game of cricket.

In 1694 Queen Mary died and barristers went into black robes of mourning. They're still wearing them.

A sixteenth-century English law permitted men to beat their wives, but only before 10 p.m.

A twenty-five-year-old man went to court to claim damages for an industrial accident involving a bulldozer, which he said had affected his sex life. The judge presiding over the court asked the young man if he was married and, hearing that he wasn't, stated that in that case he didn't see how the injury could affect him.

A fine of £500 and a ten-year prison sentence was imposed on a cleaner from the Ministry of War in Paris who was found guilty of cutting up top-secret military documents and using them to cover the tops of her jars of home-made jam.

A man has been awarded $137,000 by a New York State court for wrongful arrest after the zip on his trousers broke and he was charged with indecent exposure.

An elderly Yorkshire man was given an absolute discharge when he appeared in court on his 500th drunkenness charge. A couple of days later he was back on his 501st charge, claiming that he had got drunk to celebrate his anniversary. He was fined 50p.

An unemployed accountant appearing as a defendant in a West Country hearing was asked to confirm that he had bought a bag of manure for £3 and had later sold it for £650. He agreed, saying, 'Mark-ups are normal in my profession.'

A judge has ruled that a woman who kills her husband is not eligible for a widow's pension.

Playwright Christopher Marlowe, Italian poet Dante and Lord Byron all acted as government spies.

The longest recorded sitting in the House of Commons lasted 41½ hours, between 4 p.m. on 31 January and 9.30 a.m. on 2 February 1881. It was concerned with the question of Protection of Person and Property in Ireland. The longest recorded speech in the House of Commons was given on 7 February 1828 by Henry Peter Brougham on Law Reform. He spoke non-stop for six hours.

The heaviest MP on record is Cyril Smith MBE, Liberal member for Rochdale since 1972, who weighed in at 29 stone 12 pounds in January 1976.

Americans who are unfortunate enough to become kidnap victims can find some consolation in the knowledge that their ransom payment will be deducted from their income tax.

A student of sociology, who was working on the problem of juvenile delinquency, decided one evening to ring a number of households and ask the parents whether they knew where their children were. Accordingly at 10.30 p.m. he phoned ten families. Eight of his calls were answered by children who did not appear to know where their parents were.

Legal Briefs

In this section you'll find dozens of brief jokes, many of them just a line long. They're ideal for breaking the ice quickly when you first start your speech, and for linking your jokes and stories as you go along. When you tell one, don't labour it too hard, just drop it casually into your speech and leave it to the audience to find the humour. That way you'll build up a sense of real rapport with them.

She was only the constable's daughter, but she let the chief inspector.

Thieves broke into Scotland Yard last night and stole all the toilets. A police spokesman said, 'At the moment we have nothing to go on.'

When the boy next door joined the police force his mother told me he became very fussy about his food. All he'd eat were beefburglars and pork truncheon meat.

A police spokesman, commenting on the fact that the same house had been burgled four times in as many weeks, said that it was obvious that the criminals were feeling the effects of the housing shortage.

God moves in mysterious ways — he never leaves any fingerprints.

The police thought they'd caught the burglar who broke into my house the other week, but when they questioned him he came up with an alibi. Apparently he'd been murdering his mother for the rent money, so they had to let him go.

He found a beautiful blonde wandering lost in the street. When he took her to the police station the officer said, 'If no one claims her in a week she's yours.'

Last night somebody drilled a hole in the fence surrounding a nudist camp. Police are currently looking into it.

A villain escaped from prison by helicopter yesterday. Police have set up road blocks but so far have failed to find him.

He'd watched so many detective stories on TV that my brother used to wipe his fingerprints off the knob when he switched the set off.

Did you hear about the mad scientist who crossed a policeman with a telegram? He got copper wire.

In another experiment the same mad scientist crossed a policeman with an octopus and got a copper with eight long arms of the law.

Would you say that people who lose their budgies should send for the flying squad?

On my way here I heard a news bulletin. Apparently a lorry carrying treacle has collided with a van of golden syrup on the M6. The police have advised motorists to stick to their lanes.

What we need in today's police force are experts and all-rounders. The experts get to know more and more about less and less until at last, they know everything about nothing, and the all-rounders get to know less and less about more and more until at last they know nothing about everything.

A young driver was pulled up for speeding on the motorway, and when he enquired innocently whether he had been driving too fast he was informed by the constable that it was more a case of flying too low.

Here's a question for you all. Why did the policeman wear red and yellow striped braces? To keep his trousers up.

You hear some funny things in a police station. Just last night I heard a policeman say to a prisoner, 'Will you come quietly or do I have to put in the earplugs?'

A woman driver is one who drives in exactly the same way as a man but gets taken to court for it.

I read in the paper the other day that a man had been found drowned in a cesspit. At the inquest the verdict was sewercide ...

Would you say that a thief is just a person with a fine eye for an opportunity?

Did you hear about the man who stole a calendar? He got twelve months.

Only the other day a shopkeeper was held up by a man waving a bunch of flowers at him in a threatening manner. It was robbery with violets.

Have you heard about the man who was put away for doing his Christmas shopping early? The police found him in Harrods at 4 a.m.

Did you hear about the man who robbed the glue factory? He just said, 'Stick 'em up!'

Did you hear about the cyclist who was arrested for driving without due care and attention? They confiscated his bicycle clips.

You know you've got a suspicious contract when the first paragraph forbids you to read any of the others ...

Have you heard of the famous judge who has no fingers? He's called Justice Thumbs.

If there were no bad people, just think — there would be no good lawyers.

A judge was asked by his hostess at a dinner party whether he had ever tried rum and blackcurrant. 'No, but I've tried a lot of fellows who have,' the judge replied.

Definition of a lawyer's briefs: his underpants.

Did you hear about the accident that happened to the judge? The newspaper report says that it wasn't serious and that he hopes to resume sitting shortly.

The judge was only four feet eleven inches tall — a small thing sent to try us.

Funny things, juries. Six men and six women go into a locked room for a couple of hours and all come out shouting 'Not guilty!'

Court cases get more and more complicated every day. Only yesterday I read of a jury who'd come up with a verdict of 'an act of God under very suspicious circumstances.'

Would you agree that two mothers-in-law is a suitable punishment for a bigamist?

A judge and a barrister were involved in a heated argument on a point of law. Finally the barrister submitted with the words. 'Yes, my Lord, you are right and I am wrong, as you generally are.'

At a recent court hearing a man found guilty of jumping the red lights claimed in mitigation that he had often stopped at green lights when he hadn't had to.

As the foreman of the Irish jury said, 'We find the man who stole the car not guilty.'

She got a divorce on the grounds that her husband had spoken to her only three times in eight years of marriage. She also got custody of their three children.

'As God is my judge, I did not take this money,' swore the defendant.
    'He isn't. I am. You did,' came the implacable reply.

The difference between law and equity courts: at common law you are done for at once, and at equity you are not so easily disposed of. It's rather like the difference between prussic acid and laudanum.

Don't panic — no political party can possibly be as bad as its leaders.

A politican was being heckled by someone in the crowd. 'There's a bus leaving here in five minutes. Please make sure you're under it,' he replied.

You know that politician who's always going on about peaceful coexistence? I know for a fact he's been married five times.

Politicians today are beginning to feel concerned that there are so many elderly people in this country. They just can't work out how they can survive so long under such appalling conditions.

Would you say that a member of the SDP is a person who makes enemies left and right?

It's no good telling our politicians to go to hell until they've finished building it for us.

Have you heard that they're now building burglar-proof houses? They call them Sure Lock Holmes.

In order to remember it, everyone has to change the truth a little.

Did you hear about the old gentleman who asked the lovely young girl if she would come up to his room and help him write his will?

A burglar came home from robbing a house and started sawing the legs off his bed. When his wife asked him what on earth he was doing, he explained that he had to lie low for a while.

Did you hear about the crook who came out of prison and went straight back behind bars? He bought a pub.

A set of traffic lights have been stolen from a main road junction in Ipswich. A police spokesman said, 'Some thieves will stop at nothing.'

Did you hear about the robber who always took a bath before going on a job? It was so that he could make a clean getaway.

The Eleventh Commandment:
   Thou shalt not get found out.
The Twelfth Commandment:
   If found out thou shalt not get caught.

Comic Speeches for the Sales Force

•••••

Contents

PART ONE

How to make a comic speech

Ground Rules

Salesmen have a great advantage when it comes to making speeches, and that's because they're used to selling. What, you might ask, does a career spent selling cars or pharmaceuticals have in common with standing up in front of an audience and making them laugh? The connection is that the public speaker has to sell *himself* to his audience, just as the salesman has to sell his goods to his customer.

The very best salesmen have the gift of the gab; the others have to learn to speak persuasively — and so does the public speaker. Natural-born salesmen have an inbuilt way of sizing up customers and responding to them; the rest of us have to learn the technique — and so does the public speaker.

The similarities go even further. Every salesman worth his salt decides his goals in advance and aims to achieve them, knowing that before he can pull off a deal a lot of forward-planning and preparation has to be done. And his main aim is to leave his customer feeling pleased and satisfied with his purchase. All this the public speaker must do too!

To help you, this book contains everything needed to turn a salesman into a public speaker. In it you'll find all the information required to prepare and deliver an entertaining speech — everything from how to assess what kind of material your audience will enjoy to coping with your nerves on the day. And because this is the *complete* guide to comic speechmaking, you'll find hundreds of jokes, anecdotes and quotations to ensure that you're never at a loss for words.

Know your audience

Everyone feels nervous at the mere idea of making a speech to an audience of strangers, but one of the first things you can do to make yourself feel better about it is to realise that nerves are a good thing. Don't just try to ignore them — they won't go away. Instead, resolve to channel all that nervous energy into preparing yourself and your speech so that you please the audience. And the best way of pleasing them, as any salesman knows, is by giving them something they want.

But what *do* they want? That's the fundamental question and one you'll have to answer before you can begin to prepare yourself. Most importantly, every audience wants to hear a speech which has been created especially for them and the occasion, one that is relevant and interesting — to *them*. In a word, it must be entertaining.

There are quite a few public speakers around who, having written one speech, decide to make it do for the rest of their lives and for every occasion at which they're invited to talk. If they're feeling generous they add a few topical jokes or stories, but more often than not they just ramble over tried, trusted and tedious ground. You probably first encountered one of this breed at a school speech day and there's usually one at weddings and company dinners. They even pop up on television these days, appearing on three chat shows in a single week and telling the same stories on them all!

11

Even worse than this kind of speaker, there's the one who imagines himself to be such a naturally gifted orator that he doesn't prepare any material at all. Admittedly there are a few people who can make brilliant impromptu speeches; they tend to be rich and famous because it's such a rare gift. Those who don't have it simply drone on for as long as the fancy takes them, usually until their guests are about to pass out from boredom. Such speakers enjoy themselves, but they don't please their audiences — and pleasing your audience is the very first rule of speech-making.

The audience

Before you can start working out how to please them, you'll have to find out about them. Will they appreciate your slightly risqué stories about life as a travelling salesman, or would they prefer to hear something a little more sedate? Remember, it's the audience who will decide whether your material is funny or not. You may find it hilarious, but if *they* don't you might just as well give up. So before you do anything else, assess your audience and decide on the right kind of material for them.

Age is an important factor. A young and sophisticated audience will respond to a different kind of material than an older gathering. An audience composed of fellow sales personnel will enjoy jokes and stories that might be lost on the local Ladies Circle. Bear this in mind when you come to select your material.

Also bear in mind the sex of your audience. The kind of jokes guaranteed to go down a bomb at an all-male sales office celebration will go down less well in mixed company, so be careful. In fact it's always best to avoid dirty jokes altogether, particularly if you're in a work situation. If you embarrass strangers you at least have the comfort of knowing that you're unlikely to meet them again. The same can't be said if you upset your colleagues.

Find out from the organisers of the occasion as much information as you can — about the people on the committee, if there is one, the names and interests of any special guests, the aims of the organisation and about any other speakers and what they'll be talking on. Then do some homework to see if you can come up with any amusing stories that will tie in perfectly with the occasion — make them the basis of your speech. This may sound like unnecessarily hard work, but some topical and personal references can make all the difference between a passable and a brilliant speech. They prove that you've cared enough to do some research — and as all salesmen know, there's nothing that a customer responds to more warmly than some personal interest.

The occasion

Different occasions require different kinds of speeches. You'll find guidelines on the kind of speech to make at conferences, presentations, dinners and various functions in the last part of this section. Remember, though, that it isn't just the formal requirements of an occasion that matter. Tone is important, too, and you must anticipate and be sensitive to it. A skilled salesman judges the mood of his customer and responds to it, and so must the public speaker. What kind of entertainment is your audience expecting? A boozy evening function demands a robust kind of humour. A lunchtime speaking engagement may be more subdued and require a wittier approach. A retirement presentation may call for a gentle, nostalgic tone, while a funny speech urging the sales force on to even greater achievements might benefit from a punchy, aggressive feel. Use your judgement and bear the mood of the occasion in mind when you're selecting your material.

If you've been invited to propose a toast or make a presentation, make sure you do so — don't get carried away and forget what you're there for. At a recent dinner the speaker, who was supposed to present an award to

13

the company's best salesman, got so absorbed in what he had to say that he sat down still holding the award and had to be reminded by the chairman that it wasn't his to keep! The best way of avoiding this kind of embarrassment is to plan your speech well in advance and stick to it. Try to resist the temptation to improvise, no matter how well you're received, because it's improvisation that's likely to throw you off your stride.

Here's a check list of 10 simple Do's and Don't's which you should bear in mind as you sit down to prepare your speech.

Do's

1   Do aim to entertain and please your audience.
2   Do some research beforehand, paying particular attention to the age and sex of your audience.
3   Do find out about your role. Are you to present an award or make a toast? Make sure that you prepare the right kind of speech.
4   Do find out about any special guests or facts and refer to them in your speech.
5   Do choose the right kind of material for the occasion.

Don't's

1   Don't use old material.
2   Don't risk offending anyone with blue jokes.
3   Don't include irrelevant material that will bore your audience.
4   Don't forget to fulfil your function, be it proposing a toast or offering a vote of thanks.
5   Don't improvise or speak for too long.

Perfect Preparation

Once you know the kind of speech you're going to make and the sort of audience you'll be entertaining, you can begin to prepare your material. Preparation is absolutely vital if you're going to give a polished performance, so allow as much time as possible to work on the speech.

Start by reading through this book and jotting down all the jokes, quotes, anecdotes and so on that you like and that you feel are directly relevant to your audience. Be ruthless and cut out anything that isn't related in some way to your subject and anything that can't be adapted to fit. On a separate sheet, put down all the things that you *have* to say in the speech and all the points that you particularly want to make.

With any luck you'll begin to see the material falling into place, with the quotes leading into the points you want to make and the stories illustrating the theme. This is exactly what you're aiming for — a seamless speech with one idea moving into the next without any effort. You'll probably have to adapt some of the material if it's to fit in perfectly, so change the names and locations and details to suit the occasion. For example, if you're going to be speaking in Newcastle and you're using a joke set in London, change the location and add some Geordie colour. Most importantly of all, put everything into your own words. You'll feel more comfortable when you come to use the material if it's written in the kind of language and the style you're used to, and it will make your speech seem that much more personal to the audience.

Sir Thomas Beecham once said of his orchestra that the important thing was 'to begin and end together, what happens in between doesn't matter very much.' Pretty much the same can be said of making a speech. If you can capture the attention of the audience with your first line, you're likely to have them with you for the rest of the speech. And if they're going to remember anything when they get home, it's likely to be your final line — so make sure that it's worth remembering.

Some speakers like to work on the opening and closing lines of their speech together, linking them so that the last line finishes what the first line started. Whatever you decide to do, make sure that both the beginning and the end of your speech are absolutely relevant — both to the occasion and the central part of the speech. Nothing irrelevant should be allowed in at all or you'll begin to look as if you're rambling.

Opening and closing a speech are the two most difficult things of all. Try using one of these opening gambits.

Quotations

You'll find dozens of useful quotations in this book and one of them should be ideal for opening your speech. When you're looking for it, bear in mind that it should allow you to move straight into the main part of your speech without any stress. If you have to force a quotation to fit your theme then forget it. Always inform your audience that it *is* a quote and not your own words. It's quite likely that someone in the audience will have heard it before and they might think you a fraud if you don't name the person who said it first.

Don't use a quotation for the opening *and* closing of your speech because that would look too much like cheating, but a quote can round off a speech perfectly. Again, you'll find something suitable in the relevant section of this book — and again, make sure that it ties in completely with the main subject of your speech.

Questions

A question can be a very effective way of getting your speech off the ground. Try asking an apparently serious one and following it up with a ridiculous answer. Or ask a ridiculous question to which there's no answer. Whichever kind you choose, aim to raise a laugh from the audience and break the ice.

The 'Did you know?' gambit is also a useful one. Find an amazing fact in the relevant section of this book and ask your audience if they knew it. It's bound to start your speech off with a bang!

Jokes

A joke may seem the obvious way of starting a speech, but in fact jokes can go badly wrong. If they work you'll have the audience eating out of your hand — but if they fall flat you'll have everyone in an agony of embarrassment and praying that you finish quickly.

The best kind of joke to look out for is one that has something to do with a member of the audience or with something directly relevant to the occasion. You may find that simply by changing a few details in one of the jokes in this book you've got the ideal opening gag — in which case use it. But never use a joke simply because you think it's funny.

Exactly the same advice can be applied to ending a speech. No speech, no matter how well-received, can be counted a great success unless it ends on a high note. Looking for a new screenplay, Sam Goldwyn once remarked, 'What we want is a story that begins with an earthquake and builds up to a climax.' That's what you have to aim for too!

Never end with an apologetic, 'Well, folks, that's about it,' line. That only suggests that you've run out of ideas or that you couldn't be bothered to finish the job off properly, and there's really no excuse for that. Even if you can't find the kind of climax that Goldwyn was looking for, you can end your speech in an amusing and tidy way.

Anecdotes

There's bound to be an anecdote in this book that will encapsulate and illustrate your theme perfectly. You can use it to finish your speech in classic style, but beware of using anything too long or rambling. You don't want to lose your audience's attention in the last few moments. If you're speaking about friends, family or colleagues at work, try to uncover an amusing story about them; nothing embarrassing, of course, just something to show what nice people they are. This is *guaranteed* to bring your speech to a successful conclusion.

Jokes

Ending a speech with a joke is even more risky than opening with one. After all, even if your opening joke falls flat you have the rest of your speech to regain the audience's interest. If you end with a damp squib, no matter how good the speech the audience will remember you for only one thing — your failure to pull it off. Only finish with a joke if you can think of nothing better and if you're absolutely certain that it will work.

When you're preparing your speech, take an occasional look at this checklist of 10 Do's and Don't's just to keep your aims in mind.

Do's

1   Do check your material to ensure that it's suitable for the audience you assessed in the last section.
2   Do make sure that you have included all the things you *have* to say — your vote of thanks or the toast, for example.
3   Do adapt all the material to ensure that it's relevant.
4   Do aim to start and finish your speech on a high note.
5   Do credit any quotations you use.

Don't's

1   Don't use any material that isn't relevant to the occasion or will cause offence.
2   Don't start your speech with a joke unless you feel confident that it will work.
3   Don't tail off at the end of the speech; finish properly.
4   Don't use too many quotes or anecdotes from the lives of other people.
5   Don't speak too long; make sure that your speech is the right length.

If, when you finish preparing your speech, you feel confident that you've observed these guidelines, you can be sure that you're halfway towards success. Now all you need to know is how to deliver the speech you've written!

Successful Delivery

Preparing your speech is one thing — and the most important of all — but delivering it is something else. The best speech can be ruined by poor delivery and the thoroughly mediocre made to pass muster by good technique. Fortunately just a few simple measures will ensure that your delivery does your speech justice.

Rehearsal

You don't need to learn your material like an actor, but rehearsal will help you to become familiar with it and iron out any problems that weren't apparent on paper. For example, you may find that a particular sequence of words turn out to be difficult to say, or you might have problems pronouncing certain words — in which case rewrite them. Try to learn half a dozen key phrases which will take you smoothly from one part of your speech to the next so that you don't keep having to refer to your notes; no matter how nervous you're feeling, this will make your speech seem smooth and practised.

While you're rehearsing, experiment by using your voice to emphasise different points of the speech. Try changing your tone and volume, too, for effect. If you have a tape recorder then use it to tape the various versions of your speech — then you can play them back and decide which sounds the most interesting and lively. Don't, by the way, worry about your accent. Lots of speakers try to iron out their natural accent, but they forget that the way they speak is all part of their personality. Without it they seem very dull. As you listen to yourself speaking you'll begin to recognise the most successful ways of delivering certain parts of your speech. For example, the best way of telling your jokes is to do it casually, without labouring them too much. If you feel that there's a rather dull patch in the speech try animating it by changing your tone or emphasis, or even just speeding it up a bit. It's this kind of preparation that will give you polish on the day.

Body language

No matter how nervous you feel about speaking in front of an audience, you should try not to let them know — and it's the body which most often gives the secret away.

Begin by standing easily with your weight on both feet so that you feel balanced This way you'll look steady, even if you don't feel it. Your main problem will be what to do with your hands. If you have notes, hold them in front of you at about waist level with one hand. With your free hand, lightly grasp the note-holding wrist. If you're lucky, there will be a lectern of some sort at which you can stand. Rest your hands on either side of it and you'll look very much at ease. Only royalty can get away with holding their hands behind their backs, and you'll look sloppy if you put your hands in your pockets, so don't adopt either of these postures. If you've no notes and no lectern, just stand with your left hand lightly holding your right wrist in front of you. It looks surprisingly natural and relaxed. Next time you switch on the TV you'll notice how many presenters and comedians use the position!

Notes

The very worst thing you can do is *read* your speech. Comic speeches need a touch of spontaneity, even if they've been prepared weeks in advance and you've been rehearsing for days. Reading a speech kills it dead. It makes the material seem dull, even if it isn't, it prevents eye contact, which is very important in breaking down the barrier between speaker and audience; and it destroys that important sense of a shared occasion, with speaker and audience responding to each other. On top of all that, the very fact that you are reading will indicate a lack of confidence — and your audience will be alerted to your discomfort and share in it.

That said, it's equally inadvisable to stand up and speak without the aid of any notes at all. Nerves can affect the memories of even professional speakers, so don't take any risks. Many people like to write their notes on postcards, using a single main heading and a couple of key phrases to prompt them. If you decide to do this, make sure that you number the cards clearly. You are bound to drop them if you don't, and reassembling them in the wrong order could create all kinds of chaos! Make sure, too, that you write your headings in large capital letters. When you're standing up and holding the cards at waist level you need to take in all the information at a single glance.

If cards seem too fiddly, write the main headings of your speech on a single sheet of paper, again using a few key words underneath to jog your memory. You'll know, from your rehearsals, those things you find difficult to remember and those which come easily. Jot down the points you get stuck on.

If you're going to use quotations then write them clearly on postcards and read them when the time comes. This ensures that you get them absolutely right and, far from doubting your competence, your audience will be impressed by your thoroughness.

Don't try to hide your notes. Simply use them as

inconspicuously as possible. They prove that you have prepared a speech specially for the occasion and that you care about getting it right — and there's no need to be concerned about that.

On the day

On the day of your speech there are a number of simple precautions you can take to ensure that everything goes smoothly. Some of them may seem quite painfully obvious, but it's the most obvious things that are overlooked, particularly when you're nervous.

Electronic assistance — in the form of microphones and public address systems — needs handling with care. When you accept an invitation to speak, enquire if a microphone is to be provided. If it is, test it before the other guests arrive so that you don't have the embarrassing experience of opening your speech to find that the equipment isn't working. Make a point of checking how to raise or lower the microphone so that if the previous speaker was a giant or a midget you can readjust it without fuss, and try it out, so that you know how far away from it you need to stand. Microphones have a life of their own. You will have to speak directly into some, while others pick up sounds from several feet away. Find out which variety yours is *before* you get to your feet.

If the microphone squeals at you, or despite your preparation, booms too loudly or not at all, get it adjusted during your preliminary remarks, and wait, if necessary, until the fault has been corrected. It may seem amusing to begin with, but the audience will soon tire of it and you won't have a chance to communicate your humour and ideas if they are unable to hear what you have to say or are in constant danger of being deafened.

If you know that you tend to put your hands in your pockets while you're speaking, remove all your loose change and keys so that you're not tempted to jangle them. And make sure that you have a clean handkerchief somewhere about you. A scrap of well-used tissue isn't going to impress the audience when you need to blow your nose.

If you've worked hard to make the opening words of your speech interesting and funny, it would be a great shame to waste them by starting to speak while the audience is still talking and settling down in their seats. So wait for silence, even if it seems to take an age, and when you've obtained it start confidently and loudly so that everyone can hear what you have to say. Whatever you do, don't be hurried. Public speakers talk quite slowly and allow plenty of pauses so that the audience can respond. Take it at a leisurely pace, making sure that you're heard throughout the room, and you'll win the audience's attention immediately.

Some people, but only a very few, are at their best after a few drinks. Unless you know for certain that alcohol will improve your performance, it's probably best not to drink before you speak. Drinking tends to dull reactions and instil a false sense of confidence — and you need to be completely in control of yourself and your material if you're going to make a success of the occasion. Naturally, once you've made your speech and it's been greeted with applause and laughter, you can reward yourself!

Whether you've been drinking or not, accidents do happen. Cope with them by acknowledging them and turning them to your advantage. For example, the speaker who knocked a glass of water over himself brought the house down with the throwaway line, 'Whoops! For a moment there I thought my trousers were on fire!' If someone in the audience drops a glass or falls off their chair, acknowledge it and pause for laughter rather than ploughing on as if nothing has happened. Although you have prepared your speech in advance, you should be aware of things happening around you and flexible enough to add a topical observation or funny remark if necessary. And the better-rehearsed and more at ease you are with your material, the more confident you'll be about including the odd spontaneous line.

If you follow these guidelines you really can't go far wrong. But here, as a last-minute reminder, is a checklist of Do's and Don't's that will ensure that your delivery will do justice to all the work you've put into your speech.

Do's

1 Do rehearse your material.
2 Do work on your posture so that you look relaxed and comfortable.
3 Do prepare your notes and quotations carefully.
4 Do take simple precautions — like dressing correctly, checking microphones and checking your appearance.
5 Do anticipate any accidents and interruptions and be prepared for them.

Don't's

1 Don't read your speech.
2 Don't make any last-minute attempts to change your accent or your appearance.
3 Don't arrive late or unprepared.
4 Don't start your speech before everyone is ready.
5 Don't drink before you make your speech.

The Right Speech
for the Right Occasion

Every speech you make should be created especially for the occasion — and every occasion requires a different kind of speech. Some occasions are informal, in which case you must use your discretion to decide what will be most appropriate. For most formal occasions, however, there are basic guidelines which it's best to observe, particularly if you don't have much speaking experience. They'll help you to avoid the worst pitfalls and, at the very least, ensure that you make the right kind of speech.

After-dinner speeches

It's quite an honour to be invited to make an after-dinner speech, because it indicates that your host has confidence in your ability to entertain the audience. That said, after-dinner speechmaking strikes terror into the hearts of many speakers.

It's certainly true that standing up on your own and speaking confidently and amusingly to an audience which has very high expectations of you *can* be quite an ordeal, but there are ways of ensuring that your speech is a great success. And the first is preparation. Most wise after-dinner speakers talk for between ten and twenty minutes, and if you're not well prepared it's impossible to be entertaining for that length of time. Preparation will also give you the advantage of seeming spontaneous and at ease, no matter how you're actually feeling inside. Don't underestimate the importance of appearances, because a tense, nervous speaker can't expect to win the confidence of those listening to him. If you look as if you're enjoying yourself you're halfway to persuading the audience that you *are*.

Some very successful speakers are renowned for writing their speeches on the back of an envelope a few minutes before they are introduced to the audience. Don't try to copy them. Others have — which is why in certain circles the audience dread the after-dinner speeches even more than the speakers themselves! Above all else, be entertaining. You may have deeply held views on serious subjects but an after-dinner speech is not the best time to expand on them. Keep your material witty and light and try to pace it so that any longer stories are followed by some quick laughs.

Try also to be brief. When you are first invited to speak, find out from the organisers how long they expect you to speak for and don't exceed it by so much as a minute. It's far better to be brief and wickedly amusing than to speak for half an hour with only a few laughs. Remember that no one ever complained of a speech being too short.

If by any chance you should find that you're not being well received — though if you follow these guidelines that shouldn't happen — the best thing to do is retire gracefully. Condense your argument, get to the conclusion of your speech and sit down with your head held high. There's no point in prolonging everyone's agony.

Conferences and conventions

Humour is a vital ingredient for conferences and conventions, particularly if you're one of the last speakers at an all-day or even days-long gathering. No matter how serious your topic, a joke or amusing quotation will help to capture your audience's attention, and once you have their interest it will be easier to keep it.

If you know that you're going to be one of the last people to speak, bend one of the major guidelines of the earlier section of this book and *don't* prepare your material too thoroughly. If you're very unlucky you may find that the earlier speeches have effectively covered all that you had planned to say in your own address. It's better, in this situation, to be prepared with a good general outline — one with plenty of relevant humour and wit (because that's what will be required at the end of a long day's speeches) — and build on it as the conference progresses. Listen to the other speakers, making a note of their argument and the things you disagree with or strongly approve of. Insert all these points in your outline to prove that you've been listening, and in this way you'll ensure that your speech is completely integrated and relevant.

Energy and enthusiasm are both important on these kinds of occasion. Be positive and amusing; give people what they want to hear but also give them some food for thought. Above all, try not to look on it as too much of an ordeal. It's in fact an opportunity for you to impress fellow members of the sales force and to make your mark on the occasion.

Presentations

Presentations follow a simple formula that can be adapted for all kinds of occasions, from retirements to award ceremonies. The most important thing to include is information, so that the people watching will be able to appreciate what's going on. You can highlight your speech with a joke or an anecdote, but speak for five minutes at the most and try not to steal the show from the person being honoured.

Here's the basic presentation formula being used for an award presentation:

1   *Name the award and give full details about it*
    We're here tonight to witness the presentation of the
    1986 Golden Lemon award. As you may know, the
    Golden Lemon is awarded each year by the Lemon
    Aid Foundation to the member of the sales force who
    has done the most to promote the image of citrus
    fruit during the past twelve months. As well as this
    wonderful Golden Lemon trophy the salesman or
    woman also receives a cash prize of £1,000 as a
    reward for their efforts.
2   *State the name of the recipient and what he or she has done
    to win the award.*
    Pippa Passmore is this year's winner, and the news
    will come as no surprise to those who work with her.
    It was Pippa who devised our latest sales strategy,
    which has been a resounding success and has revital-
    ised the image of citrus fruit.
3   *Present the award.*
    I'm very pleased, Pippa, to be able to present you
    with the 1986 Golden Lemon trophy and this cheque
    for £1,000.

   If you ever find yourself in the lucky position of receiving an award, this is the pattern that your answer should
follow:
1   *Say thank you to the person making the award and to the
    organisation he or she represents.*
    I'd like to express my thanks both to Mr Jones and to
    the Lemon Aid Foundation for this lovely award.
2   *Say what the award means to you and what you'll do with
    it.*
    I'm very proud to have been chosen to receive this
    honour. I shall keep the trophy on my desk so that it
    will urge me on to even greater efforts next year.

   Don't be tempted to go into great detail about all the
teamwork and effort that went into your career or award;
it's likely to bore people. Also resist the temptation to be
modest and say that you can't think what you've done to
deserve the honour. Accept it with good grace and be as
amusing and brief as you can.

Toasts

If you find yourself asked to propose a toast at a light-hearted and informal occasion, a few witty words often go down well. Two minutes is the optimum length for a toast, so jokes are not in order. You may find that you can adapt a one-liner from the last section of this book to make an appropriate toast for the sales force, but whatever you end up doing, make sure that everything you say is relevant, amusing and leads up to your main purpose — that of encouraging people to raise their glasses.

These guidelines should ensure that you make the right kind of speech at most formal occasions. If, however, you are invited to speak on an occasion that is not dealt with here, find out from the organisers exactly what they require of you and try to give it to them.

This is a final checklist of Do's and Don't's to be considered when you're working out what kind of speech to make on a particular occasion.

Do's

1   Do assess the audience and the formal requirements of the occasion.
2   Find out how long you will be expected to speak for and on which subject.
3   Are you expected to propose a toast or fulfil a function of some kind?
4   Do your research.
5   Do it *now*!

Don't's

1   Don't leave anything to the last minute.
2   Don't leave out a vital part of the proceedings.

Make sure you know what you'll be expected to do.

3 Don't forget to rehearse your material when you have prepared it.

4 Don't try to revamp an old speech; start something completely new.

5 Don't forget to include your thanks and acknowledgements.

PART TWO

The material

Just Jokes

You'll find a joke suitable for every sales-oriented occasion here. Remember that once you've chosen something suitable you'll need to adapt it by adding your own details and observations. That way the joke won't be one you've borrowed from a book, but your own.

A husband came storming home to his wife. 'I was in the pub,' he said, 'and got talking to a door-to-door salesman who's been down this road. He said he'd seduced every woman in the street except one.'

His wife thought for a moment. 'I bet it's that snooty cow at number eight,' she said.

'I hope these sheets are clean,' said a travelling salesman who had spent the last couple of nights in extremely seedy lodgings.

'Of course they are!' protested the landlady. 'I washed them myself. If you don't believe me, feel them. They're still damp.'

A certain travelling salesman had made his reputation by taking his dog with him on calls. One day one of his customers asked him why the dog always accompanied him.

'He talks to me during my journeys,' he said. The customer refused to believe this.

'I'll give you odds of ten to one that you can't make that dog talk,' he laughed. The salesman got down on his hands and knees and tried to coax the dog to talk, but nothing happened. Shrugging, the salesman handed over his money and he and his dog left the premises.

'Why the hell didn't you say something?' he demanded as soon as they were outside.

The dog winked. 'Think of the kind of odds you'll get next time.'

The salesman was spreading something in the middle of the road. 'What on earth do you think you're doing?' said a passing policeman.

'I'm just spreading alligator powder,' said the salesman.

'But there aren't any alligators around here,' said the policeman.

'Which just proves how well it works. Want to buy some?'

The Irish salesman was accompanied on his rounds by a trainee. They stopped for lunch and both took out their sandwiches. The salesman took the top one and his face fell. 'Cheese and pickle,' he said. He looked at the second one. 'More cheese and pickle,' he sighed. The bottom sandwich was cheese and pickle too. His face fell further.

'Why don't you get your wife to give you something else for a change?' asked the trainee gently.

'I don't have a wife,' spluttered the salesman. 'I have to make these myself every morning.'

A female sales representative was travelling home one night after an evening spent with the area sales manager. On her way down the motorway she was stopped by a police patrol and breathalysed. She blew into the machine and it immediately changed colour.

'Oh dear,' said the policeman. 'You've had a stiff one tonight.'

'Good grief!' exclaimed the girl, looking embarrassed. 'Does that show too?'

A travelling salesman raced breathlessly onto a station platform in Northern Ireland.

'When is the next train to Belfast?' he asked the porter.

'Sorry, sir,' came the reply. 'The next train has just left.'

A salesman raced into a country pub one evening and asked the landlord, 'Does anyone in this village have a large black dog that wears a white collar?'

'I don't think so,' said the landlord, scratching his head. 'Does anyone here have a black dog with a white collar?' The occupants of the bar all shook their heads.

'Oh my God!' cried the salesman. 'I'm sorry, then, but I've just run over your vicar.'

A company rep was stopped the other day for drinking and driving. The police officer went up to him and asked him to blow into the balloon. 'Certainly, sir,' said the salesman. 'Who's playing in goal?'

A salesman was stopped by a policeman one dark November night. 'Are you aware you have no rear light showing, sir?'

The salesman leapt out of the car and dashed round to the back, where he began to hold his head and mutter distractedly.

'Don't worry, sir, it's not all that serious,' the policeman said sympathetically.

'What do you mean, not serious?' cried the salesman. 'When I set off I had an exhibition caravan on that towbar.'

A salesman was up in court for disorderly behaviour. One of his colleagues was, in his defence, explaining that he and the accused had called in at a pub on the way home to 'steady' themselves after receiving a rocket from their boss.

'You don't think you both had too much to drink?' asked the magistrate.

'Oh no. The only problem was that we both ended up so steady we couldn't move.'

A salesman was travelling in a railway compartment with an American who engaged him in conversation. 'In the States we can board a train in the morning and travel all day and still not reach our destination before nightfall,' he boasted.

The Englishman smiled. 'We have those over here too.'

In the 1930s commercial travellers were held in some esteem. They wore bowler hats and travelled around the country by train. A rather pompous member of the species arrived in a northern town and, gazing condescendingly on the railway porter asked, 'What's the situation in this town regarding hotels?'

The porter sniffed and looked the salesman up and down before saying, 'I don't think you'll have too much trouble getting a job.'

The salesman was up in court for having defrauded his employer out of several thousand pounds — a crime which had led to the bankruptcy of the business and the ruin of his employer.

'How on earth could you have cheated a man who trusted you?' asked the judge despairingly.

'Because it doesn't work with people who don't trust you, your worship,' came the reply.

A salesman developed a fault in his new rear-engined car while out on his calls. As he stood by the side of the road an identical car pulled up to offer assistance.

'What's wrong?' asked his would-be rescuer.

'I don't know,' sighed the salesman, lifting the bonnet, 'but it looks as if my engine's dropped out.'

'You're in luck,' said the other man. 'I don't know about cars either, but I *do* know that there's a spare engine in my boot.'

A salesman had just been presented with his new company car, so he was disappointed to get into it and discover that the engine was dead. After peering under the bonnet for a few moments he decided he needed expert help and called a mechanic. The mechanic took one look and just twiddled a small wire. Immediately the engine started.

'That'll be twelve pounds fifty, please,' he said.

'But that's outrageous!' said the salesman. 'All you did was twiddle a wire.'

'Look,' said the mechanic, 'it's fifty pence for twiddling the wire but it's twelve pounds for knowing which wire to twiddle.'

A sales manager was giving some of his tips to his new door-to-door encyclopaedia salesmen. 'I owe most of my success to the first eight words I uttered whenever a woman opened the door.'

'What were they?' asked an eager young recruit.

'Excuse me, miss, but is your mother in?'

A salesman's car broke down and left him stranded overnight in a remote little town with only one hotel, a sleazy, seedy place. The TV was broken and there was no one in the bar, and he was just wondering what he could do for the evening when, passing an open door, he saw a snooker table and decided to have a solitary game.

The receptionist managed to find him a cue and a set of balls, but everything was so old and grubby that the balls were a uniform grey colour. 'How do you expect me to play with these?' he asked. 'I can't even tell the white from the black.'

'Don't worry,' said the receptionist. 'You'll soon get to know them by their shape.'

A haberdashery salesman was requested to call on an Irish nudist camp. 'What can I do for you?' he asked the manager.

'We need 250 pink ribbons and 250 blue ribbons so that our members can tell who's male and who's female.'

Two young salesmen met up in a sleepy town where there was nothing much going on. They had a few drinks, then one of them leapt to his feet and said, 'I saw a Catholic church up the road, so I'm going to confession.'

'You're crazy,' said the other, but off went his friend.

In the confessional the salesman confessed to the priest that he had made love with a local girl. Naturally concerned, the priest questioned him. Who had it been? The salesman stubbornly refused to say, and although the priest named a number of girls he did not get a satisfactory reply. Eventually the salesman left and returned to his friend in the bar.

'Well,' he asked, 'did you get absolution?'

'No,' said the other man, 'but I got some useful names and addresses. Come on, we're going to have a good evening.'

A salesman called at the office of a major potential customer with the intention of landing a massive sales coup. He handed his card to the great man's secretary and requested a meeting, but when she took it through to her boss he just tore it up and threw it in the bin. Unfortunately for him, the secretary had left the door open a few inches and the salesman saw what happened.

When she returned and told him that her boss would not see him, he politely requested whether he might have his card back. A minute later she emerged from the office with a pound note which she offered to the salesman with an apology. He took it, then pulled out another card. 'The cards are fifty pence each,' he explained, 'so here's another for your boss to keep.'

The great man was so taken by his cheek that he agreed to meet him.

The salesman knew that his company car was getting old and scruffy, but he only realised *how* old when he had a puncture as he was heading up the A1. Pulling onto the hard shoulder, he got out the jack and the spanner and proceeded to take off the wheel. As he was rolling the spare round, he discovered another man with the bonnet up, just about to disconnect the battery.

'What do you think you're doing?' he asked indignantly.

'Look, mate,' the man replied, 'if you're going to have the tyres I'm going to have the bloody battery.'

A salesman found himself marooned in the Orkneys by bad weather and contacted his HQ in Aberdeen with the news. Back came the reply. 'No problem. Take a week's holiday as from yesterday.'

The sales manager was accompanying a nervous newcomer on a tour of the latter's new territory. Unfortunately they experienced some car trouble and they ran out of petrol at the bottom of a steep hill. 'You'll have to walk a mile up the hill to get some petrol,' said the manager. 'Damn it, this is going to hold us up for ages.'

'Why don't I push the car up the hill?' volunteered the salesman, trying to seem eager. The manager agreed, and so the new man pushed the heavy car all the way up the steep hill and to the nearest garage, which was about a mile away. As they pulled into the forecourt the manager wound down his window and looked out at the sweating and gasping salesman.

'Do you smoke?' he asked.

'Yes, I do,' said the salesman, anticipating a large cigar at the very least.

'I'm not surprised,' said the manager. 'You seem to be in a very poor state of fitness.'

Two salesmen were travelling together, the older introducing the younger to his patch, when they had trouble with their car and had to stay for the night at a beautiful manor house. The place was owned by a very attractive mature lady who, they discovered, had been widowed and left with this amazing house and estate.

She was very kind and showed each of them to their rooms where they spent a comfortable night. In the morning they said goodbye and went on their way. More than a year later the two men met at a sales conference.

'Tell me,' said the younger man, 'when we spent that night at the manor, did you by any chance sneak into that lady's bedroom?'

'I did,' admitted the older man.

'And did you use *my* name?'

'I did — you see you're unmarried, and I didn't want my wife getting to hear about it . . .'

'I've just heard from her solicitor,' said the young man.

'This is terrible!' cried the other.

'Not at all. She died last month and left me the house and the estate in her will.'

A group of businessmen were up late one night at their conference hotel discussing a new promotional idea. About midnight they began to feel hungry, so they asked room service to send up some sandwiches. These duly arrived, but they were rather dainty and they didn't last long. The sales manager phoned down again and requested more.

'Just how many do you want?'

The manager counted his colleagues, then picked up the bill. 'Judging from what we got last time for our money, I'd say about sixty pounds' worth.'

The new salesman was attending the company dance and spotted his boss, the sales director, across the room. Turning to a pretty girl next to him, he said, 'Look at the mean old devil. He's the most awful man I've ever met.'

'Is he really?' replied the girl. 'I'll have you know that I'm his daughter.'

The salesman blanched. 'Do you know who *I* am?' he asked.

She shook her head. 'Well thank God for that,' he said.

A young salesman was hauled up before the managing director, who had received complaints about his mounting debts. 'What do you *do* with your salary?' he demanded.

The salesman shrugged. 'Some goes on drink, some on women, some on the horses. The rest I squander.'

A multi-national company booked an entire hotel for its sales conference. On the second day one of the delegates died and the hotel manager sent the undertakers to remove the body. 'It's in room 301,' he told them.

Half an hour later the undertaker called into the manager's office to confirm that the job had been done and the occupant of room 103 had been taken away.

'You idiot!' cried the manager. 'I said room 301. Was the man in 103 dead too?'

'He said he wasn't,' shrugged the undertaker, 'but we all know what terrible liars these salesmen are.'

Two salesmen were discussing the shorthand typist who worked for them both. 'I took her out the other night,' said one, 'and we went back to her place. I've got to tell you, she's terrific in bed, much better than my wife. Why don't *you* take her out? I know she fancies you.'

The other salesman duly did this and reported back to his friend the next day. 'She's certainly good in bed,' he agreed, 'but I wouldn't say she's any better than your wife.'

The son of a company chairman was placed in the sales office in order to learn the business of selling. The office manager was concerned that there should be no ill-feeling among the staff due to the young man's relationship with the owner of the firm. He asked if he might speak to the Chairman on the matter.

'Don't worry,' said the top man. 'I want you just to

treat him as you would anyone else who was to take over the company in the future.'

The Sales Director and his wife were at the company Christmas party, and he was making liberal use of the free bar. 'That's the tenth time you've been to the bar this evening,' his wife wailed. 'What on earth will people think?'

'It's all right,' he told her. 'Every time I get a drink I say it's for you.'

The company dance was in full swing and a very small and young-looking salesman who had had rather a lot to drink went up to the chairman's wife and asked her to dance with him. She gazed down at him disapprovingly and said, 'I would never dance with a child.'

'I'm sorry, I wasn't aware of your condition,' said the salesman.

The Sales Manager called a meeting of all his male staff. 'Have any of you been sleeping with my secretary?' he demanded. His secretary being a stunningly attractive girl who was fairly free with her favours, there were a lot of embarrassed glances and stifled coughs.

'All right, let's try it another way,' he said. 'Is there anyone here who *hasn't* slept with my secretary?' More embarrassed looks. Then one of the salesmen raised his hand.

'I haven't,' he confessed.

'Right,' said the sales manager. '*You're* going to fire her.'

A sales director with a reputation for toughness sent for one of his sales force, a young man who had failed to secure a large order. 'This is the second time you've failed to make an easy sale,' he lectured. 'I should have no hesitation in firing you right now. However, I'm a sporting man and I'm willing to give you a chance to redeem yourself. One of my eyes is a false one. If you can tell which it is I'll allow you to remain on the staff.'

Taking a long look into the sales director's eyes, the young man said, 'The right one is false.'

'You're right. How did you guess?'

'It has a more sympathetic look than the other one.'

The sales manager was giving a dressing-down to one of his young computer salesmen, and he got carried away with himself.

'Don't talk to me like that!' protested the young man. 'I take orders from no one.'

'*Precisely.*'

At a sales conference a famous salesman had been invited to talk about his success. 'I'm sure we can all learn from him,' said the speaker who introduced him. 'For example, he sold two million books in Africa, a continent not normally thought of as a major book market. May we ask you how you did it?'

'That's easy,' said the salesman. 'I sold them as aids to family planning.'

A surprised gasp travelled around the audience. 'Perhaps you'd explain,' said the chairman.

'All I told them was that to prevent pregnancy they just had to take the book and grip it firmly between the knees . . .'

Everyone knew that the sales manager liked a few drinks, but they were all pretty stunned when his wife phoned the office one morning to say that he wouldn't be coming in to work for a month or two.

'He's gone to Canada,' she explained.

'Family troubles?' enquired his deputy.

'No. He saw a notice saying DRINK CANADA DRY, so he thought he'd have a go.'

The sales manager walked into his office and discovered one of his sales reps and his secretary making passionate love on his desk. 'Jenkins!' he screeched. 'Miss Peabody!

What do you think you're doing? And keep still while I'm talking to you.'

In many ways a company is like an orchestra. The string section is like the sales force, fiddling their overtime, expenses and lunches. The Managing Director is the euphonium pumping away in the background all the time. The wind section are the shop stewards. The percussion section is the typing pool, constantly banging away, and the conductor is the chairman, trying to make them all pull together and forever glancing over his shoulder to see the reaction from customers.

'Could I speak to your boss, please?' a man asked the dumb secretary.
    'Are you a salesman, a creditor or a friend of his?' she asked.
    'I suppose you could say I'm all three,' he smiled.
    'Oh.' She thought hard. 'In that case, I'm afraid he's in a meeting. He's away on business. Would you like to come this way?'

What's the difference between an overseas sales director and a wealthy yacht owner and his girlfriend? One is abroad with sales, the other is sailing abroad.

The area manager sat looking through the sales figures for the previous month. Steam seeped from his ears as he noted that one salesman had, yet again, sold less than half that of anyone else on the team.
    'That's it, Robinson,' he yelled. 'You're fired!'
    'Surely not, sir,' Robinson replied equably. 'Slaves are *sold*, not fired.'

A certain salesman's performance seemed to be suffering and he'd been involved with a number of incidents which had caused complaints from customers, so the company sent him off to see a psychiatrist. 'Tell me about your early life,' said the psychiatrist, so the salesman did, at some length.

After an hour the psychiatrist interrupted. 'There doesn't seem to be anything out of the ordinary in your background. In fact I'll be honest with you and say that you seem as normal and sane as I am.'

'But doctor,' said the salesman, 'what about all these little bugs crawling over my skin? I can't bear them!'

'Aaah!' shrieked the psychiatrist. 'Don't start flicking them all over me!'

A disgruntled salesman overheard one of his bosses mention that he and his family were going on holiday to Wales. 'Wales is good for only two things, prostitutes and rugby,' he muttered as he walked past.

'What was that?' said the boss. 'I'll have you know that my wife was born and bred in Wales.'

The salesman did some quick thinking. 'Really? And what position did she play?'

The marketing manager at a big company became increasingly worried as his colleagues dropped dead around him. First it was his chief salesman, then the overseas buyer, followed in quick succession by the chief executive and the finance director. Stress and good living all seemed to be taking their toll, so he tried to regulate his work and his drinking habits.

One evening he took a rather timid young salesman to the local pub to try and talk a bit of confidence into the boy over a large glass of orange juice. Instead of opening up, the young man just seemed to become more and more subdued. Suddenly the manager became agitated. 'My God, I'm paralysed!' he cried. 'It's my turn next. I'm going to die!'

'What's wrong?' asked the salesman.

'I've been pinching my leg while we've been talking and I can't feel a thing.'

'Thank goodness for that,' blushed the young man. 'It's my leg you've been pinching.'

A British salesman who had been working in a tiny African state got into a bit of local bother and needed to leave the country in a hurry. Unfortunately he couldn't get out over the borders, so he turned for help to a man who was trapping wild animals for export to an English wildlife park.

'Just slip into this gorilla suit,' said the trapper, 'and we'll slip you out in a crate in a day or two.' The salesman did so, and was put in a cage like the other animals. During the night, however, he heard a noise and found that a lion from the cage next door had slipped in with him. As it approached he began to scream with fright.

'Just shut up,' said the lion. 'Anyone would think you were the only person trying to get out of the country.'

The sales director had a new secretary who, though she had seemed very impressive at the interview, was now making awful mistakes in his letters. One day, after he'd given her back another batch for retyping, he snapped, 'I can't think what's wrong. Don't you know the Queen's English?'

'Of course I do,' she protested. 'If she wasn't, she wouldn't be our queen, would she?'

Four salesmen from the same company were sitting together during a lunch break at a conference. As the wine flowed they began to admit their weaknesses.

'I'm fond of the odd bet,' said the most senior. 'Don't tell the boss, but I sometimes put the money I collect for goods on the horses. So far I've won every time, but I know that sooner or later I'll lose the lot.'

'My problem's booze,' said his assistant. 'I've had a few close shaves recently. I live in fear of being banned from driving.'

'It's women that are my little weakness,' said the third. 'In fact I think I've got the boss's daughter pregnant.'

There was a long silence. The three of them turned to the trainee who was sitting silently. 'You must have a fault,' they said. 'What is it?'

'I suppose,' he said, 'that my great weakness is my over-ambition. But,' he smiled, 'I've got a funny feeling that I'm on my way to the top.'

For many years the assistant sales manager was fond of nipping out for a couple of whiskies each lunchtime. To hide the fact from his boss, he always sucked a strong peppermint on his way back to work. One day, in a tearing hurry to get back to his desk, he found he'd run out of mints, so he had a pickled onion instead.

Later, as he leaned across the manager's desk with the latest figures, his boss asked. 'How long have you been working with me?'

'Five years,' said the assistant, surprised.

'That's right,' agreed the manager. 'For five years I've put up with the smell of whisky and peppermints every afternoon. But I warn you, if it's going to be whisky and pickled onions from now on, you're fired!'

The salesman went to his doctor complaining that he was having difficulty sleeping.

'Are you sleeping at night?' asked the doctor.

'Yes,' said the salesman. 'And I'm not having too much trouble nodding off in the mornings. It's just the afternoons that are a bit of a problem.'

The puzzled salesman was talking to a man who ran a local newspaper in a small country town. 'I don't understand how you sell it,' he said. 'After all, in a place as small as this everyone knows what everyone else is doing.'

The newspaper man just smiled. 'They may know what everyone else is doing, but they have to read the paper to find out who's been caught doing it.'

The estate agent was showing a young couple around a house. 'There's something very special about this property,' he told them. 'To the north is the sewage works, to the south the brewery, to the east the gasworks and to the west the abattoir.'

'That isn't special,' cried the woman. 'It's awful!'

'Yes it is special,' said the estate agent. 'It's the only house in the area where you can always tell which way the wind's blowing.'

The salesman took his small son to the zoo. 'Well,' said his mother when they arrived home, 'did you like the zoo?'

'Oh yes,' said the boy. 'And Daddy did too, especially when one of the animals come home at a hundred to one.'

The salesman, letter in hand, entered the office of his secretary, who happened to be very pregnant. 'I think we have a typist's error, here,' he said.

She blushed slightly and patted her tummy. 'Well I won't tell anyone if you don't!'

The sales manager called his team into his office. 'I've got good and bad news for you,' he announced. 'The bad news is that they've cut our commission by three per cent. The good news is that I've persuaded them to backdate it for six months.'

A salesman who had been invited to attend a conference at his company's northern HQ decided to travel by train so that he would be fresh when he arrived first thing in the morning. His secretary duly booked him a sleeper, but he was warned that he would have to share a compartment with another passenger.

He boarded the train on the night and found himself sharing with a middle-aged woman who made eyes at him. Ignoring her, he went to bed, only to be woken in the early hours of the morning by a persistent tapping on the bottom of his bunk. 'Are you awake?' she asked.

'Yes,' he muttered.

'I'm awfully cold,' she said. 'Could you let me have a spare blanket?'

'I've got a better idea,' replied the salesman. 'Let's pretend we're married.'

'There's nothing I'd like more,' she giggled.

'Right,' said the salesman. 'Get your own bloody blanket.'

A salesman was trying to sell a housewife a freezer. 'It'll pay for itself,' he told her. 'You'll save so much on your food bills that you'll soon be making money on it.'

'I appreciate that,' she agreed. 'It's just that at the moment we're paying for our car on the fares we're saving, and our mortgage on the rent we're saving. We honestly can't afford to save any more.'

The young mother was looking at a very sophisticated toy that had been recommended by the salesman for her little boy. 'Isn't it a bit complicated for him?' she asked.

'In fact it's a very educational toy,' said the salesman, 'guaranteed to prepare the child for coping in the modern world. You see, whichever way he puts it together is bound to be wrong.'

In the fabric department of a large store a customer asked one of the sales girls to cut her a metre of material. This the girl did, and asked the customer for three pounds. She also pointed out that, if the customer was interested, there was now a remnant of one and a half metres which she could have for two pounds fifty pence.

'Keep the metre you've just cut,' said the customer. 'I'll take the remnant.'

A newsagent had a shop next door to a bank. One day one of his customers came in and asked him if he could lend him ten pounds, just till the end of the month.

'I'd like to, honestly,' said the newsagent, 'but I've come to an arrangement with the bank. They've promised not to sell cigarettes and newspapers and I've promised not to lend any money.'

A young shopkeeper was explaining business ethics to his girlfriend. 'It's like this,' he said. 'If a customer comes into the shop, buys something that costs ten pounds and gives me a ten pound note which I later discover is *two* ten pound notes stuck together, should I tell my partner?'

A woman raced into a butcher's shop late on Christmas Eve. 'I need a large turkey,' she panted. The butcher had only one bird left, which he was anxious to be rid of, but when he showed it to her she asked for a bigger one.

'I'll just check the cold store,' he said, and disappeared behind the scenes where he wrapped the bird in plastic and put it in a box, which made it look bigger. 'Is this any good?' he asked, emerging again.

'That's fine,' said his customer. Then she paused. 'Look, just to be on the safe side, I'd better take both.'

A lady asked her fishmonger the price of his cod fillets. 'One pound twenty pence a pound,' he told her.

'But it's only one pound a pound down the road,' she exclaimed.

'You'd do better to buy it there, then,' said the fishmonger.

'Oh, they're out of cod,' his customer replied.

'That explains it,' the fishmonger said. 'When I'm out of it *I* sell it for eighty pence a pound.'

Did you hear about the Irish salesman? When he was trained he was taught that personal grooming and cleanliness were very important if he was to impress his clients, so he had clean socks and underwear every day. By Friday he couldn't fasten his trousers or get his shoes on.

A salesman who worked in a gents' outfitters went to confession and told the priest that he had stolen a roll of cloth from the shop.

'I hope you're not going to make a habit of this,' said the priest.

'Actually,' said the salesman, 'I was going to have a jacket made.'

A young man who went on a course,
To learn all about the sales force,
Gave too much concentration
To client penetration,
Now his wife is seeking a divorce.

A brain salesman had called at the house of a man who was going to have a brain transplant. 'I've got two for you to choose from,' he said. 'This one is a teacher's, and it costs £1,000. And this is a politician's, which will cost you £10,000.'

The potential buyer thought a bit. 'Does that mean the politician's brain is better than the teacher's?'

'No,' the salesman shrugged. 'It's just that the politician's is unused.'

The wife of the chief salesman of a major international company was invited to launch a ship that had been built for the company. She was delighted to oblige, but not so happy when she saw an account of the occasion in the company's internal newspaper. It read: 'Mrs Brown smashed a bottle of champagne against her side and then slowly her enormous bulk slid down the slipway to tumultuous cheers from the watching crowd.'

The dictator of a small African country that was experiencing civil unrest arrived unexpectedly at a company manufacturing tanks and armaments somewhere in the Midlands. 'I'm looking for something that will help me to keep my workers in line,' he told the sales manager.

Together they toured the factory looking at the various products, and while they were doing this a hooter sounded and the workforce all leapt up and dashed out. 'Insurrection! Revolution!' cried the visitor. 'This is what they do in *my* country. But look, we can use your tanks to round them up and bring them all back ...'

'No, no, you don't understand,' interrupted the sales manager. 'In an hour the hooter will sound again and they'll all come back.'

'Well in that case,' said the statesman, 'I'll take five hundred hooters.'

A sales manager received a request for a reference from a company which was considering employing a salesman whom he had fired for laziness. He considered the problem for a long time before writing, 'Dear Sir, If you can get Martin Jones to work for you you will indeed be fortunate ...'

At the end of a long day the buyer of a major retail chain at last had a few moments free and agreed to see a salesman. 'You're very lucky,' he commented as the man entered. 'I've been so busy I've had to refuse to see a dozen reps today.'

'I know,' said the salesman. 'I'm them.'

Some people are born salesmen. Take the Jew who was travelling on a train with a stranger. The stranger guessed his companion's religion and asked him why the Jews were considered such brainy people. 'It's fishcakes that give us our brains,' came the reply, and to prove the fact the Jew took out his lunch of fishcakes.

'In that case, if you've got a fishcake to spare, I'd like to purchase it from you,' said the man.

'Yes, I've got one spare. It will be a pound,' said the Jew, and the man paid up.

'Delicious,' he exclaimed, tucking in. Suddenly he paused. 'You sold me a fishcake for the price of a packet of fish and chips,' he murmured.

'You see,' said his companion. 'It's beginning to work already.'

The sales force of a local company had a very boozy Christmas lunch party the other year, and one of their number ended up being sick down his trousers. Rather than risk a lecture from his wife, on his way to the station he popped into a discount clothing store. 'A pair of trousers,' he said. 'Thirty-six inch waist and plain grey in colour.' The assistant stuffed the trousers into a paper bag and handed them to him. He managed to find an empty compartment on the train home, and as it pulled out of the station he removed his smelly old trousers. Not knowing where to put them, he rolled them up and threw them out of the window. Then he opened the paper bag — and found that he'd bought a red nylon polo-necked sweater ...

Did you hear about the salesman who had three successive jobs? He started out selling elastic but was sacked for being too tight. Then he travelled in ladies' underwear, but was arrested for indecency. Eventually he ended up selling All Bran because he liked the regular hours.

An insurance salesman was approached by a man of ninety-seven who wished to take out a life insurance policy. The old chap filled out a form and had a medical, despite all attempts to put him off, but eventually his application was turned down.

'I'm afraid the risks are just too great,' the insurance man told him.

'You're mad,' protested the old boy. 'Just check the mortality figures and you'll find that very few men die over the age of ninety-seven.'

During a long sales conference an invited speaker gave a long and dreary speech at a mid-week dinner. Unfortunately he droned on and on and showed no signs of stopping. There was a lot of coughing and shuffling of feet, but still he didn't stop. One young employee, who had had far too much to drink, was spotted creeping up behind the speaker with a port decanter, apparently intending to hit him on the head with it. Unfortunately he missed his target and instead hit the head of the guest alongside him. As he slumped forward in a daze, the man was heard to beg, 'Hit me again, I can still hear him.'

A sales manager who had often used a certain hotel when he had been a salesman in the area, took his new bride there for their honeymoon. On their first morning he and his new wife came down to the dining-room for breakfast.

'Where's my honey?' the salesman asked the waiter when he brought the toast. The waiter cast an embarrassed glance at the blushing new wife and whispered, as quietly as he could, 'I'm afraid she doesn't work here any more, sir.'

A salesman used to pass his son's school on the way to work in the mornings, so he always dropped the child off. One day he had some paperwork to complete before he went to the office, so his wife took the little boy to school instead. That evening the salesman asked his son if he had enjoyed the novelty of being driven to school by his mother.

'Oh yes, and we didn't see a single silly bastard on the whole journey,' replied his son.

A salesman who had been feeling unwell went to see his doctor and had an extensive check-up. The doctor seemed very subdued. 'Would you like the good news or the bad news first?' the doctor asked.

'The good news,' said the salesman.

'The good news is that by the time you receive my bill you'll be dead.'

A salesman who was a keen golfer decided he would pay for a lesson from the club professional in an attempt to iron out his problems. Having watched his pupil's swing several times, the pro said, 'Why not play golf like you behave at work?'

'What do you mean?' asked the man.

'Well, I'm told by your colleagues that you always take

every opportunity to get your head down and keep it there.'

The estate agent was checking his little son's homework.
    'Daddy, what's six times four?' the boy asked.
    'Are you buying or selling?' his father replied.

A group of immigrants landed in Australia in the early part of this century. The party contained three men who had been salesmen in their home lands. One was American, one German and one English. Ten years passed and the American owned three hotels, the German had three factories and the Englishman was still waiting to be introduced.

The sales manager of a large company arrived in a small town to attend a dinner at which he was to be principal speaker. Since he was to make a speech the following day to the Chamber of Commerce in the town he asked the local newspaper reporter not to print any of his jokes. The speech went well, but the reporter must have felt disgruntled, because when an account of the occasion appeared it read, 'the principal speaker told several stories which we were unable to print.'

The sales manager had been out with his wife at a company dance and on the way home he was stopped by the police for reckless driving. Instead of cooperating he was awkward and belligerent and refused to get out of the car to be breathalysed. 'I'm awfully sorry, officer,' said his poor wife, trying to defuse the situation. 'He always gets like this when he's drunk.'

On his way home from work a salesman bought some flowers for his wife as a surprise. As she opened the door to greet him he handed her the bouquet — and she immediately burst into tears. 'Whatever is the matter?' the husband asked.
    His wife sobbed. 'I've had a terrible day. The washing-

57

machine leaked on the floor, the cat got run over, the freezer's defrosted, and now here you are, *drunk*!'

A speaker at a sales dinner droned on interminably and when he eventually sat down there was a great surge of relief all round. One of the diners, noted for his optimism, said to his neighbour, 'Never mind, there's a good side to everything. After that the winter won't seem so long.'

The managing director of a large company owned a race-horse and used to invite his staff to watch it run. One day he took his sales director with him to Newmarket. In the saddling enclosure he stood and watched the trainer help-ing the jockey saddle up. The sales director noticed the trainer give the horse something to eat.

'What's that?' he asked curiously.

'Just a sweet, sir,' replied the trainer. 'Would you like one?' The sales director accepted the offer.

As he gave the jockey a leg-up the trainer murmured quietly 'Hold him back for the first six furlongs, then let him go. If anything passes you in the final quarter mile it'll be the sales director.'

A group of salesmen who had been urged to get fit by their boss were in the habit of working out and having a sauna at the end of the day. Several of them were sitting naked in the sauna one evening when two ladies opened the door and, not realising their mistake, stepped inside the cabin. All of the salesmen grabbed their towels and wrapped them around themselves except one, who covered his head.

When the embarrassed ladies had gone, the other salesmen demanded an explanation of his strange behaviour. 'I don't know about you lot,' he said, 'but around here I'm known by my face ...'

One evening a good-looking young salesman was driving to Birmingham in a company van packed with exhibition equipment and goods. A few miles from home he picked up a stunningly beautiful girl who was hitch-hiking, and after a few minutes conversation and meaningful glances he pulled off the main road and parked on a quiet grass verge.

The front of the van being very cramped, there wasn't much room for manoeuvre, so they climbed out, intending to make love on the grass. Unfortunately it was raining, so they crawled under the van. They were hard at it when the salesman looked up to find a policeman looming over him.

'What do you think you're doing?' asked the policeman.

'I'm mending my van,' replied the salesman quickly.

'No, you're not,' said the constable. 'I'll give you three reasons why. First, you're the wrong way up. Second, a small crowd that has just turned out of the pub is cheering you on. And third, someone's nicked your van.'

Everyone tried to be polite about the launch of the new product, but things didn't go very well. In fact, according to one of the people present, 'The product was as useless as the sales manager, the sales manager was as wet as the tea, the tea was as tasteless as the chairman's wife, the chairman's wife was as old as the office furniture, the office furniture as stylish as the toilet seat, the toilet seat as clean as the manager's collar, the manager's collar as tight as the designer, the designer as attractive as his product, the product was as useless . . .'

The shoe-shop manager had had several pairs of a certain brand of shoe returned with complaints that it fell apart after a few months' wear. 'We'll cover ourselves by putting up a sign,' he told his staff. And he produced a notice, which he placed in the window by the shoes, reading: THIS SHOE IS FIT FOR A QUEEN.

'But it's one of the worst-made shoes we stock!' gasped an assistant.

'And just how much walking does a queen have to do?'

Yorkshire cricket lovers raced to the paper kiosk, where the paper seller was yelling 'Yorkshire do it again! Read all about it!' On close inspection one customer discovered that Yorkshire's score was a measly 53 for 7. Having expected more successful news he asked the paper-seller to explain his sales pitch.

'Well it's the fifth disaster they've had,' said the seller, quite unabashed.

Sales Stories

Every salesman knows that real life is far funnier than any joke — so here's a selection of true anecdotes and stories covering all aspects of the sales force, from retailing to advertising.

A travelling salesman brought up for speeding in Lechlade, Gloucestershire in 1974 told the court, 'I forgot myself. But at the far end of town they were screaming for toilet rolls.'

Salesmen beware! A Dutch computer firm recently displayed its wares at a British exhibition. Fifteen-year-old Simon Kaye took a look at their product and proceeded to suggest ways of making it cheaper and more competitive.

The salesmen took notes and sent them to head office, who confirmed that young Simon's advice was correct. As a thankyou they offered him a free computer but he declined, saying that he already had seven.

A thirty-two-year-old carpet salesman from Maryland, USA, was told by his doctor that he was suffering from Crohn's disease and had only three months to live. Deciding to make the most of it, the man embezzled $30,000 from the company and went on a spending spree, drinking, dining and generally enjoying himself. Only one thing bothered him, and that was the fact that his health didn't seem to be deteriorating. In fact, as the weeks

61

passed, he was beginning to feel better.

Worried, he sought a second opinion — and it was revealed that, far from suffering Crohn's disease, he had a simple hernia and an allergy problem.

A German campaign to boost sales of washing-powder quoted a housewife as saying, 'I wouldn't swap one packet of my favourite powder for two of any other make.'

The company was inundated with letters from housewives saying that *they* certainly would accept the deal, and one man even tried to swap a ton of their product for two tons of a rival brand.

Asked to comment on the fact that sales of mistletoe were falling, a salesman said, 'It's a fast disappearing thing now people have sex all the year round.'

Questioned about the presence of a black girl clad in a feather boa on his stand at the Motor Show, the then Sales Director of the Lotus sports car company said, 'You have to understand what our car is all about. I won't say that the man who buys one of our yellow dropheads is running a mistress, but he wants to make his friends wonder if he is running one. A coloured girl is the great status symbol in mistresses at the moment. It's a subliminal message we're putting across.'

A South Humberside man who was applying for a job described his present post as 'transport manager' at a supermarket. He was in fact in charge of the trolleys in the shop.

Always think before you speak. Brian Johnston, the cricket commentator, didn't. Which was why, during a Test Match between England and the West Indies he uttered the line 'The bowler's Holding, the batsman's Willey.'

In the heyday of Hollywood one salesman found himself with a sales pitch that covered some of the most remote parts of South America. Arriving in a small town in Venezuela he went to the local cinema owner and offered him the latest Clark Gable picture.

'But Clark Gable is dead,' said the man.

'No, he's not,' said the salesman.

'Yes he is,' insisted the cinema proprietor. 'Didn't you see his last film?'

'Yes,' said the salesman.

'He died in it. If you saw it, you must know.'

'But it was only a film, he was acting!' protested the salesman.

'Can't a man believe the evidence of his own eyes?' responded the cinema owner. 'We saw him die. There would be a riot if we showed another Clark Gable picture.'

In 1948 British and American car manufacturers visited the Volkswagen plant to take a look at the Beetle. 'The Volkswagen,' they decided, 'does not meet the fundamental technical requirements of a motor car.'

They went on to invest $350 million in a new car, the Edsel — which went out of production, one of the worst failures in manufacturing history, only two years later.

In 1897 the Remington Company turned down the offer of a patent writing machine, an early typewriter, with the words, 'no mere machine can replace a reliable and honest clerk.'

A London amusement arcade manager went all the way to Paris in 1970 to investigate a new and very expensive fortune-telling computer. When he tried it out, the machine produced for him a lengthy prediction which included the warning, 'If you are contemplating signing any contracts today, do not.'

He chose to ignore the advice and bought the computer. It was a mistake. Five weeks later, having cost him thousands and brought him little custom, it was returned to the manufacturer.

The council of a Canadian town was having difficulty in selling its cemetery plots, so a resolution was passed cancelling a previous regulation which said that people had to be dead before they could purchase a plot. 'That could explain why they're not selling too well,' commented the mayor.

Sometimes a company is so concerned with producing and selling its product that it ignores problems close to home. Take, for example, the wood preservative firm, Cuprinol Ltd, which was disturbed to find that while its products were preserving thousands of homes, the floor of its company canteen was riddled with wet rot . . .

Alfred Bloomingdale, owner of the world-famous department store, once produced a musical which opened in Boston before moving to Broadway. The critics didn't like it, and when Bloomingdale asked George S. Kaufman for his advice he told him, 'If I were you, I'd close the show and keep the store open at night.'

Mr Arthur Cox, who owns a shop, hates VAT so much that he refuses to stock anything that carries VAT. So he sells ordinary biscuits but not chocolate ones, and canned fish but not cat food. However, he has to be registered for VAT so that he can claim back VAT-rated items such as paper bags that have to be used in the shop. This means that the VAT man has to pay him, but he doesn't have to pay a penny.

A Nottingham travel agent was interviewed by the local paper on the problems of selling holidays in Belfast. He insisted that the troubles were having little effect on his trade. 'It's going on every day in Belfast. I don't think bombs have the same sort of "feel" about them that they might have done some years ago.'

In Moscow in 1983 a brand new ophthalmic centre, packed with all the latest technology and diagnostic measures to advise on people's sight problems was opened. Unfortunately its opening coincided with a national shortage of spectacle frames and lenses, though more were promised in a year or two.

An elderly Chicago lady got lost one day in one of the city's huge department stores. She claimed that, unable to find her way out, she spent a month living in the shop until she was eventually found in the bedding department. She had opened an account and lived off the things she bought, even eating in the restaurant!

A dress manufacturer was faced with an angry customer who had only discovered *after* she had got her new dress home that it could be neither dry-cleaned nor washed.

His reply was dismissive. 'I don't expect my clothes to be worn more than once.'

A nun found leaving an Oxford Street store with two cardigans in her bag was charged with shoplifting. When she appeared in court she explained that her misdemeanour had been 'the work of the devil'.

The vice-president of sales for an American corporation had been on a business trip to St Louis and promised his wife to arrive home on an early evening plane. Unfortunately he missed it, and by the time he managed to call her she had already left for the airport.

Finding her husband wasn't on the plane, she left messages on the answerphones of four of his friends in St Louis, asking if he'd decided to change his plans and was staying the night with them. Then she went home.

A couple of hours later her husband arrived and explained what had happened. But throughout the evening his friends called one by one to assure his wife that he was staying with them ...

Salesmen are rarely popular. The nineteenth-century poet Thomas Campbell once shocked his fellow guests at a literary dinner by drinking to the health of Napoleon Bonaparte. Cries of horror greeted this action but he turned them to laughter by reminding them that Bonaparte once shot a book salesman.

Always have confidence in your product, that's what the sales force is told. And the team that sold the Thermofax copier did have confidence. What was more they sold thousands of the machines. Everything looked bright. Then came the bad news. After a week or two in the files, Thermofax copies turned black.

You don't just have to have the right product. It has to work, too. In 1983 a Norwegian health club owner 'discovered' a revolutionary new diet that went down a treat with his customers. It included beer and ice cream and was very popular — until members noticed that their waistlines were growing. In protest at his behaviour, they burned down his club.

Have faith in your products. The BBC did when they imported *The Thorn Birds*, an American TV show, in 1984. Every critic who saw it panned it; few programmes have ever received such appalling reviews. Despite that, the people who really count loved it so much that 22 million of them switched on their sets for one episode — and an extra power station had to be brought into operation to cope with the power demand.

One of the first things salesmen have to learn is to keep copies of their documents. Sam Goldwyn believed in keeping copies, too. Someone once asked him if he would allow the disposal of all correspondence files over six years old in order to save space. He gave his permission, but said, 'Make copies first.'

In 1975 Smirnoff launched an advertising campaign for

their vodka. One of their famous adverts showed a dusky lady and the line. 'I thought the Kama Sutra was an Indian restaurant until I discovered Smirnoff.'

Then some market research was done — and it was shown that sixty per cent of those questioned *did* think that the Kama Sutra was an Indian restaurant . . .

Sales promotions and free offers can get horribly complicated, as a Worcester man found when he posted off 2,000 cigarette coupons with a request for a free watch. Before long he received a golf bag, a pressure cooker, a doll, two electric blankets, various records, a number of pots, pans and tape recorders and a number of other items, including a wristwatch.

Being an honest man, he kept the watch and sent back the other stuff. In gratitude the tobacco company sent him 10,000 more coupons. With these he ordered some household tools and a bedspread. Back though the post came a plant stand and two stepladders . . .

Looking for a macho-sounding name for their pork and beans product, which was to be launched on the Canadian market, an advertising agency settled on 'Gros Jos.' Fortunately a French-speaking member of the team was able to stop them in time. The colloquial translation of 'Gros Jos' was 'big tits'.

The Parker Pen Company produced a pen which contained new ink which would not leak and would 'prevent embarrassment' caused by black stains. In the course of the overseas selling promotion the word 'embarrassment' was mis-translated as *embarazar* — which means 'to prevent pregnancy'.

The company was inundated with demands for the new wonder contraceptive and had to make swift changes to their claims for the pen's powers.

A sales campaign for a new soap powder didn't work as well as expected in Saudi Arabia. Executives puzzled over it but simply couldn't understand why. It was a simple enough advert. On the left of the poster was a pile of grubby washing. In the middle a smiling lady was shown bundling the washing into a machine. And on the right was a heap of gleaming white garments. Then some bright spark remembered that the Arabs read from right to left ...

Advertising can help sales — but sometimes it's more of a hindrance. Take those famous adverts in which the late Leonard Rossiter poured a drink over Joan Collins. They became classics, loved by everyone. But can you remember the name of the product they were promoting? If you can, you're in a minority. Follow-up research showed that viewers loved the adverts so much they didn't take any notice of the drink itself, and so they were scrapped.

Sometimes even bright-sounding ideas don't sell. Like the American newspaper that was set up to publish nothing but good news, its owners thinking that everyone would like to hear something cheerful for a change. Unfortunately headlines like, 19,459,483 CITIZENS WERE NOT KILLED IN AUTO ACCIDENTS THIS YEAR were not what people wanted to know.

Sponsorship can backfire — as it did on Benson and Hedges during their tennis tournament at Wembley. Their star player, John McEnroe, called for a ban on smoking. 'Can't breathe this side of the net,' he protested. 'It's like a London fog.'

The manufacturers of a certain brand of male contraceptive couldn't understand why the small and medium sizes of their product were consistently outsold by the large size. After all, they had done a great deal of careful research and they knew there was a market.

In an attempt to solve the problem, they called in a team of marketeers to find out what was going wrong. After a great deal of time and money spent pondering the problem, the product was relaunched — still in three sizes but this time labelled Large, Super and Giant ...

Birds Eye's new product, Cod Pieces, had been fully developed by the time someone began to wonder whether the name was well chosen.

In the 1950s the Pepsodent toothpaste company decided to move into South East Asia and began an aggressive advertising campaign promising whiter teeth. Nothing happened, and an investigation discovered the inhabitants of the area enjoyed chewing betel nut, which stains the teeth. Betel nut is expensive, and the richer the locals, the blacker their teeth. No one *wanted* white teeth.

Determined to exploit his brother's popularity as president of the USA, Billy Carter launched 'Billy's Beer' in 1977. Unfortunately he got the timing wrong. Jimmy's career began to sink fast, and so did sales of Billy's beer. And things weren't helped by Miss Lillian, their mother who, far from endorsing the product, told the world, 'I tried it once, but it gave me diarrhoea.'

A manufacturer of a foot deodorant known as Pulvapies decided to cash in during an election in Ecuador and devised an advertising campaign which included slogans such as 'Vote for any candidate. But for well-being and hygiene — vote Pulvapies,' and 'For Mayor — Honourable Pulvapies'.

So impressed were the locals that they duly elected a foot deodorant to be their mayor ...

Don't believe adverts. You think that's a bit strong? Giovanni Martinelli, a famous Italian opera singer who joined the New York Metropolitan Opera, was asked by a reporter how he managed to smoke and sing so brilliantly.

'I would not think if it!' the singer replied.

The reporter pointed out that Martinelli had asserted in

an advert that a certain brand of cigarettes did not irritate his throat.

'Of course I gave that endorsement,' Martinelli said. 'How could they irritate my throat? I have never smoked!'

One of the biggest flops in advertising history was that for Strand cigarettes. It featured a trench-coated man standing alone in the rain on a street corner and lighting a cigarette to comfort himself. Although it wasn't explicit, it looked as if he had been stood up by his girlfriend — and no one wanted to identify with the kind of man who got stood up!

You sometimes have to adapt a product to ensure that it will sell in your market. Take the case of Radclyffe Hall's book *The Well of Loneliness*. When Sam Goldwyn heard how well it was selling he decided to buy the film rights.

'You won't be able to film the book,' an assistant warned him. 'It's about lesbians.'

'No problem,' Goldwyn replied. 'Where the book's got Lesbians we'll use Austrians.'

Sales Line

Whether you're looking for a provocative quotation on which to base a conference speech, words of wisdom from unexpected sources, or hilarious examples of bad commercial judgement, you'll find something suitable here.

Rolls Royce announced today that it is recalling all Rolls Royce cars made after 1966 because of the faulty nuts behind the wheel.

Walter Cronkite.

I have heard of a man who had in mind to sell his house, and therefore carried a piece of brick in his pocket which he shewed as a pattern to encourage purchasers.

The Irish way of selling, described by Jonathan Swift.

It's not the employer who pays the wages — it's the products.

Henry Ford.

When you are getting kicked from the rear it means you are in front.

Bishop Fulton Sheen.

Naturally enough for a company the size of Beecham, the year brought its problems. The pharmaceutical side of the business, including proprietary medicines, was clearly not helped by the very low level of winter sickness through-out the northern hemisphere.

Annual report of the Beecham Group chairman.

No one has endurance like the man who sells insurance.

Traditional insurance maxim.

It is well known what a middle man is; he is a man who bamboozles one party and plunders the other.

Disraeli.

These eggs aren't all they're cracked up to be.

My tool has given considerable satisfaction.

Our Bristol factory went bust in 1981.

My wife is much happier with the carpet now that she has her underfelt.

Extracts from letters sent to sales departments.

When I sell liquor it's called bootlegging; when my patrons serve it on silver trays on Lake Shore Drive, it's called hospitality.

Al Capone.

It used to be that people needed products to survive. Now products need people to survive.

Nicholas Johnson.

Business is simply other people's money.

Alexander Dumas.

Cars new and pre-owned.

Sign in a car dealer's window.

Nothing is as irritating as the fellow who chats pleasantly to you while he's overcharging you.

Kim Hubbard.

Dear Madam,

With reference to your blue raincoat, our manufacturers have given the garment in question a thorough testing, and find that it is absolutely waterproof. If you will wear it on a dry day and then take it off and examine it, you will see that our statement is correct.

Letter from a rainwear manufacturer to a dissatisfied customer.

The basis of optimism is sheer terror.

Oscar Wilde.

Customers giving orders will be swiftly executed.

Sign in a Hong Kong tailor's shop.

A man without a smile must not open a shop.

Proverb.

Closed until we open.

Sign in a Polish bicycle shop.

Experience is a name everyone gives to their mistakes.

Oscar Wilde.

Experience is a marvellous thing. It enables you to recognise a mistake whenever you make it again.

Saturday Evening Post.

When a man comes to me for advice I find out the kind of advice he wants and I give it to him.

Josh Billings.

He that travels knows much.

Thomas Fuller.

Tact is the ability to describe others as they see themselves.

Abraham Lincoln.

The true concept of business is: do other men for they would do you.

Charles Dickens.

The trouble with being punctual is that nobody's there to appreciate it.

Franklin P. Jones.

If at first you don't succeed, try, try again. Then quit. There's no use being a damn fool about it.

W.C. Fields.

Advertising may be described as the science of arresting the human intelligence long enough to get money from it.

Stephen Leacock.

I do not read advertisements — I would spend all my time wanting things.

Archbishop of Canterbury.

The consumer is not a moron. She is *your* wife. And she is grown up.

David Ogilvy.

We don't think the Beatles will do anything in this market.

Jay Livingstone, Capitol Records.

Next to the American corpse, the American bride is the hottest thing in today's merchandising market.

Kitty Hanson.

Some are born great, some achieve greatness and some hire public relations officers.

Daniel Boorstin.

THE HITE REPORT ON MALE SEXUALITY
£12.50 (cased)   £9.95 (limp)

Book advert.

SALES STAFF REQUIRED. NO OBJECTION TO SEX.
Card in employment agency window.

It is our job to make women unhappy with what they have.

B. Earl Puckett.

Public relations is the art of winning friends and getting people under the influence.

Jeremy Tunstall.

You can fool all the people all the time if the advertising is right and the budget is big enough.

Joseph Levine.

There are a million definitions of public relations. I have found it to be the craft of arranging the truth so that people will like you.

Alan Harrington.

A good advert should be like a good sermon; it must comfort the afflicted, it must also afflict the comfortable.

Bernice Fitzgibon.

The philosophy behind much advertising is based on the old observation that every man is really two men — the man he is and the man he wants to be.

William Feather.

An advertising agency; eighty-five per cent confusion and fifteen per cent commission.

Fred Allen.

Doing business without advertising is like winking at a girl in the dark. *You* know what you're doing but no one else does.

Stewart Britt.

If advertising encourages people to live beyond their means, so does matrimony.

Bruce Barton.

Statistics are like a bikini. What they reveal is suggestive but what they conceal is vital.

Aaron Levenstein.

There are too many one ulcer men holding down two ulcer jobs.

Prince Philip.

If the British people liked work as much as they like sport and were as interested in economics as in, say, gardening, we should be at the top of all world tables of industrial nations.

John Hill.

A genius is one who can do anything except make a living.

Joey Adams.

The trouble with the rat race is that even if you win, you're still a rat.

Lily Tomlin.

Work is the curse of the drinking classes.

Oscar Wilde.

The reason why worry kills more people than work is that more people worry than work.

Robert Frost.

My father taught me to work; he did not teach me to love it.

Abraham Lincoln.

I like work. I can sit and look at it for hours. I love to keep it by me; the idea of getting rid of it nearly breaks my heart.

Jerome K. Jerome.

Anyone can do any amount of work provided that it isn't the work he is supposed to be doing at the moment.
Robert Benchley.

I'll give you a definite maybe.

Sam Goldwyn.

You can dismiss from your mind that we are holding back technical developments. As far as we are concerned, there is no consumer demand for a long-life bulb.
Thorn Lighting spokesman.

The two great tragedies of life — not getting what you want and getting it.
Oscar Wilde.

If you are wishful, to do your business with us the movements of our staff will be reserved for your inspection.

The contents of our wine bottles have been individually passed by our manager.

If you should show an interest our representative will be welcome to expose his briefs to you at any moment.
Translated sales brochures sent to English salesmen.

It is a project which, as far as I can see, has a viable marketing opportunity ahead of it.
Giles Shaw, Northern Ireland's Minister of Commerce, on the De Lorean car.

You should make a point of trying every experience once, except incest and folk dancing.
Arnold Bax.

Anything that won't sell, I don't want to invent.

Thomas Edison.

If they're going to get anywhere, it will have to be without the vile-looking singer with the tyre-tread lips.

TV producer after the Rolling Stones' first TV performance.

There's a sucker born every minute.

P.T. Barnum.

A verbal contract isn't worth the paper it's written on.

Sam Goldwyn.

Competition brings out the best in products and the worst in people.

David Sarnoff.

Nothing that costs only a dollar is worth having.

Elizabeth Arden.

Electric light will never take the place of gas.

Werner Von Siemens.

It's a Fact

Which Roman god represents both salesmen and thieves? Which best-selling board game was turned down for having '52 fundamental errors?' Find out in this selection of strange facts and bizarre sales stories!

The first woman ever to place a lonely-hearts advert in a British newspaper was a spinster from Manchester called Helen Morrison. Her advert appeared in the *Manchester Weekly Journal* in 1727. When the mayor of Manchester saw it he committed her to a lunatic asylum for a month.

The first coin-operated slot machines for dispensing products were invented by a Greek in the first century AD.

The safety razor was invented and marketed by King C. Gillette. At first it looked as if his development was a dud. When it went on sale in 1903 only 51 razors and 168 blades were sold. Things picked up the following year, though. 90,000 razors and 12,400,000 blades were sold!

It's true, someone *has* sold refrigerators to Eskimos. They use them to prevent food from freezing solid. And the Saudi Arabian government has bought several snow-ploughs — to clear sand off the roads.

The author of a book called *Nutrition for Health* was not a good advert for his ideas. He died of malnutrition.

An American record company had such a success with their release 'The Best of Marcel Marceau' that they are planning a follow-up. Monsieur Marceau is, of course, a mime artist, and the record contains nothing but silences followed by applause.

A British firm once landed an order to export 1,800 tons of sand to Abu Dhabi — one of the most desert-covered countries in the world.

The Scottish distillery of Bruichladdich launched a fifteen-year-old malt whisky in 1982. To make it different from all the others on the market they commissioned special crystal decanters and a lockable Victorian-style tantalus to hold them. The job of the salesmen was to persuade people to part with £1,000 for each of them ...

The Roman god of merchants and salesmen was Mercury, who was also the god of thieves.

Arthur Ferguson has to be one of the most successful salesmen of all times. In 1923 he sold Big Ben and Nelson's Column to an American couple who paid £1,000 and £6,000 respectively. So smooth-talking was he that he also convinced would-be buyers into parting with a deposit of £2,000 for Buckingham Palace.

When Harrods introduced the very first escalator in Britain, they stationed attendants at the top to administer brandy and smelling salts to any customer who was overcome by the experience.

One of the biggest bargains of all time? In 1626 an anonymous Indian chief sold the island of Manhattan to Governor Peter Minuit for $24 worth of supplies. These days

Manhattan land and real estate prices are among the highest in the world.

It's a fact that extroverts sleep better than introverts. So the more outgoing a salesman, the better he sleeps at night.

You can fool some of the people some of the time ... A physician called Dr Koch made a substantial fortune in the first half of this century with a patent medicine said to cure cancer and TB. When analysed in 1943 it was said to be indistinguishable from distilled water.

Even the sales potential of some of the world's most successful products wasn't at first realised. Take Monopoly, for example. When it was first offered to Parker Brothers in the USA they rejected it, saying that it had '52 fundamental errors'.

They say that there's always room for an improved product in the market. Take mousetraps, for example. An American inventor designed one that was smart and re-usable and retailed at only twice the price of the old throwaway variety. Use it to catch two mice and after that you were saving money!

Unfortunately no one 'bought it. The inventor had overlooked one thing. No one wants to remove a squashed mouse from a trap; they'd rather throw the whole thing away.

'Come alive with Pepsi' was a successful advertising slogan in America, but translated into German its effect wasn't quite the same. 'Rise from the grave with Pepsi' was one translation.

General Motors couldn't understand why their Chevrolet Nova wasn't selling well in Spanish-speaking America. Then someone pointed out that in Spanish 'No va' meant 'won't go'.

A nine-year-old visitor to a museum in County Durham politely pointed out to one of the curators that an exhibit they had labelled as a Roman *sesterce* coin was in fact a plastic token given away in a sales promotion by a soft drinks company.

A woman who fainted at a supermarket check-out in Nuremberg, West Germany, was discovered to have a frozen chicken under her hat — presumably she was attempting to smuggle it out of the store. She ended up in hospital with suspected brain damage.

A Parisian grocer was jailed for two years in 1978 for stabbing his wife to death with a wedge of cheese.

Public relations exercises can cause headaches — and even before PR was invented there were problems. Take the inaugural run of the railway that went from St Louis to Jefferson City in 1955. Two hundred passengers had embarked, and it was only when they failed to arrive at their destination that someone remembered that they hadn't yet connected the track across the bridge over the Gasconade River . . .

Advertisement in a New Zealand paper: OTAGO STUD FARM REQUIRES SINGLE YOUNG MAN.

Anxious to boost the number of passengers on their buses, an East Anglian bus company decided to promote the service with bus bingo. Numbers were displayed on the sides of buses and bingo cards were distributed to people living in the area. When they spotted numbers they just crossed them off their cards.

A car dealer in Coventry bought a twenty foot high fibreglass statue of King Kong as a sales gimmick and then renamed his company the King Kong Car Company. The Department of Trade were not keen on this marketing strategy. They wrote to him forbidding the use of the term King Kong because it implied 'royal patronage.'

When petrol companies first introduced fully automatic petrol pumps, the sort that accept notes and dispense petrol, they tried the idea out in a few selected garages and watched customer reaction.

Few people got the hang of it to begin with. One lady stuffed a pound note down the pump's nozzle and proceeded to shout her order into it. One man wrote his name and address on a piece of paper and inserted it in the slot intended for his one pound note. Asked why, he told observers, 'It said "Insert a note" so I did.'

Bright ideas are invaluable when it comes to selling, but careful research is even more important. Some plucky salesman must have persuaded a Scottish council to buy special protective clothing for its lollipop ladies. In theory it was a great idea — special jerkins that lit up at night to warn drivers. But no one thought to consult the lollipop ladies themselves, and they were none too keen on having their flashing bosoms lit up for all to see.

The Royal Melbourne Golf Club decided to sell off some bushland bordering the course for a building development. Unfortunately the person in charge of the sale got the deeds confused and sold off the eighth, ninth, tenth and eleventh fairways.

Cyril Lord's carpet company thought they'd have a huge success with their British version of 'Astroturf' artificial grass carpeting. Unfortunately the product turned out to have a built-in problem. After a few weeks it turned from green to blue . . .

Advertisement: Fashionable Chiswick Village. Set in attractive communal grounds with trees (tenants have their own small private parts).

Give your customers something that sounds really good. When the stage show of *Grease* went to Mexico it was retitled *Vaseline*. In Paris it was *Brilliantine*. And in Tokyo it was *Glease*.

In China they've found a way to boost the sales of dull books. They package them up with sex manuals, so that along with the facts of life purchasers can also learn the joys of subjects like *How to Repair Electrical Goods*.

Sales Brief

In this section you'll find dozens of brief jokes and wry observations to slip into your speech. They're ideal for breaking the ice quickly when you start and for linking your themes and jokes as you go along. Don't labour these one-liners, just drop them casually into your speech and allow the audience to spot them.

Did you hear about the table linen salesman who signed a contract to supply Barry Manilow with tablecloths to blow his nose on?

One of our salesmen was held up the other week by a man who waved a bunch of flowers at him. It was robbery with violets.

A friend of mine used to be a clock salesman until his company was wound up.

Who wants to be a success anyway? All success involves is making more money to pay the taxes you wouldn't have to pay if you didn't make so much money in the first place.

A friend of mine used to sell bras, but then the company went bust.

There was an advert for gardening services in the local

paper. It read, DON'T KILL YOURSELF IN THE GARDEN, LET US DO IT FOR YOU.

Another advert read, FOR SALE. MANURE £1 A BAG. DO IT YOURSELF 50P.

People do live in the strangest kind of houses. The estate agent had one in his window the other day. COTTAGE, TWO BEDS, it said. SITTING/DINING ROOM, KITCHEN, TOILET 6 MILES FROM BRISTOL.

My friend the bra salesman decided to get out of the business and form a holding company of his own.

Success as a salesman is just a matter of luck — ask any failure.

If you hype something and it sells, you're acclaimed as a genius — it couldn't have been hype. It you hype something and it doesn't sell, then it was just hype.

Did you hear about the head salesman with a firm of dungaree manufacturers? He was congratulated on his overall performance.

There are two ways in which young salesmen thrown in at the deep end survive. One is by crawling and the other is breast stroking.

Every salesman should read the *Sun* — it's the best way of keeping abreast of the market.

Door to door salesmen are like fitted carpets. Everyone walks over them.

Did you hear about the Irish paint salesman who was dismissed from his job for stealing some cans of yellow paint? He was caught red-handed.

Experience is what you get when you fail to get what you really wanted.

FOR SALE: Set of drawers belonging to a lady with bandy legs due to past misuse.

Life as a book salesman has its surprises. Only the other day someone asked for *Tess of the Dormobiles*.

The salesman who can smile when things go wrong has just thought of someone else he can blame it all on.

A proverb for our times. People who live in glass houses are constantly pestered by double-glazing salesmen.

Always remember that no matter how much you sell, you'll never sell enough. And the things you don't sell will be far more important than those you do.

If you can't get a day's work done in twenty-four hours, try working nights.

When lunching with a client, remember that if you can lie on the floor without holding on, you're not drunk.

Remember, if you're not fired with enthusiasm you'll be fired with enthusiasm.

Have you noticed how the efficiency of saleswomen varies in direct proportion to their ugliness?

Our sales manager defines zeal as a certain nervous disorder affecting young and inexperienced salesmen. Fortunately they soon get over it.

Remember, all work and no play makes Jack a dull boy and Jill a rich widow.

When it comes to giving, my firm stops at nothing. You

can do your best to make your product foolproof, but you'll never make it damn foolproof.

Our salesmen work such irregular hours that they get a free bran bonus in their pay packets.

I know a salesman who says he's the most successful in the world. He even claims to have sold Adam the first loose-leaf system.

Only the other day they put this notice up in the office. OWING TO A STAFF SHORTAGE TYPISTS WILL HANDLE SENIOR SALES MANAGEMENT BETWEEN 9 a.m. AND NOON AND SALESMEN IN THE AFTERNOON.

My boss keeps telling me that anything is possible if I only try hard enough. Personally I prefer to think anything is possible if you don't know what you're talking about.

Office notice: IN THE INTERESTS OF EFFICIENCY WILL ALL SALESMEN PLEASE TAKE ADVANTAGE OF THEIR SECRETARIES BEFORE 3 p.m.

Teamwork is essential in a sales force. That way you always have someone else to blame.

Selling is just like being a greengrocer. You have to know your onions, always dangle a carrot, and make the customer glad you've been (bean).

Confucius he say that man selling doughnuts will boast about the size of the doughnut, but the customer will consider the size of the hole.

You need to think your ideas through before you market something. The Irish may well have invented the toilet seat but it was the English who put the hole in it.

An optimistic salesman is one who believes he can sell himself to the world. A pessimistic salesman is one who thinks he already has.

Never travel without your expense account. After all, one should always take something sensational to read on a journey.

A friend of mine used to sell roller blinds but then the company was wound up.

The next time someone tells you he got rich by hard work, just try asking him whose ...

The business of life is living — not business.

A sales conference is a gathering of people who singly do nothing and together decide that nothing can be done.

Sales meetings are where minutes are kept and hours are lost.

Looking through a brochure of hotels offering conference facilities I noticed one which read: CASUAL JACKETS ACCEPTED BUT NOT TROUSERS.

If you're buying a house, make sure you understand the language of the estate agent:
A house of old world charm No bathroom
Quiet, exclusive situation Miles from anywhere
Will benefit from improvement About to fall down
Needs refurbishing Hasn't fallen down *yet*
Ripe for development It just fell down

At a recent sales conference one of the speakers talked about Customer Rights in Advertising Policy. He called it C.R.A.P. for short, and the salesmen all agreed.

A lecherous old salesman was admitted to hospital the

other week. He lay on the sheets staring at the nurses and wishing it was the other way round.

My boss has a tray on his desk containing letters of complaint from dissatisfied customers. It's labelled OMCST — that stands for Only a Miracle Can Solve These.

Our new sales manager was like all new brooms. He made some sweeping changes and left most of us standing in the dirt.

Our sales manager is so appallingly bad at his job that his contribution to our figures last year was about the same as Arthur Scargill's to Conservative garden fêtes.

Our sales manager has the same advice for expense claims as he has for the man who delivers our parcels — 'Stuff 'em in the back passage.'

Selling any kind of goods is like selling beer. The less froth it contains, the more you'll sell.

People find some strange excuses for not buying perfectly good products. For example: The car salesman was told 'I can't aFORD it.'
The camera salesman was told 'I don't LEICA it.'
And the Paxo rep was told to stuff it . . .

Two secretaries in the typing pool were discussing the handsome new salesman.
    'He dresses so smartly,' said one.
    'And so quickly, too,' said the other.

Sign in a shop window. IN ORDER TO MAINTAIN THE HIGH STANDARD OF SERVICE OUR CUSTOMERS HAVE COME TO EXPECT, THIS SHOP WILL BE CLOSED ON MONDAYS, THURSDAYS AND SATURDAY AFTERNOONS.

Why is it they always have the sales when the shops are so crowded?

I've asked the chairman to let me know when to stop as I've been known to reach the end and still carry on.